Is the Goddess a feminist?

Is the Goddess a feminist?

the politics of south asian goddesses

Edited by

Alf Hiltebeitel & Kathleen M. Erndl

Sheffield
Academic Press

Published by Sheffield Academic Press Ltd
Mansion House
19 Kingfield Road
Sheffield S11 9AS
England

http://www.shef-ac-press.co.uk

Typeset by Sheffield Academic Press
and
Printed on acid-free paper in Great Britain
by The Cromwell Press
Trowbridge, Wiltshire

British Library Cataloguing in Publication Data

A catalogue record for this book is available
from the British Library

ISBN 11-84127-157-8 pbk

Contents

List of Contributors   7

Introduction: Writing Goddesses, Goddesses Writing,
and Other Scholarly Concerns
     Alf Hiltebeitel and Kathleen M. Erndl   11

'*Sa Ham*—I Am She': Woman as Goddess
     Rita DasGupta Sherma   24

Dancing with Prakriti: The Samkhyan Goddess as *Pativrata*
and *Guru*
     Alfred Collins   52

Battles, Brides, and Sacrifice: Rajput *Kuldevis* in Rajasthan
     Lindsey Harlan   69

Is *Shakti* Empowering for Women? Reflections on Feminism
and the Hindu Goddess
     Kathleen M. Erndl   91

Is the Goddess a Feminist?
     Rita M. Gross   104

Draupadi's Question
     Alf Hiltebeitel   113

Is the *Devi Mahatmya* a Feminist Scripture?
     Cynthia Ann Humes   123

Power in its Place: Is the Great Goddess of Hinduism a Feminist?
     Usha Menon and Richard A. Shweder   151

Is Vajrayogini a Feminist? A Tantric Buddhist Case Study
     Miranda Shaw   166

In Our Image: The Feminist Vision of the Hindu Goddess
    Stanley N. Kurtz   181

Is the Hindu Goddess Tradition a Good Resource for
Western Feminism?
    Tracy Pintchman   187

Seeking Ma, Seeking Me
    Brenda Dobia   203

A Garland of Talking Heads for the Goddess: Some
Autobiographical and Psychoanalytic Reflections
on the Western Kali
    Jeffrey J. Kripal   239

Real and Imagined Goddesses: A Debate
    Rajeswari Sunder Rajan   269

Index of Authors   285

List of Contributors

Alfred Collins Following undergraduate studies at the University of Chicago, Al Collins earned two PhDs at the University of Texas at Austin, in Indian Studies and in Clinical Psychology. He was a Fullbright scholar in Madras in 1971–72. His paper 'Selfhood in Context: Some Indian Solutions', written with Prakash Desai, received Honorable Mention for the Bryce Boyer award from the American Anthropological Association in 1986. Trained in Jungian and psychoanalytic self psychology and Sanskrit literature, he has written on Samkhya, Vedanta, and Kashmiri Saivism; on the father–son relationship in Indian and Western literature and society; and on Western and Indian fairy- and folk-tales. For years he has pursued the aim of uncovering and/or reconstructing an Indian self psychology from Yogic, Samkhyan, and Buddhist materials and tracing this back into earlier Indian cosmogonic and psychophysiological thought. He is a practicing clinical psychologist in Anchorage, Alaska.

Brenda Dobia has a background in psychology and yoga. Her special interests are in the areas of women's health, women's spirituality and contemporary female rites of passage, and she has authored a number of articles in these fields. Brenda currently works as a lecturer in the Department of Social Ecology at the University of Western Sydney, where she is also completing her PhD. In addition she teaches in the Diploma of Health: Yoga at Naturecare College in Sydney, Australia.

Kathleen M. Erndl is Associate Professor of Religion at the Florida State University. She is the author of *Victory to the Mother: The Hindu Goddess of Northwestern India in Myth, Ritual, and Symbol* and other works on goddesses, women and religious experience in Hinduism. The recipient of fellowships from the National Endowment for the Humanities and the Guggenheim Foundation, she is currently at work on a book entitled *Playing with the Mother: Women, Goddess Possession, and Power in Kangra Hinduism*.

Rita M. Gross is the author of two award-winning books on Buddhism, *Buddhism After Patriarchy: A Feminist History, Analysis, and Reconstruction of Buddhism* and *Soaring and Settling: Buddhist Perspectives on Contemporary Social and Religious Issues*. In addition to several other books which she has written or edited, she has written many articles on various aspects of the study of women and religion and feminist theology.

Lindsey Harlan, Associate Professor at Connecticut College, is the author of *Religion and Rajput Women* and co-editor with Paul Courtright of *From the Margins of Hindu Marriage*. She is currently finishing a book project on possessions in contemporary hero cults. She has written various essays on gender and heroism. She holds a PhD from Harvard University.

Alf Hiltebeitel is Columbian School Professor of Religion and Human Sciences and Director of the Human Sciences Program at the George Washington University. He has authored two volumes on *The Cult of Draupadi: Rethinking India's Oral and Classical Epics: Draupadi among Rajputs, Muslims, and Dalits*; and *Rethinking the Mahabharata: A Reader's Guide to the Education of Yudhisthira*, and is co-editor with Barbara D. Miller of *Hair: Its Power and Meaning in Asian Cultures*.

Cynthia Ann Humes is Associate Professor of Religious Studies at Claremont McKenna College. Her publications concern contemporary use of Sanskrit literature, modern ritual in North Indian goddess worship, political and economic dimensions of Hinduism, and issues of gender in world religions. Recently, she has co-written a book on the history of the Transcendental Meditation movement in the United States and translated and annotated the popular discourses of Shankaracharya Brahmananda Saraswati.

Jeffrey J. Kripal is the Vira I. Heinz Associate Professor of Religion at Westminster College (New Wilmington, PA). His publication include *Kali's Child: The Mystical and the Erotic in the Life and Teachings of Ramakrishna*, which won the American Academy of Religion's History of Religions Prize, and *Vishnu on Freud's Desk: A Reader in Psychoanalysis and Hinduism*, which he co-

edited with T.G. Vaidyanathan of Bangalore, India. He has also co-
edited a third volume with G. William Barnard titled *Crossing
Boundaries: Essays on the Ethical Status of Mysticism*. His most
recent research and writing focus on the mystical experiences of
historians of mysticism and the manner in which these ecstatic,
unitive and erotic experiences are hermeneutically reflected in
scholarly writing. He is presently Visiting Associate Professor of the
History of Religion at Harvard Divinity School.

Stanley N. Kurtz received his PhD in Anthropology from Harvard University, has taught at Harvard, and is currently a Fellow of
the Committee on Human Development and the Center for Research
on Culture and Mental Health at the University of Chicago. He is
the author of *All the Mothers Are One: Hindu India and the Cultural Shaping of Psychoanalysis*.

Usha Menon is Assistant Professor of Anthropology at Drexel University. Her research site has been the temple town of Bhubaneswar
in Orissa, eastern India. She writes on popular, contemporary understandings of the goddess Kali, on family dynamic and gender
relations in Oriya Hindu society, and on Hindu morality. She is
currently studying the supposed militancy of Hindu women vis-à-vis
Muslims—a relatively recent phenomenon on the subcontinent and
one that is potentially troubling. She is also completing a book on
the life experiences of Oriya Hindu women and the relevance of
Western feminist thought to their lives and experiences.

Tracy Pintchman is Director of the Program in Religion, Culture
and Society and Associate Professor of Hindu Studies and Religious
Studies at Loyola University of Chicago. Her publications include
The Rise of the Goddess in the Hindu Tradition (1994), a forthcoming edited volume titled *Seeking Mahadevi: Constructing the
Identities of the Hindu Great Goddess*, and various articles and
book chapters. She is currently working on a book on Hindu
women's rituals.

Rajeswari Sunder Rajan was until recently a Senior Fellow at
the Nehru Memorial Museum and Library, New Delhi, and will
shortly be taking up an appointment at the University of Oxford.
She is the author of *Real and Imagined Women: Gender, Culture*

and Postcolonialism. She has edited *The Lie of the Land: English Literary Studies in India, Signposts: Gender Issues in Post-Independence India*, and was guest editor of the special issue on 'Gender in the Making: Indian Contexts' of *Thamyris: Mythmaking from Past to Present*. Her work on feminist theory and politics has appeared in numerous journals.

Miranda Shaw, Associate Professor of Religion at the University of Richmond in Virginia, is the author of *Passionate Enlightenment: Women in Tantric Buddhism* and of *Buddhist Goddesses of India, Tibet, and Nepal*, forthcoming from Princeton University Press.

Rita DasGupta Sherma holds a Masters in Women's Studies in Religion from Claremont Graduate University (CGU) and is a doctoral candidate in the PhD program in Theology, Ethics, and Culture at CGU. She is a multi-media artist, and has lectured widely on Asian religious art and iconography. She has written articles on tantra and ecofeminism, and is currently working on a volume on 'The Ecotheological Reconstruction of Hindu Tantra'.

Richard A. Shweder, a cultural anthropologist, is Professor of Human Development at the University of Chicago. He is the author/editor of several books, including *Thinking through Cultures: Expeditions in Cultural Psychology*; *Culture Theory: Essays in Mind, Self, and Emotion* (with Robert A. LeVine); and *Welcome to Middle Age! (and Other Cultural Fictions)*. He is a past president of the Society for Psychological Anthropology and is currently co-chair of the Social Science Research Council/Russell Sage Foundation Working Group on Ethnic Customs, Assimilation, and American Law. For the past thirty years, Professor Shweder has been conducting research on moral foundations of family life practices in the Hindu temple town of Bhubaneswar on the east coast of India.

Alf Hiltebeitel and Kathleen M. Erndl

Introduction: Writing Goddesses, Goddesses Writing, and Other Scholarly Concerns

Of all the world's religions, Hinduism has the most elaborate *living* Goddess traditions. Hindu conceptions of female deities and the over-arching Great Goddess stem from the supreme cosmic power, Shakti, from whom all creation emerges and by whom it is sustained. The worship of the Goddess, of the divine as female, has a long history in India and continues to become even more popular today. By virtue of their common feminine nature, women are in some contexts regarded as special manifestations of the Goddess, sharing in her powers. Thus, the Goddess can perhaps be viewed as a mythic model for Hindu women. Western religious traditions, on the other hand, while not totally devoid of feminine imagery, lack any true parallel to the Hindu Goddess. This perceived deficiency has inspired some Western religious feminists to recover and revive goddesses and feminine images of the divine from the ancient past. Nevertheless, some feminists and scholars of religion have argued that the existence of the Hindu Goddess has not appeared outwardly to have benefited women's position in Indian society.

The question of the relationship between Indian (primarily Hindu, but including Buddhist and Jain) goddesses and women is multi-faceted and complex, frequently leading to contradictory answers, depending upon how the question is framed and who is doing the asking—and answering. To provide just a taste of this complexity, we relate two brief encounters experienced by one of the editors of this volume. Over twenty years ago, when I (Kathleen Erndl) was a young graduate student visiting campuses to explore their PhD programs, I sat nervously in the office of a prominent Indian male professor at a prestigious university in the US, trying to appear intelligent and scholarly. Having just returned from a year and half of study and travel in India, the highlight of which was a pilgrimage to the mountain temple of the famous goddess Vaishno Devi, I spoke with enthusiasm about the possibility of researching Hindu goddess worship for my PhD dissertation and even intimated that it might be worthwhile to explore the relationship between goddesses and women. The august professor squinted slightly, stroked his chin, seemed to ponder for a moment, then distractedly remarked, 'Ah, yes. We like them as goddesses, but not as people.' After that conversation-stopper, the interview ended abruptly.[1] Fast forward about two decades. Now myself an established academic, I was in a small village in the foothills of the Himalayas, seated with a group of local women outside the temple of a holy woman, a goddess-possessed healer whom people referred to as Mataji or 'Respected Mother'. She was one of many such women I had come to know in researching my second book (Erndl forthcoming). The devotees and I were waiting for Mataji to return from a doctor's appointment in nearby Dharamsala. When she finally appeared, looking strong and vibrant in an orange salwar-kameez outfit in spite of her rather serious chronic medical condition, her face glowing, I spontaneous-ly blurted out to the woman next to me, 'How beautiful Mataji looks!' The woman smiled knowingly at me and said, 'And why not? She has the *shakti* [power, energy] of the Goddess. She is the Goddess herself.' These two perspectives, one from a Westernized Indian male academic, the other from an Indian village woman steeped in local oral traditions, represent just two of the multiple perspectives on the relationship between women and goddesses, perceptions which range from emphasizing identity to continuity to disjunction to paradox to irrelevance.

When the two of us, Alf Hiltebeitel and Kathleen Erndl, first start-ed talking some years ago about the possibility of editing this book, we were interested not so much in solving once and for all the woman/goddess question as playing with it, formulating it in differ-ent ways, and taking into account multiple perspectives.[2] The idea was that writing about goddesses in India had taken a number of

1.   I never found out, as I matriculated at another university, what exactly he meant by 'we' and 'them'. I did, however, produce a PhD dissertation and subsequently a book (Erndl 1993) on Hindu goddess worship.

2.   We note with pleasure that our preoccupation with this question is not simply the pastime of the academy but is also being engaged in a self-conscious public way in India. For example, a recent photographic exhibit entitled 'Woman/Goddess', curated by artist Gayatri Sinha, explores many facets of this relationship over the last 50 years. This exhibit toured several Indian cities in late 1999 and early 2000. Like the present collection, the exhibit does not

distinct forms and had generated a corresponding number of interpretive positions but that little had been done to spur thinking about
the issues that drive these formations. So, we decided to bring the
question of goddesses and feminism out into the open to be addressed, discussed, debated, and pondered over by scholars from
different disciplinary perspectives and with varying degrees of in-
sider and outsider status with respect to both Indian goddess traditions and feminism. Our central question has struck a chord not
only with the authors, but also with our colleagues, some anxious
to find out the answer, others spurring us on with answers of their
own or with further questions. As the book bears out, there are
many interrelated issues, but its contributors have had no difficulty
in recognizing the question, 'Is the Goddess a Feminist?' as posing
the single driving issue behind their own and others' writings on
South Asian (and other) goddesses; nor in recognizing that it is
timely and exciting to bring these positions into open debate.

The reader will notice that among the essays, there is no uniform
definition of 'feminist' or even of 'goddess' (with either a small or
capital g). We feel that an imposed definition would stifle rather
than foster the kind of reflection we wanted to elicit and that each
contributor should define feminism in the way which best makes
sense in relation to her or his approach to the study of Indian goddesses and gender issues. Furthermore, the agreement to debate
rests on a felt need that the question makes apparent: the need for
scholarly reflexivity. The question brings its authors to think about
the relation one has to what one studies, and the complicity of
scholarship with its subjects and objects. Reflexivity has come to
be considered a 'good' thing, although, to be sure, it can be tire-
some when authors end up writing mainly about themselves. Complicity, however, is generally considered a 'bad' thing. But in theology, where one speaks out of a community of shared experience,
or in psychology, where shared images can be counted as strategies
of healing, or in anthropology, where shared experiences are counted as participant observations, the point is problematic. And in post-
colonial South Asia, where it can be a question of which groups
and individuals choose the goddess to represent themselves, it

come to any general conclusion but rather raises more questions through the
examination of multiple perspectives.

is politically problematic in ways that have not been sufficiently acknowledged or thought through.

The question locates stances within what Rajeswari Sunder Rajan calls a discursive field. But it is a field in which, until recently, the discourse has been almost uselessly fragmented. On the one hand, we have a virtual goddess industry—nourished in the West by New Age goddess spirituality and what Usha Menon and Rick Shweder call ecological feminism, and in India by Hindu chauvinist spiritualizations of Mother India (Bharat Mata)—which makes it trendy to write about goddesses and the Goddess.[3] And on the other hand, we have the contributors to this volume who may relate positively or negatively to one or another of these agendas, but who in either case benefit from the atmosphere while writing about goddesses in and for very different camps. This is not to point fingers, since all the contributors have happily joined in some of the camping. But it does serve to indicate what this book is not about.

It is not written from within either the spirituality or Hindu nationalist wings of the industry. It is not a work about a single goddess, or about the Indian Great Goddess, although some of its contributors have written such books. And it is not a collection of essays about a sample of South Asian goddesses, although several of its authors have written for such collections. Such works are typical products of the field of religious studies, and mark the outcome of recent decades in which mainly Western scholars have combined textual and field study of Indian goddesses to produce contributions to the academic study and teaching of religion. It is not a book devoted to refining interpretive strategies, whether feminist, theological, anthropological, post-colonial, Marxist, Freudian, Jungian, Lacanian, Foucauldian, or Spivakian—although, again, each of these perspectives is reflected, as are others, in one or more of this book's essays, and in the wider works of its authors. And it is not a book with a corrective agenda, particularly with regard to readings of South Asian prehistory and history, through which many authors

---

3.   For an overview and critical discussion of this industry as it bears on Western interpretations and appropriations of the Hindu goddess Kali, see McDermott (1996). On promulgation of Bharat Mata by the Indian 'guru business', see McKean (1996a; 1996b). On women and goddess imagery generally in the Hindu Nationalist movement, see Bacchetta (1993) and Basu (1993).

have made goddesses and ancient Indian women their handmaidens to primordialist claims about matriarchy, Dravidians, Tamilttay (Mother Tamil), a Sarasvati civilization, or the putative higher status of women in the Vedic age. Rather, it is a book that airs a needed and overdue debate about 'interests' among authors who value an interdisciplinary framework of discussion backed by historical, textual and anthropological rigor. What is surprising is how readily the contributors with differing interests and approaches saw rewards in rethinking their own work on South Asian goddesses around a question where disagreement is inevitable, but likely to be stimulating. The rapid-fire format of the initial American Academy of Religion panel that brought some of us together around this topic is retained to the extent that most of the essays are short and focused on the question. The result is a fast-paced, lively, text-usable, focused, debate-centered, transnational, gender-bending, and multi-issue group of essays.

A persistent issue underlying the essays is that of writing: writing about goddesses (in the scriptures, in current scholarship, etc.), goddesses writing, women writing, men writing. Indian scriptures yield a memorable figure of a writing god: Ganesha the elephant-headed son of Parvati and Shiva, who broke off one of his tusks to write down the *Mahabharata*, India's 'great epic', as it was dictated to him by its 'author' Vyasa. But we can think of no writing goddesses. Goddesses are more associated with speaking than with writing. At most, goddesses and gods get to instruct each other and their worshipers orally in certain esoteric tantric texts, which, it has been assumed, have been mostly written by men. Till now, one might only hear that the highly Brahmanical and Sanskritic goddess Sarasvati, also known as Vac, the personification of sacred speech and wife of the creator Brahma, is the patroness of the arts, including Sanskrit speech and only secondarily writing. Or one might hear that Mother Tamil (Tamilttay) is herself a goddess, though more as 'mother tongue' (*taymoli*) than for any connection with writing;[4]

---

4.   See Ramaswamy (1995), especially pp. 711-19 on 'The Gendering of Language: Tamil as Woman, Goddess, and Mother'. Ramaswamy attributes an 'over-writing of the erotic and sensuous by the compassionate and nurturing' to 'socialist and nationalist reformers', replicating the 'dominant paradigm' of Bharat Mata on the 'sub-national level' (p. 713). Most of the 'tracts on Tamilttay' are 'written by men and are in general addressed to the Tamilian male'

or that while Durga blesses the military weapons of Ksatriya warriors at the fall festival of Dashahara, she would also bless the writing implements of Brahman scribes and accountants, since for these men, the stylus was their weapon. Or, one might hear Amritanandamayi, a woman from Kerala also known as Ammachi whom her international movement of devotees regards as the self-realized supreme Mother, while she is on tour in America, and see two of her red-robed Indian male translators fervently writing down her talk so that one of them can 'translate' it from Malayalam into English, and then take six times as long as she did in his oral amplification. Or one might hear of an illiterate village woman, a Mataji through whom a goddess speaks and whose divinely inspired words are tape-recorded and transcribed by an American scholar to serve as raw material for her next book.[5] Yet goddesses do come of age. For instance, there was a poster, spotted by some of our colleagues in the early 1980s in Delhi, showing a goddess holding a typewriter in one of her multiple upraised weapon-bearing hands, making it clear that writing was now one of her weapons. We are told that the poster is out of print. Now that the typewriter is obsolete, we can look forward to the goddess with a computer.

So 'writing goddesses' could mean that goddesses have now started writing themselves, for and about themselves and others, or, more matter-of-factly, that some women in South Asia have ceased to let men, both male gods and their human incarnations, be their inscribers. The project of 'writing goddesses' thus overlaps with the recuperation of forgotten Indian women authors, to which Miranda Shaw has contributed by showing that writers about tantra—both South Asian (including Tibetan) practitioners and modern scholars—have by various means suppressed the fact that certain foundational Vajrayana Buddhist tantric texts were authored by women, in the Tibetan case in part by the dropping of gender-

---

who is called upon to rescue the endangered mother, while women 'ought to produce such heroic sons who would go off' to do Tamilttay's battles. But women's groups also mobilized in the 1930s to save Tamilttay from Hindi (p. 718). The classicist Raghavendra Iyer praised her in a 1933 Tamil Conference poem as a nourisher of the great Tamil poets and scholars, and one who 'caused learning to grow among women!' (pp. 715-16).

5.   See, for example Erndl (1997) and Erndl (forthcoming) for examples of how wise but illiterate women can become 'writing goddesses'.

specific endings in the translation of Sanskrit names (Shaw 1994: 75-76). Indeed, in tantric terms, where a woman practitioner visualizes herself as a deity, an authoress like Sahajayoginicinta *was* a writing goddess (Shaw 1994: 179-94).

But the image of writing goddesses also has critical and ironic edges. As Tracy Pintchman reminds us, writing about South Asian goddesses and women, and the relation between them, calls not only for a hermeneutic of recovery but a hermeneutic of suspicion. Sunder Rajan and Stanley Kurtz insist that patriarchy and hierarchy, respectively, explain the seeming contradictions between Indian goddesses and Indian women. Menon and Shweder argue that rather than promoting resistance to 'the system', goddesses serve to keep it standing. Sunder Rajan points out that in one Indian state, there appears to be no correlation between women's literacy and the worship of goddesses. Pintchman argues that there is no necessary correlation between a symbol and its interpretation: the goddess can be interpreted to empower women or to disempower them— or, for that matter, to overpower them, as in the case of the *sati*, a woman who immolates herself on her husband's funeral pyre (Hiltebeitel 1999). Pintchman questions whether a deity's gender makes any difference at all in these respects. Kathleen Erndl would agree with all these points but in her essay for this volume focuses on examples of Hindu women, both 'traditional' and 'modern', who experience nurturing and empowerment through identification with female divine imagery or the worship of female deities. All of these authors agree that a necessary correlation between powerful goddesses and empowered women would imply simplistic theories of role models and uni-gender projections.

As to the symbol itself, Sunder Rajan mentions that not all goddesses get written about equally. Until recently, goddesses of low and Untouchable castes and tribals—or as some call them, folk goddesses—have tended to be virtually invisible to India's literary establishments unless their worship was Brahmanized, or they were written up in a Sanskrit Purana, or until they were written about by Westerners.[6] Sunder Rajan also sees feminine divinity shaped not

6. For an important 'subaltern' study of the goddess, see Hardiman (1987). Also, it is not uncommon among both Western and Indian commentators to consider folk goddess traditions to be relatively non-sexist and to equate Brahmanical influence with patriarchy. See, for example, Berreman (1993); Mohanty

by 'the elevation of strong or aberrant women or by women's actual material and historical conditions', but by 'the embodiment of desired qualities in the female figure'. That male desire defines the most typical expressions can hardly be doubted. Several essays track South Asian concepts of authority (*adhikara*), power (*shakti*), and control (particularly women's self-control over their own emotions), and find that they routinely underwrite male dominance. Menon and Shweder consider the image of Kali's trampling of Shiva—a favorite of both Indian and Western feminists for her indicators of female power, independence and dominance—in which, according to the interpretation of contemporary high-caste Orissans and contradicting traditional tantric interpretations (as discussed by Jeffrey Kripal), Kali's true moment is her show of 'shame' or respectful self-restraint before Shiva: a confirmation of gender inequalities as 'natural moral facts', and of the idea that women's power lies in their 'voluntary' self-subordination. As Humes observes, whereas goddesses can dominate, control their own *shakti*, and order female forms by emanation, ordinary women are dominated and generally lack these controlling and ordering capacities. On the other hand, as Kripal demonstrates, male desire may not only be about domination, but about intimacy.

As several authors remark, Shakti is linked up with the non-hierarchical axis of auspiciousness/inauspiciousness rather than with the caste-stratifying and women-subordinating axis of purity/pollution.[7] But as Rita Gross observes, there seems to emerge another axis of power/authority. Here women have power and men authority or control, except when men lose control and women voluntarily, or through their 'natural moral' constitution, control themselves to return it to them. Such power is not power to do but power to be tapped. Males do not have it, or much of it, of their own, but they know its value in maintaining, or if necessary restoring, their authority. Ordinarily, as Erndl observes, women's power and auspiciousness are acknowledged to be controlled for patriarchal pur-

---

(1998). In the introduction to the latter, the author states, 'It is also important to mention here that this story has been influenced by the Brahmanical tradition which considers a wife to be inferior' (p. 9).

7.   Several authors cite the path-breaking works of Frédérique Apffel Marglin on these two axes.

poses (as in some famous verses of the *Laws of Manu*). But the myths and rituals often suggest that goddesses dominate only when men have lost control *temporarily*. The myth or ritual usually finds some way for the goddess or heroine to return power to them, as exemplified in Lindsay Harlan's essay. When 'the system' or 'symbolic order' breaks down—when demons conquer the gods and take over the universe, or when the patriarchal family falls apart— goddesses and heroines can become the last resort, but only for the time being. Traditionally, only tantra (Hindu and Buddhist) seems to admit forcefully the durable reversals that allow for authorizing goddesses and women. However, as Rita Sherma indicates in the first essay, which also serves as a general orientation to the roles and images of women in several varieties and historical periods of Hinduism, one also finds a few role-reversing authors among the women saint-singers of the bhakti tradition. In any case, as Humes observes, *stri shakti*, 'the power of women', does not fit Western concepts of power, in that it is not a power that 'connotes the ability to control and dominate'—and women who have it do not necessarily control it, nor are they deemed to be consciously aware of it. It is not agency but, rather, potentiality. For Erndl, then, a task for Hindu feminists would appear to be to 'rescue shakti from its patriarchal prison'.

Several of our authors also address the question of 'who speaks' for the goddess. Pintchman finds that women who serve as priestesses of a goddess consider their role appropriate because they do not intrude upon her when seeing her icon naked, rather than because of any identification with her or with her power. Humes finds that most women express devotion to the goddess in vernaculars, relying on males who know the authoritative texts in Sanskrit. She finds one exception: a woman who draws on the Sanskrit texts for her mostly women disciples. But this woman acknowledges the authority of male pandits over the texts, and stresses the values of the *pativrata* or devoted wife in her teachings. Kurtz finds that women who worship goddesses are more prone to express concerns about the males in their lives than they are about themselves and other females.

Yet our authors, even if they define them rather differently, also note that there are multiple Western and South Asian feminisms, and that even if one hesitates or refuses to call the goddess a feminist, she raises feminist questions. Occasionally, she even does this herself, in the written and oral texts. Two stories treated boil down to virtually the same question. When the male gods in one case and male heroes in the other have put them into compromising situations that demand their stripping, the goddess Durga (in Menon and Shweder's article) asks, 'What kinds of gods are these?' and the epic heroine and incarnate goddess Draupadi (in Alf Hiltebeitel's article) asks (to paraphrase), 'What kinds of men are these?' Likewise, the goddess also raises feminist questions for those who study her. For Gross, the goddess is a 'theological resource' with whom to counter Abrahamic monotheism's long struggle to exterminate the goddess. For Brenda Dobia, the Goddess is not merely a symbol to be studied or interpreted but is rather a living presence who reveals Herself across a cultural and religious divide, challenging Western social constructions of a monotheistic deity and an autonomous individual self. Shaw, Collins and Hiltebeitel explore the hermeneutical possibilities of reading even patriarchal texts against the grain. Similarly, Dobia, although acknowledging that the feminist critique of religion is valid, argues that 'this need not require us to discard Hindu Goddess mythology as male-derived and therefore inherently unusable'. She quotes Wendy O'Flaherty as observing that it is possible

> to extract an 'operational code' from a myth, a code whose pattern may be suggested by similar patterns elucidated in the fields of psychology, philosophy, and even the natural sciences. We *can* see the patterns that are obscured by the mythmakers' view of themselves (O'Flaherty 1980: 8).

As Humes puts it, the goddess and the texts that glorify her make certain things 'thinkable'—both for and about women: for instance, heroic martial women (Viranganas) and the 'phallic feminine'. Although heroic martial women are no less thinkable in the biblical Song of Deborah or the history of Joan of Arc, the fact that some martial heroines are 'thinkable' in relation to goddesses would seem likely to make a difference. Humes argues that the goddess's female ascription can subvert male dominance and 'sublate' the masculine through symbols of castration and power over the regeneracy of male sacrificial blood.

Several authors also notice symbolic representations of women's outrage and anger, and suggest that these expressions are not entirely second-hand.[8] Collins questions whether a language of female anger is subtly coded, and perhaps also suppressed, in the abstract and impersonal philosophical principles of *purusha* (male spirit, pure 'witnessing' consciousness) and *prakriti* (feminine matter/energy). He interprets the scene in which *prakriti*'s highest aspect, the faculty of intellect (*buddhi*), sees through and dissolves the (implicitly male) ego (*ahamkara*) as akin to the beheading scenes of bhakti myths and tantric icons—a violent scene that in the abstractions of Samkhya philosophy leaves no room to affirm that *purusha* could be, in psychoanalytic parlance, *prakriti*'s reciprocating 'self-object'. *Ahamkara* or ego is the self that can be represented as a head cut off physically so that *purusha* can be its own self-witness in an 'onanistic' spiritual isolation (*kaivalya*). *Prakriti* is thus seen to have been pleasurable and liberating in acting for the 'purpose of *purusha*'. Yet ultimately she is dark and dangerous to the ego, a sword-wielding embodiment of blind, unconscious ignorance. Collins asks whether *prakriti* deludes out of rage at being unrecognized in her wholeness. But could it not also be that she is enraged at being 'witnessed' in her insentient wholeness without being able to 'consciously' witness back? Hiltebeitel finds that a dynamic of similar open questions operates in the *Mahabharata*'s portrayal of Draupadi, and that the Bengali short story writer Mahasweta Devi has noted this and drawn out the epic scene's potential for an explicitly feminist reading that subjects such questions to a political critique. In the epic Draupadi's case, her words and actions seem to call the ascription of unconscious blindness under narrative question. Draupadi raises the question of gendered and ungendered self in a way that exposes male authority as powerless to answer it in its own terms. And it seems that she knows this from the moment she asks.

Moreover, as Pintchman points out, goddesses as symbols are not tied to their primary cultural matrices. They are fluid with respect to both place and time. They can start to migrate, across South Asian

---

8.   See the essays by Erndl and Menon and Shweder, in addition to those of Collins and Hiltebeitel discussed below. See also Shaw (1994: 31, 41, 48-49) on the tantric goddess Vajrayogini (the subject of her essay in this volume), who is also called Dvesavajri, 'Diamond of Hatred', and whose consort Candamaharosana 'singles out' for the direst punishments 'those who transgress against women'.

geography, up and down the caste system, even across the seas, and can take on new 'looks'. Menon and Shweder's myth about Kali is from a particular region of India, Orissa. Although other regional Kalis can be found who have been 'tamed' or 'self-controlled' in similar but different ways, one can also find more autonomous Kalis with both power and authority.[9] Erndl's essay calls attention to ways in which women's movements have begun to 'mobilize' this mobility to generate a sense of identity and common cause among women across caste, class, region, language, and kinship lines. And goddesses, like people, do change with the times. As Gross reminds us, in the final analysis it matters not so much whether the Goddess is a feminist as whether her devotees are, and what they mean to do about it.

Is the Goddess a feminist? This question, we believe, can never be answered definitively and for all time. But by framing the question and responding to it in different ways, the authors of this volume hope not only to provide some lively and informative reading but also to provoke further thought and debate on the matter.

Bibliography

Bacchetta, Paola
 1993   'All Our Goddesses Are Armed: Religion, Resistance, and Revenge in
                the Life of a Militant Hindu Nationalist Woman', in Amrita Basu (ed.),
                Women and Religious Nationalism in India, *Bulletin of Concerned
                Asian Scholars*. 25.4: 38-52.
Basu, Amrita
 1993   'Feminism Inverted: The Real Women and Gendered Imagery of Hindu
                Nationalism', in *idem* (ed.), *Women and Religious Nationalism in
                India*, *Bulletin of Concerned Asian Scholars*. 25.4: 25-37.
Berreman, Gerald D.
 1993   'Sanskritization as Female Oppression in India', in Barbara Diane Miller
                (ed.), *Sex and Gender Hierarchies* (Cambridge: Cambridge Univer-
                sity Press): 366-92.
Dehejia, Vidya
 1999   *Devi: The Great Goddess. Female Divinity in South Asian Art* (Wash-
                ington, DC: Arthur M. Sackler Gallery, Smithsonian Institution, in
                association with Mapin Publishing, Ahmedabad and Prestel Verlag,
                Munich).

9.   Ankalamma, a regional multiform of Kali from the southern state of Andhra Pradesh, demands worship and authority for herself in Shiva's Lingayat sectarian bastion of Kalyan (see Roghair 1982: 194-99).

Erndl, Kathleen M.
1993   *Victory to the Mother: The Hindu Goddess of Northwest India in Myth, Ritual, and Symbol* (New York: Oxford University Press).
1997   'The Goddess and Women's Power: A Hindu Case Study', in Karen King (ed.), *Women and Goddess Traditions in Antiquity and Today* (introduction by Karen Jo Torjesen; Minneapolis: Fortress Press): 17-38.
forthcoming   *Playing with the Mother: Women, Goddess Possession, and Power in Kangra Hinduism.*

Hardiman, David
1987   *The Coming of the Devi: Adivasi Assertion in Western India* (Delhi: Oxford University Press).

Hiltebeitel, Alf
1999   'Fathers of the Bride, Fathers of Sati: Myths, Rites, and Scholarly Practices', *Thamyris* 6.1: 65-94.

McDermott, Rachel Fell
1996   'The Western Kali', in John Stratton Hawley and Donna Marie Wulff (eds.), *Devi: Goddesses of India* (Berkeley: University of California Press): 281-313.

McKean, Lise
1996a   'Mother India and Her Militant Matriots', in John Stratton Hawley and Donna Marie Wulff (eds.), *Devi: Goddesses of India* (Berkeley: University of California Press): 250-80.
1996b   *Divine Enterprise: Gurus and the Hindu Nationalist Movement* (Chicago: University of Chicago Press, 1996).

Mohanty, Bidyut
1998   'Lakshmi and Alakshmi: The Kojagari Lakshmi Vrat Katha of Bengal' (trans. Dulali Nag), *Manushi* 104: 9-11.

O'Flaherty, Wendy Doniger
1980   *Women, Androgynes, and Other Mythical Beasts* (Chicago: University of Chicago Press).

Orr, Leslie C.
1999   'Recent Studies of Hindu Goddesses', *Religious Studies Review* 25.3: 239-46.

Ramaswamy, Sumathi
1995   'En/gendering Language: The Poetics of Tamil Identity', *Comparative Study of Society and History* 35.4: 638-725.

Roghair, Gene H.
1982   *The Epic of Palnadu* (Oxford: Clarendon Press).

Shaw, Miranda
1994   *Passionate Enlightenment: Women in Tantric Buddhism* (Princeton: Princeton University Press).

Wulff, Donna Marie, and John Stratton Hawley (eds.)
1996   *Devi: Goddesses of India* (Berkeley: University of California Press).

Rita DasGupta Sherma

'Sa Ham—I Am She': Woman as Goddess

Worship of the divine feminine has always been a distinctive feature of the Hindu tradition. Village goddesses, worshiped for millennia, still have currency today. Female divinities, such as Sarasvati, Vac, Aditi and Viraj, populate the earliest vedic literature. Later,
different facets of the feminine principle are mentioned in philosophical literature; these include *prakriti/pradhana* (the natural
world and the material substance of the universe); *shakti* (the creative power of a supreme being); and *maya* (the divine power of
morphogenesis, differentiation, and veiling of the underlying
unity). Texts of the puranas (scriptures that form the basis of much
of Hindu theogony, mythology and ritual) such as the *Devi Mahatmya* and the *Devi Bhagavata* create a single Great Goddess (Devi)
by melding together various regional goddess theologies, the different aspects of the feminine principle, and the notion of an ultimate reality. The Devi, who is transcendent and immanent, is the
material cause of creation as well as the Self in all beings. In this
capacity, the Devi is fully involved in the current of the cosmic
drama; though formless, she manifests herself to vanquish evil each
time it threatens the universal order. But she is also the quiescent
ground of the Absolute. The full unfolding of the feminine principle occurs in the texts of the tantric tradition (*tantras, agamas,
nigamas, pancharatra samhitas*) with the complex systemization
of the functions of Shakti.

At first glance, however, this triumph of the divine feminine does
not seem to have had an uplifting effect on the secular or religious
lives of Hindu women. It seems that a society giving rise to *sati*, a
culture in which women do not receive the rite of religious initiation (*upanayana*), and in which a woman's primary mode of religiosity has traditionally been the worship of her husband as her
spiritual lord (*pati*) cannot be expected to pass the acid test of feminist analysis. Yet one still wonders how the presence of feminine
divinity has affected the self-consciousness of the Hindu woman in
the private world of her own inner spiritual life. To be sure, abuse,

neglect and cruelty continue to pervade the lives of many Hindu women, especially the poor and low-caste. But there have also been women in every era of Hindu history who have left an indelible mark on the religious legacy of India. How were these women luminaries able to circumvent or subvert the orthodox institutions which governed all social behavior? How did they succeed in setting their own course and mapping their own spiritual destiny? I would suggest that it was their self-understanding that set them apart from other women. It was their ability to interpret their own relationship with female divinity as one of identity which often enabled them to go beyond the boundaries of normative religious and social behavior for Hindu women. It is my contention that the availability of models of the divine feminine has been instrumental in the emergence of female spiritual adepts throughout Hindu history.

While Hindu goddess worship in general does not seem to have explicitly endowed the human female with greater authority or autonomy, the ubiquitous presence of female deity has colored the notion of Hindu womanhood in subtle ways and has led to an identification with the celestial feminine on many levels. Some of the ways in which Hindus relate women with goddesses are not in keeping with Western feminist concepts of female power and autonomy. For example: every Hindu wife and mother is explicitly referred to as the 'Lakshmi of the house', Lakshmi being the devoted and subservient wife of the God Vishnu, as well as the goddess of good fortune. A loyal, self-sacrificing wife is identified with Sita, the long-suffering wife of the god Rama; a widow about to commit *sati* is considered the goddess Sati incarnate and, in a reversal of cultural norms, her elders touch *her* feet and request *her* blessings. Other forms of identification between woman and goddess, however, reflect a profound degree of self-assurance and independence that mirrors contemporary feminist spiritual longings. A well-known example would be Mira Bai; the famed Vaishnava poetess-saint yearned for her beloved Lord Krishna in the mode of Radha, his celestial consort. Tantric *yoginis* (female ascetics) went further still, and identified with the fierce and autonomous goddesses of tantric lore, and thereby felt empowered to diverge from social stereotypes.

Thus, it seems that the problem lies not in the inability of Hindu women to identify with divine models, but rather, in the choice of models. Those women who identified with powerful models were able to subvert orthodox norms, while those who identified with non-autonomous, submissive models were destined to remain in the restrictive social structure.

I would contend that the greatest flowering of women's religious aspirations can be seen in periods of Hindu history which emphasize the divine feminine, and in movements which provide women with maximum access to celestial feminine models. Among these movements, those that were most significantly influenced by tantric theology—which endows the feminine principle with full autonomy and ontological equivalence with (or primacy over) the masculine principle—were the most likely to be amenable to the development of women's religious self-agency and spiritual authority. Conversely, one finds scarce evidence of women of spiritual eminence in Hindu traditions that devalue the feminine principle and emphasize a philosophy of transcendence.

This chapter will attempt to show that there is a markedly positive relationship in Hindu history between the rise of movements that emphasize the feminine divine and the emergence of female religious teachers and preceptors. Further, I will place special emphasis on tantric sects since it is here that one finds the greatest number of women who were not only spiritual adepts, but whose lives shatter the stereotypes of submissive Hindu women. Finally, we will examine, from the perspective of women's status, the difference between conventional, temple-centered, priest-mediated worship of the Great Goddess, and personal worship and communion based on a theology of identification.

Identification and Realization: The Importance of Feminine Divine Models

In the early vedic period, women were active participants with their husbands in the sacrificial rites and rituals that were the foci of vedic religion. During this period, great importance was attached to the notion of the 'complementarity of male and female roles for the wellbeing of the family, society, and cosmos' which was reflected in the 'idea of the divine couple' (Young 1987: 100). Religious initiation (*upanayana*) and subsequent vedic studies (*brahmacharya*) were considered necessary prerequisites for marriage (*Atharva-Veda* 2.5.18) for both men and women. The husband and wife were, theoretically, joint owners (*dampati*) of the household and

property, and both partners were equally necessary for full participation in religious rites.

Although the male gods Agni, Soma and Indra dominate the vedic
religion there are numerous passages that invoke the various goddesses of the vedic pantheon. While vedic goddesses such as Sarasvati, Usas, Prithivi, Aditi, Vac and others do not occupy the center
of the textual sacrificial tradition, it is quite likely that they were
central to women's household and riverine rituals, especially if we
consider the divergence between canonical textual tradition and
worship of regional and village goddesses in modern India.

During the post-vedic period, a greater rigidity regarding gender
roles seems to have developed—much to the detriment of women.
From the time of the Brahmanas, there occurs a distinct diminution
in the status of women. There seems to be 'no trace of any great
woman in the desert of desolate theological speculation of the
extensive Brahmana literature' (De 1982: 138). And in the entire
corpus of upanishadic scripture, only two names merit attention—
those of Gargi and Maitreyi. This period saw the rise of the ascetic
tradition which excluded women and identified them with sexuality, impurity, desire (in its broadest sense), and embeddedness in
societal structures—all of which had to be renounced by the *moksha* (liberation)-seeking ascetic.

At this time, the pure (*shaucha*)/impure (*ashaucha*) dichotomy
grew in importance, with women increasingly perceived as impure,
especially during menstruation, and the period following child-
birth. During these times of impurity, women were barred from
participation in religious rites. The adverse effect on the status of
women from the loss of the opportunity for religious education and
resulting social demotion was now compounded by the increasing
ascendancy of the ascetic ideal.

The earliest systematized elaboration of ascetic disciplines was
the *Yoga Sutras* of Patanjali (c. 200 CE). Patanjali uses the ontology
of the Samkhya system which posits two ontological principles:
purusha and *prakriti* (spirit and matter). Suffering arises because
individuals identify the self with the body-mind complex (the realm
of *prakriti*); freedom from suffering is achievable by an inner realization of the self as *purusha*, eternally pure and free, attainable
through the complete disjunction of the self from this body-mind
complex which is manifest material nature—i.e. the feminine prin-

ciple. The phenomenal world, its activities, life forms and material substance are all manifestations of *prakriti*. The fabric of *prakriti* is woven with the three essential characteristics of matter (the *gunas*): *sattva* (luminosity, purity), *rajas* (passion, dynamism), and *tamas* (inertia, darkness). The goal of Yoga is to strengthen and enhance the *sattva guna* while diminishing the prevalence and influence of the *rajas* and *tamas*. The diminution of the *rajas guna* is a particularly daunting task since it involves the taming of the passions, emotions and all desire—considered the arena of the feminine, and symbolized by women. Patanjali's worldview afforded ample opportunity for the development of a discriminatory perspective on women due to their biological functions (Sherma 1999) .

Throughout the post-vedic era Hindu religious life has developed in two spheres: *dharma* (duty to family, social class, and world), which governed the life of the householder, and *moksha*, the aim of the renouncer-ascetic. The concept of *varnashrama-dharma* (one's dharmic duty according to caste, stage of life, and gender) eventually came to be foundational to the Hindu way of life, resulting in a rigid demarcation of gender and caste roles and undermining opportunities for religious autonomy for women and lower castes. As we have seen, the emergence of the renouncer tradition, with its emphasis on asceticism, had already diminished women's status.

The *bhakti* (devotional) movement, which began with the classical era, saw a popularization of accessible models of the feminine divine. *Bhakti* implied the devotional ritual worship of, and an intense, passionate longing for one's chosen deity (*ishta devata*, usually a form of Shiva or Vishnu), without requiring severance from normative societal obligations. *Bhakti* attempted to reconcile the familial religion of the Vedas with the aim of mystic union found in the ascetic traditions. With the advent of *bhakti*, new avenues of religious expression opened up for women; history records the emergence of numerous women saints belonging to the *bhakti* schools (*sampradayas*). For women, who already tended the family altar, *bhakti* was a convenient path for religious self-expression.

In *bhakti*, the revitalization of the 'divine couple' provided a structure that was conducive to women's identification with the feminine half of the celestial couple which had been so prevalent in vedic times. This, combined with an emphasis on an intensely personal and emotional form of worship, provided women with an outlet for intimate—and independent—connection with deity. Female *bhaktas* often expressed the desired mystical union with their chosen deity in rapturous prose redolent with erotic imagery. The deity, whether a form of Vishnu or Shiva, was most often cast in the role of celestial husband or lover. The intense longing of the devotee for the chosen deity was the longing of Parvati for Shiva; or the yearning of Radha for Krishna.

However, while *bhakti* brought with it a release from gender constraints for religious practice and affirmed family life as compatible with spiritual endeavor, it often continued to uphold the institution of *varnashrama-dharma*. The *smriti* literature, foundational to Hindu codes of conduct, recognized only *stri-dharma* as the proper duty for women. *Stri-dharma* stipulates that the focus of a woman's entire religious devotion should be her husband/*pati* (Lord). Her domestic chores, the bearing of children, prayers for the well-being of the husband, were all seen as devotional service to her *pati*. In essence, he was her human *ishta devata*. This was seen as problematic by women who wished to embrace the devotional path (*bhakti-marga*) and follow it to its logical conclusion, that is, complete mystic absorption in the divine embrace of their sole beloved, the celestial Lord, the 'true' *ishta devata*. Such devotion, however, could be considered contradictory to the tenets of *stri-dharma* since it could undermine a woman's loyalty to and ability to perform *seva* for her earthly lord, the husband. For some of the poetess-saints of the classical and medieval period, the conflict between *stri-dharma* and *sva-dharma* (duty to self) was irreconcilable.

For female Vaishnavite mystics (those who worship the god Vishnu), the problem was compounded by the fact that Vaishnavism strongly upholds *varnashrama-dharma* and elevates *stri-dharma* to celestial proportions—Lakshmi, the consort of Vishnu, is the model of a subservient Hindu wife. Sita and Radha, the ever-devoted consorts of Vishnu's two major incarnations, Rama and Krishna respectively, certainly do not offer liberating models of feminine self-determination. The absence of autonomous models of the divine feminine and social pressures to conform to *stri-dharma* placed obstacles on the path of Vaishnava women *bhaktas*.

Women saints of the Shaiva tradition (worshippers of the god Shiva), however, were often able to subvert the social norms of *stri-dharma* with less struggle by identifying with the strong and autonomous divine feminine models of Shaivism. This, as I will show, was due in large part to the Goddess theology (*shaktivada*) of the *tantras* that has greatly influenced Shaivism. It encouraged women's spiritual aspirations and respected the self-agency of women sages (Gupta 1991).

The Virashaiva dictum '*Sarana sati, Linga pati*' (the devotee is the wife, Shiva is the husband) reflects an emphasis on the feminization of the devotee and an identification with Shiva's *shakti* which made the role of *sarana* a completely natural path for women, where female gender is not a hindrance, but an asset. The Kashmiri Shaiva *yogini* Lalla Ded reveled in the freedom of a life absorbed in Shiva and as a wandering ascetic, roamed about unencumbered by clothes, which, for her, symbolized attachment to ego-consciousness (i.e. social approval/disapproval). Lalla describes her own ecstatic spiritual experience as follows:

> Passionate, with longing in my eyes, searching wide, and seeking night and day, Lo! I beheld the Truthful One, the Wise (Shiva). Here in mine own house to fill my gaze! (Ghanananda and Stewart-Wallace 1979: 45).

As we have noted, Vaishnavite women *bhaktas* often had to overcome great obstacles to obtain the freedom to live as they pleased, and faced considerable pressure to remain within the confines of the traditional social structure. This is evidenced by the initial harassment faced by Mira Bai and the difficult compromises accepted by Bahina Bai and others. In contrast to the obstacle ridden environment that faced most Vaishnava female mystics, medieval Bengal Vaishnavism provided more amenable circumstances for the emergence of women *acharyas* (religious teachers) and *gurus* (spiritual preceptors). The growth of the cult of Radha as a divine feminine principle in medieval Vaishnavism was foundational to the emergence of Vaishnava women of spiritual authority.

The concept of Radha was not clearly developed in the *Bhagavata Purana* (c. tenth century CE), but by the time of the *Gitagovinda* of Jayadeva (c. twelfth century CE), Radha had been established as a prime focus of Vaishnavism. The fully developed concept of Radha is the hallmark of the Vaishnava movements founded by

Nimbarka, Vallabha, and most importantly, Chaitanya. Sukumar Sen notes the significance of the rise of Radha in Chaitanya's movement:

> Chaitanya's faith put new life into the people, and by raising the position of Radha above that of Krishna (in popular devotionalism), *it indirectly put a premium on the merit of womanhood as such*. It is no wonder that from the middle of the sixteenth century, women spiritual leaders or gurus made their sporadic but unmistakable appearance in Bengal Vaishnavism (Sen 1982: 373) (Italics mine).

The first two Vaishnava female *acharyas* in Chaitanya's movement were Jahnava, who had the vision and leadership to strengthen relations between the Bengal movement and the Vaishnava leaders (*goswamins*) of Vrindavan, and Sita, the wife of Advaita (a leader of Bengal Vaishnavism following the death of Chaitanya), who was the *de facto* leader of the movement even during her elderly husband's lifetime and possessed a large school of devotees in her own right (Sen 1982: 369-77). Other women *acharyas* in the movement include Ichchadevi, who wrote devotional verses and sermons in Bengali, and Hemlata (c. 1600 CE), one of the most important women in late medieval Vaishnava history, who was involved in the esoteric Vaishnava Sahajiya movement. We will later discuss the influence of Tantra on this movement.

Thus, from the early to the late medieval *bhakti* period, the inclusion and elevation of the feminine divine was foundational to the fulfillment of women's religious aspirations. As we shall see, however, nowhere is the autonomous and powerful presence of female divinity more pronounced than in the theology and soteriology of Hindu Tantra; and nowhere is the identification between woman and Goddess more explicitly affirmed than in the sacramental rituals and meditations of the tantric tradition.

The Tantric Paradigm

The texts of Tantra evince an attitude of reverence towards women inasmuch as they enjoin the worship of women as representations of Shakti, free women from the religious restrictions imposed by the purity/impurity dichotomy, accept women aspirants on the tantric path, and acknowledge the right of female gurus to confer *diksha* (initiation). However, the tantric texts are written by males for males and, consequently, manifest an androcentric viewpoint.

The presence of this male-oriented perspective has led some scholars to conclude that female spiritual empowerment and tantric practice are incompatible, that women in Tantra are only instruments for the furtherance of male religious goals, and that 'For the *tantrika*...physical women are merely spiritual batteries...' (McDaniel 1989: 274). This view is not shared by all authorities on Tantra and is not borne out by a hermeneutical approach that takes a female aspirant's perspective into consideration. Nor is it supported by the numerous references to women's initiation in the tantric texts, or by the existence of female tantric adepts, past and present. To understand the tantric perception of the nature of the feminine, it is necessary to first explore the tantric conception of the divine feminine. We therefore begin with an examination of the notion of Shakti, the feminine principle in Tantra. In order to delineate Tantra's unique viewpoint, I have juxtaposed the normative Shakta (tradition of the Great Goddess) notion of the Devi—as epitomized by the *Devi Bhagavata*—with the tantric perspective on the same.

The Concept of *Shakti* in Tantric Theology

The concept of *shakti* is found as far back as vedic literature, but *shakti* as a fully systematized cosmogonic and cosmological feminine principle arises primarily on the margins of orthodox vedic-Brahmanical tradition, in the tantric and Shakta scriptures. Pintchman (1994: 97-98) identifies three primary foci in the development of the *shakti* concept: (1) a creative ability, perceived as feminine and described as the consort or aspect of a male divinity; (2) the notion of a cosmogonic power possessed by a single, supreme being, signifying creative ability but not necessarily identified as female; and (3) an all-pervasive divine power inherent in creation.

These various perspectives on *shakti* eventually fused and gave rise to the notion of a female divinity who represented the power of her divine male consort to manifest the cosmos. The further development of the principle of *shakti* into the Great Goddess first occurs in the sixth-century text *Devi Mahatmya* or 'Glorification of the Goddess' (Coburn 1991), encased in the *Markandeya Purana*. In the *Devi Mahatmya*, various conceptions of the feminine principle (*prakriti, maya, shakti*) combine with the notion of an ultimate reality to create a Great Goddess who is the power inherent in creation and dissolution, the primordial material substance (*mula-prakriti*), as well as the creative impulse, formless yet the matrix of all forms, transcendent as well as immanent. In this text, many mythic representations of female deity are merged into the Great Goddess as her aspects.

Thus, in the *Devi Mahatmya*, the distinct theologies of regional goddesses melt into the universal theology of the Great Goddess. An important development in this text is its departure from the normative understanding of *shakti* as an aspect of a male supreme divinity; here, the feminine principle has self-agency and complete autonomy. She is not merely the power of the Absolute, She *is* the Absolute. While the entire cosmos is the material form of the Goddess, she is specifically identified with women (v. 11.4). However, this identification was not emphasized in the Shakta tradition. While the emergence of the Shaiva *bhakti* movement allowed women a certain degree of spiritual self-agency, the Shakta tradition (devotionalism directed towards Shakti) developed into a male-dominated sphere. It is only in Shakta-tantra that the Goddess–woman identification is stressed, and women's right to religious self-determination is affirmed. As Payne noted, Shaktism and Tantra form 'two intersecting but not coinciding circles' (Payne 1979: 72).

Tantric theology is undergirded by the concept of *Shiva-Shakti-samarasa*, the masculine and feminine principles in a state of primordial, transcendent, blissful unity. With the first creative impulse, there arises a determination (*samkalpa*) which is the first vibration of Shakti and disturbs the primal quiescence. Shakti then awakens from her absorption in the unified state and develops the triple functions of will (*iccha*), knowing (*jnana*), and activity (*kriya*)—represented symbolically by the three corners of the *yoni*, an inverted triangle which is the symbol of Shakti. Shakti, having awakened from a state of pure potentiality to one of active cosmogenesis, undergoes several devolutions in the process to become *maya-shakti* (the power of differentiation and veiling), *chit-shakti* (the power of consciousness), and *prakriti-shakti* (the primordial material substance of the universe). Thus Shakti is not only the morphogenic matrix of creation; she *is* creation—both the process and the product. But in union with Shiva, she is also the ground of the Absolute from which the process emanates.

S.B. DasGupta (1982: 72-73) has identified three viewpoints on the relationship between Shiva and Shakti: (1) that Shiva and Shakti are two aspects of the same truth—static and dynamic, transcendent and immanent, male and female, and absolute reality is a state of unity between the two (*samarasa* or 'one flavor'); (2) that Shiva is the Ultimate Being to which Shakti eternally belongs, but nevertheless, neither is real without the other; Shiva is *shava* (a corpse) without the dynamic power of Shakti and she has no existence without Shiva; and (3) that Shakti is the highest truth, and Shiva is merely her support—she is the ultimate power of which he is merely the container (*adhara*), her male aspect. It is in this third aspect that she is often referred to as Lalita Devi (in the *puranas*) and Tripurasundari (in the *tantras*). The Shaiva *agamas* tend to support the second viewpoint and the Shakta *tantras* present either the first or the third perspective.

Since the power of Shakti is conceived of as feminine, her different aspects are meditated on as female deities, also known as the *Mahavidyas*. Each *Mahavidya* is a goddess with her own system of ritual, a particular *mantra* (her specific energy in the form of sound), and *yantra*, which is a geometric representation composed of triangles with a distinct design for each deity, representing the three functions of Shakti as well as the *yoni* (womb, vulva) of the genetrix of the universe.

Shakti permeates the universe and as *kundalini-shakti* she is immanent in the individual as life force and latent spiritual consciousness coiled and dormant in the subtle or etheric body at a location corresponding to the base of the spine in the gross or physical body. When the *kundalini-shakti* is fully awakened and ascendant, the life force of the aspirant unites with the higher self—that is, self-realization occurs. This ascent of the *kundalini* towards the higher levels of consciousness is visualized in tantric *sadhana* as the journey of Shakti towards union with Shiva. Thus, the final realization is seen as the blissful embrace of Shiva and Shakti (*Shiva-Shakti-samarasa*). This pairing of opposites is common in tantric ritual visualization and forms the basis of tantric attitudes towards gender.

In puranic Shaktism, this bipolarity is not emphasized to such an extent. In major puranic texts such as the *Devi Mahatmya*, or the *Devi-Bhagavata Purana*, the Supreme Being, though represented

as female, actually contains both male and female. This is evidenced by certain epithets used to describe the Goddess such as
virya (lit. virile), *bija* (usually used to denote the male 'seed'), *tejas*
(a luminescence that is often associated with males and the reten-
tion of *ojas* or semen, and a corollary development of *sattva*) and
so forth (*Devi Mahatmya* 11.4). In the *Devi Bhagavata*, the Goddess declares:

> Think over what it meant, fool, when you said I have the nature of a
> woman (*stri-svabhava*). I am not a man (*puman*) [in appearance]
> but I have that nature [i.e. male nature], having donned the guise of
> a woman (10.32-35).

According to the commentator Nilakantha, the Goddess is not denying her aspect as *prakriti* (feminine principle as materiality) in this
verse, but affirming her own nature (*svabhava*) as containing both
masculine (*purusha*) and feminine principles.

To be sure, when the Absolute is envisioned as one supreme
being, it is appropriate for this principle of highest reality to encompass all dualities, including gender. But this transcending of gender
by the Goddess—when she is perceived as the sole reality—effectively subsumes the feminine under the rubric of the neuter. Moreover, the neuter is often presented in masculine terminology, as I
have shown above, and in the *Devi Bhagavata* (XII.14.24-25) the
spiritual status of women becomes even more tenuous since the
Goddess advises that women and *shudras* should only hear the text
from the mouth of a *brahmin* and never recite it themselves.

Tantric theology, on the other hand, approaches the notion of
the feminine principle in a different fashion. The Samkhyan conception of the masculine principle as a transcendent witness, and the
feminine principle as the immanent, material cause and substance
of the cosmos, is retained. However, unlike Samkhya, which views
purusha as conscious and *prakriti* as unconscious (*acit, jada*),
Tantra endows both principles with consciousness and, at the highest level, unifies them as the ground of ultimate reality. But, unlike
the unitary supreme being of the two Shakta texts mentioned above,
Tantra posits a bipolar supreme reality (Shiva and Shakti) in which
all pairs of opposites—including gender—are seen as manifestations
of the two principles. Thus, the two genders are neither diamet-
rically opposed dichotomies (such as female = weak, male = strong),

nor merged into a distinction-negating unity, but affirmed as a manifestation of either Shiva or Shakti.

As a result, the male aspirant (*sadhaka*) does not feel the discomfort and ambivalence that he clearly seems to feel in Shaktism about the existence of a supreme divinity who is represented as female. In the tantric ethos, he can visualize himself as Shiva, though his spiritual awakening is only complete when he recognizes and integrates the masculine and the feminine—both of which are within him. On the other hand, the envisioning of the Absolute not as bipolar, but only as feminine, seems to produce various forms of anxiety in the non-tantric male worshiper. As C. Mackenzie Brown observes:

> [there is] a traditional masculine bias and a fear of women, especially of their sexual, reproductive, and erotic powers. While the composer of the *Devi Bhagavata* is willing to explore in depth the erotic play of the Devi with the demons, he is generally unwilling to allow himself to approach the Goddess except as a child, and even then, not so much as a suckling infant, but as an older child whose mother keeps her breasts well-covered (Brown 1990: 200).

A negative attitude towards human femaleness is clearly reflected in *Devi Bhagavata* verses IV.2.18-26, for example, which describe the womb as a hell, where the fetus must hang head down, entombed in feces and urine, eating and drinking the same, tortured by worms, and so forth; in verse III.20.35, 37, the term *svabhava* (inherent nature) refers to female nature (*stri-svabhava*) which is then described as reckless, foolish, deceitful, and cruel (see Humes, this volume, for an analysis of the distinction made by male Shaktas between the femaleness of the Goddess and the female nature of women).

There seems to be little doubt that there was a sharp delineation in the minds of male Shaktas between the feminine divine and the human female. But how did women Shaktas see themselves in relation to the Goddess? Since the textual and commentarial tradition was in the hands of male scholar-priests, it certainly cannot be expected to yield testimony about women's spiritual affiliation with the divine feminine in conventional Shaktism. The scholar, seeking evidence of female empowerment founded on identification with the Goddess, must look at folklore, devotional songs, and poetry to cull glimpses of women's relationship with the Goddess.

Unlike conventional Shakta literature, tantric texts contain numerous references to the initiation of women into lineages, female religious preceptors, and women as embodiments of the Goddess.

The Influence of Tantric Philosophy on Various Hindu Schools

The influence of tantric theology on particular schools is often accompanied by an elevation in the status of women and an advance in female religious autonomy, stemming from Tantra's unequivocal identification between woman and Goddess. We have seen, for example, that Bengal Vaishnavism was notable for its inclusion of women in religious leadership. This development went hand-in-hand with the rise of tantric influence on Vaishnavism in this region, clearly reflected in the Vaishnava Sahajiya movement. Sahajayana was, in fact, a Buddhist tantric school characterized by a thoroughgoing iconoclasm, anti-scholasticism and the belief in the value of the human body, not only as the medium for realizing the highest truth, but as the repository of that truth. The Buddhist Sahajayanists harnessed human nature itself to the goal of realization and thus called their path *sahaja* (natural). The union of two facets of a bipolar reality, the male and female principles, was to be actualized by the union of man and woman, but with the prior knowledge of themselves as *prajna* (wisdom) and *upaya* (skillful means) respectively, combined with the practice of intense and complex mandala visualizations during union. *Prajna* is embodied by every woman and *upaya*, by every man. The bliss obtained from the meditational-sexual ritual was to be transmuted to a profound realization of the emptiness (*sunyata*) of self and all phenomena. N.N. Bhattacharya (1974: 114) notes that Bengal Vaishnavism was significantly influenced by the tantrism of Buddhist Sahajiya, and S. DasGupta maintains that 'A close study of the literature of the Vaishnava Sahajiyas will leave no room for doubting the clear fact that it records...the spirit and practices of the earlier Buddhist and Hindu Tantric cults' (DasGupta 1969: 134-35).

As we have seen, historically many Shaiva sects have proffered amenable circumstances for the emergence of female spiritual adepts. And it has been the ability of Shaiva women to identify with the *shakti* of Shiva, as envisioned in tantric literature—independent and self-willed—that provided the basis of their religious autonomy and leadership. The Shaiva understanding of *shakti* is significantly influenced by tantric literature and practices. To be sure, the Shaivas perceive Shiva as the supreme reality, but his *shakti* is more than a mere aspect or a power. Ultimately, the ground of the Absolute is the blissful union of Shiva and Shakti. Thus, Shiva and Shakti are ontologically equivalent but in some branches of Shaivism, Shakti has iconographic and ritual prominence. Dyczkowski has observed that:

> The *Saivagamas*, even those most Saiva-oriented, accommodated within themselves the concept of Sakti. This trend developed within the *Saivagamas* towards such a female-oriented view that at a certain stage…the *Saktatantras* took over (Dyczkowski 1988: 13).

Another important medieval esoteric sect which was significantly influenced by Tantra was the Nathism of the Kanphata *yogis*. The Nathas had a great impact on the development and survival of hatha yoga. The roots of Nathism may lie in indigenous goddess-worshiping sects:

> The origin of Nathism is covered with mystery. Fragments of medieval Natha literature are preserved in [the] Bengali language, a critical examination of which must show that Nathism was originally a primitive Mother Goddess cult (Bhattacharya 1974: 129).

The Kanphata Natha *yogis* trace the founding of their order to Gorakhnath, who is believed to have composed the *Gorakshashataka* in which Yoga and Tantra doctrines merge. The *Gorakshashataka*, which eventually became one of the major yoga texts of the medieval period, places a great importance on the control and channeling of the breath as life force (*prana*). And, to this end, Kanphata Natha *yogis* place great stress on the purification of the body to better enable the *prana* to flow without obstruction. When the internal *nadis* (etheric channels) are cleansed and pure, the *kundalini* energy (dormant *shakti*) can be aroused by yogic techniques, and channeled to flow freely through the body. The great emphasis on physical purity in the Natha doctrine is a clear indication of the influence of Patanjali's *Yoga Sutras*. But unlike the *Yoga Sutras*, Gorakhnath's aim is not a negation of and disassociation from the body, but the divinization and transmutation of the body and its physical functions through the arousing and channeling of the immanent feminine principle—this reflects the tantric perspective.

Keeping in mind that Gorakhnath's teachings drew on ideas from classical Yoga as well as Tantra, we can begin to examine the Natha perspective on women. Although women's purity was viewed as lower than men's in the *Gorakshashataka*—as in the *Yoga Sutras* —Natha women still received initiation, had ascetic orders of their own, and could embark on the *yogic* path whether they were unmarried, married or widowed. And, as Coward notes, such an initiation afforded Natha women 'a higher status than they [women] received elsewhere in India' (Coward 1989: 30).

How can one explain this apparent contradiction in the Natha approach to women's religious status? I would suggest that the tantric heritage of the Kanphata *yogis*, which contains an egalitarian perspective on caste and gender, was able to overcome the extreme inequity inherent in Patanjali's *guna* theory on which the *yogic* emphasis on purity is based. The tantric heritage of the Nathas is also evidenced by the Natha rejection of caste and their practice of partaking of meals in assembly. Such intimate concourse with others would be anathema for the strict followers of the *Yoga Sutras*, due to the contact with impurity that such involvement with others would bring.

The tantric perspective on gender and caste is summarized in this warning from the *Mahanirvana Tantra*:

> That low Kaula [a Kula tantric aspirant] who refuses to initiate a *chandala* [a very low-caste person, whose very gaze was thought to be polluting], or a *yavana* [foreigner, lit. a Greek] into the Kula-Dharma [a tantric sect], considering them to be low, or a woman out of disrespect for her, is himself low and goes the downward way (*Mahanirvana Tantra* XIV.187).

Various Kanphata sects also offered women greater freedom in personal life as they sanctioned widow remarriage and allowed divorce at a time that these rights were unavailable to the vast majority of Hindu women (Briggs 1982). Young girls were entitled to initiation at age twelve, as were boys. All of this was a far cry from *stri-dharma*, the horrors of widowhood, and denial of *upanayana* to young girls in orthodox Hinduism.

Yoginis—Celestial or Human?

The term *yogini* can be used to define a human female *yogi* or a feminine celestial entity who is usually an attendant of the Goddess, often in her aspect as Durga. The concept of celestial *yoginis* is of great antiquity. The Jain tradition, which worshiped various groups of goddesses including the *Sasanadevatas*, the *Vidyadevis* (forerunners of the *Mahavidyas* of tantric lore), and the *Saptamatrikas*, also adopted the already-existing cult of the sixty-four *Yoginis* (Bhattacharya 1974: 66). In Sanskrit literature, the *Yoginis* are presented as aspects of Durga who emanate from her and comprise her attendant troops as she battles the demons Shumbha and Nishumbha. Often, the most important *Yoginis* are identified with the *Saptamatrikas*. The period between 700–1000 CE saw the re-emergence of the worship of the *Saptamatrikas* and a corollary rise in the cult of the sixty-four *Yoginis*. Regarding the relationship between human and celestial *yoginis* Bhattacharya maintains that:

> Originally the *yoginis were probably human beings, women of flesh and blood*, priestesses who were supposed to be possessed by the Goddess, and later they were raised to the status of divinities (Bhattacharya 1974: 104) (Italics mine).

As we have seen, human *yoginis* do exist in the Virashaiva and other Shaiva traditions, and Gorakhnath's tantric Kanphata sects have a long tradition of female *yogis*. During his field research on the Kanphata *yogis* in the 1930s, G.W. Briggs observed that:

> Women who have been initiated into the sect are numerous. Those who are wives of *yogis* are of two classes, those who are themselves *yoginis* [in their own right] and those who are not (Briggs 1982: 48).

Briggs also found that married, unmarried and widowed women had equal access to initiation as *yoginis*. Here, as in the Vaishnava Sahaja and the Virashaiva traditions, the goal of worship is self-identification with the divine feminine. In the case of the Kanphata sect, the aim is the homologization of one's consciousness with the dormant *kundalini-shakti* within—deemed a much easier task if the aspirant is herself female. Briggs (1982: 170) notes that 'the Yogi attempts to identify the self with Tripurasundari (an ultimate form of Shakti) by thinking of himself as a woman'.

Female *siddhas* (adepts) have a long history in the Gorakhnathi sects. The earliest reference to a female Natha mystic is the legend of Queen Mayanamati, a disciple of Gorakhnath, who came to be regarded as a highly advanced *yogini* with mystical insight and magical powers. Mayanamati's son Gopi-candra, guided to the yogic path by his mother, renounced his throne, was initiated by a guru chosen by Mayanamati, and became a legendary Natha *yogi* himself. Here again, the tantric attitude of acceptance towards women is clearly evident.

Although relatively little is known of the lives and teachings of Hindu tantric *yoginis*, there are numerous textual references in the tantras regarding female initiates and aspirants. For example, in the Shaiva *Kaulatantras*, which belong to a broad and important category of tantric scripture, women adepts are considered to be specially revered transmitters of tantric doctrine (Dyczkowski 1988: 63). As the *Tantraloka Tantra* (vol. I, 35, cited in Dyczkowski 1988: 63) states, 'one should place wisdom in the mouth of a woman and take it again from her lips'. The same *tantra* also advises that the lone *yogini* who is a wandering ascetic and can be encountered at sacred pilgrimage places should also be sought out by the aspirant for her wisdom and knowledge regarding esoteric ritual (vol. xib, 19, cited in Dyczkowski 1988: 64). The *Kularatnoddyota* states that the y*ogini* who is the master's (*siddha*'s) tantric consort (*duti*) can instruct the student/disciple in the same way as the *siddha* himself, is his equal in every way and thus is entitled to the same respect (4/30a, cited in Dyczkowski 1988: 64). The *Manthanabhairava Tantra* also asserts that there is no difference between the *yogini* and a male *guru*, and that she is to be venerated as the Supreme Power which bestows the bliss of the innate nature of all things (*sahajananda*), and as the embodiment of the Bhairava's (Shiva's) will (fl. 51b, cited in Dyczkowski 1988: 64). Another text proclaims that the secret of all scripture, the supreme essence of the oral tradition, is on the lips of the *yogini* (*Cincinimatasarasamuccaya*, fl. 14b, cited in Dyczkowski 1988: 64).

The *Krama* school of Kashmir Saivism, which exhibits a distinctly tantric Shakta-orientation (in contrast to systems such as the *Pratyabhijna* and *Trika* which are strongly Shiva-centric), is traditionally thought to have been founded entirely by *yoginis*. As N. Rastogi notes:

> It may not be entirely out of point to connect this tremendous emphasis on the Shakti aspect [in *Krama* schools] with the spiritual activity undertaken by the female preceptors [that is prevalent in the *Krama* lineages]... It is difficult to establish a 'cause and effect' relationship between the Shakti orientations and the early preachings by female ascetics, yet it is a factor to be reckoned with (Rastogi 1996: 4).

The identification between the *yogini* and Shakti is explicitly suggested by the *Tantraloka Tantra* which presents the *yogini* as the
womb from which the enlightened *yogi* is born and her mouth
(source of wisdom) as the *yoni* (symbol of the universal matrix,
womb of the Goddess), the three corners of which, as noted earlier, represent consciousness of Shakti as a triune of will, knowledge and action (*iccha, jnana, kriya*) (Dyczkowski 1988: 64).

Thus, a tradition of enlightened women who acted as preceptors
and revered teachers is textually affirmed by tantric scriptures. That
these women had their own lineages and ascetic orders is evidenced by the existence of two parallel—though interconnected—
schools of the Kaulatantra which are the *Yoginikaula* and the *Sid-
dhakaula* sects. As Dyczkowski observes:

> The *Yoginikaula* is so-called because *yoginis* heard it from Siva's
> mouth and kept it within their own line of transmission. The *Sid-
> dhakaula*…is transmitted by *siddhas*, male counterparts of the
> *yoginis*… (Dyczkowski 1988: 65).

Here again, a profound identification of the human woman (*yogini*)
with the feminine divine model is evinced by the revelation of
tantric esoteric knowledge by Shiva to the *yoginis*. It is Shiva who
is the Lord of ascetics and thus it is he who usually reveals the
tantric doctrines, whereas Shakti—usually as Parvati—is the one
who requests this revelation and receives it on behalf of her 'children' (humanity). The revelation of tantric wisdom to a human
woman (*yogini*) by Shiva renders her divine—on a par with Shakti
as recipient of the tantric doctrine (*Tantrashastra*). This identification with Shakti is stressed repeatedly in tantric texts. The *Kularnava Tantra*, for example, states, regarding the relationship between the male and female aspirants (*sadhak* and *sadhika*), that it
is the *sadhak* who must serve, wait upon and attend to the *sadhika*, for she is the inner Shakti (IV, 52).

The Tantric Perspective on Women

To be sure, Tantra distinguishes itself from other religious sects by
its maverick attitudes towards the forbidden, including sexuality,
and tantric reverence for woman as Goddess incarnate is perhaps
most concretely expressed in *maithuna* (the sacrament of sexual
union). However, sacramental sex, although important for certain

tantric schools, generally represents a very small part of the overall *sadhana* of the aspirant. It is the mastery of yogic disciplines such as *pranayama*, various *asanas*, *mudras*, single-pointed concentration (*ekagrata*), and the intense meditation on the inherently pure nature of all phenomena—due to the omnipresence of Shakti—that form the basis of *sadhana* and allow for the transmutation and divinization of the entire spectrum of embodied experience, including sexuality.

An exclusive focus on the sexual elements of tantric *sadhana* can tend to obscure the foundational philosophical premise of Tantra—a premise that has advanced the cause of women's spirituality far more than have the mechanics of *maithuna*. That premise is the assumption of the radical immanence of the divine, most dynamically manifest in our human embodiment, and least concealed in the feminine form. The belief in the omnipresence of the divine feminine on the physical as well as the spiritual plane has the effect of reversing the anti-embodiment bias so prevalent in the philosophies of transcendence.

Tantric philosophy is based on a valorization of the feminine principle as mutable, morphogenic and material, and it envisions woman as the most natural expression of this feminine principle. But the divine feminine in Tantra is not limited to the maternal or nurturing aspects of the Goddess as demure wife of a celestial Lord. Tantra embraces the fierce, majestic, willful, and autonomous aspects of the Goddess and by corollary, allows women access to nuanced and multifaceted divine feminine models.

The Brahmanical tradition and the ascetic schools used, as their major tool for the suppression of women, the purity/impurity polarization. Another point of departure for the ascetic tradition's denigration of women was the 'problem' of female sexuality. The eschewal of all contact with women—who represented a danger to male vitality (*tejas*), the restrictions of family life, the dangers of impurity, and also symbolized carnality—became pivotal for the successful practice of ascetic disciplines. Since physical purity-consciousness (*sauca*), and the negative view of embodiment and sexuality that characterized the renouncer tradition, had such a negative impact on the lives of women, we will examine tantric perspectives on these issues and the resulting difference in attitudes towards women.

One belief firmly embedded in the orthodox consciousness was the notion that the loss of semen entailed the loss of vital energy which could have been used instead for spiritual ascension (see Coward 1989: 29). In Tantra, however, if sexual union was accompanied by ejaculation (which was not always the case, since the purpose was existential realization of oneself and one's partner as Shiva–Shakti, i.e. union as meditative action, not sexual pleasure) it was considered to be analogous to the vedic sacrifice. The vedic sacrifice involved the pouring of oil or butter on to a sacred altar fire, in which other things may also be offered, received by the purifying fire (Agni) and transmitted to the gods. The symbolism of the tantric identification of vedic sacrifice with ritual sexual union is elaborated by P. Rawson:

> Tantra equates the male ejaculation with the oil poured out; the friction involved with the rubbing of sticks to light the fire; the vulva of the female adept...with the altar on which the offering is poured; the fire with the enjoyment, and the woman with the Great Goddess (Rawson 1978: 31).

Such a conflation of the highly sacred concept of vedic sacrifice and the polluting act of sexual intercourse would be anathema to traditional Hindu mores. Tantric texts often seem to target orthodox concepts of purity and impurity for ridicule, in an attempt to emphasize the tantric dictum that 'for the pure, all things are pure'.

The tantric viewpoint on embodiment is distinctly different from other Indian traditions. A primary characteristic of tantrism is its anti-speculative and anti-ascetic stance which stems from a reification of embodiment as the phenomenal form of the noumenal. It is not only the vehicle for realization, it *contains* the truth that is to be realized. Saraha, the great *siddha* of Sahajayana—the Tantric Buddhist sect that profoundly influenced later Hindu Tantra—extolled the body in the exuberant style of the *sahaja yogis*:

> Here [within this body] is the Ganga and the Jumna... Prayaga and Benares—here the sun and the moon. Here the sacred places, here the *Pithas* and the *Upa-Pithas*—I have not seen a place of pilgrimage and an abode of bliss like my body (DasGupta 1969: 103).

The *Kularnava Tantra* unabashedly mocks the ascetic lifestyle, declaring that those who think that freedom can be achieved by 'punishing the body' need to ask themselves whether 'asses and (other animals)...who go about naked', homeless, and covered in mud, become *yogins* thereby? The text continues, 'Truly, such privations are for deceiving the world' (IV, 52). In Tantra, purification does not consist of elaborate ablutions, pilgrimage to purifying sites, and extreme measures for cleansing the 'impure' body. Rather, it consists of the experiential realization of the inherently pure, divine nature of the body and indeed, all things.

Thus the purification referred to in tantric texts involves a multi-layered visualization process whereby the aspirant envisions the presence of the divine Mother in every part of the body/mind complex (*bhuta-suddhi*). Since women are Shakti incarnate, their self-identification with the inner Shakti is considered easier and more natural. According to the *Aharabheda-Tantra*, 'One may be a *vamacari* [left-handed tantric] only if one can worship *vama* [in the *vama* style] being oneself a woman' (in *Karpuradi Stotra*, 8).

Sir John Woodroffe suggests that this is on the principle that

> a worshiper should always be like the object of his worship. Woman is Devata, and the embodiment of the Supreme Shakti, and is as such, honored and worshipped, and is...never [to be] the subject of enjoyment (in *Karpuradi Stotra*, 8).

The female body which, according to orthodox norms, is the epitome of impure materiality, becomes, in Tantra, the highest means for realizing wisdom—both for the woman herself and for her spiritual partner. Her physiological functions and fluids, on which Samkhya-Yoga philosophy projects the imprisoning chains of the lower *gunas* (especially *rajas*) and the stamp of impurity, are envisioned in many sects of Tantra as the material manifestation of the power of the Goddess. The *Yoni Tantra* declares:

> A devotee should worship [offer *puja*] with the *yoni tattva* [female sexual fluids], of the form of the *yoni*, to the deluder of the world (*maya-shakti*), at night when it is full moon, at a crossroads (II.6).

> Having [envisioned] the *yoni*...after bathing and reciting the mantra 108 times, a person becomes a Shiva on earth (II.8).

The *Yoni Tantra* goes on to describe the reverential attitude with which the *sadhaka* must approach the *shakti* (here, the female aspirant or adept) and states that the given mantra must be recited during the entire process of union. The *shakti*'s *yoni* is analogized to the 'great *yoni*' (matrix of the universe) and the *sadhaka* is enjoined to worship her as 'the essence of Devi (Goddess), the Shakti in the form of a *shakti*' (II.10).

Many tantric texts state that the woman who receives this Shakti
puja (she is often called *bhairavi, yogini,* or most commonly *shakti,* indicating in every case an explicit identification with the Goddess) should be the *svashakti or adyashakti* (the *sadhaka*'s wife).
According to the *Kaulikarcanadipika,* 'Without the adyashakti,
worship [becomes] just evil magic' (in *Karpuradi Stotra,* 7). And
the *Kulacudamani Nigama* II.30 describes in detail the worship
of the *sadhaka*'s wife who must be an aspirant herself, and offers
instructions for her initiation if she is not yet a *sadhika.* If the
female participant is *Parashakti* (not the wife of the *sadhaka*), she
must be an adept herself (*adhikari*) and an 'associate in the worship on the principle stated in the *Guhyakalikhanda* of the *Ma-
hakala-Samhita*', which insists:

> As is the competency of the *Sadhaka* [male aspirant], so must be that
> of the *Sadhika* [female aspirant]. In this way only is success attained
> and not otherwise... (in *Karpuradi Stotra,* 10).

Often, tantric texts use *sandhya bhasa* (intentional language) to
convey doctrines in a manner that only the initiated will understand
in order to avoid indiscriminate dissemination of esoteric practices.
In this system, there can exist three levels of meaning: supreme
(*Para*); subtle (*Sukshma*) and gross (*Sthula*). Thus *Parashakti* can
mean a woman other than one's wife, or it can mean supreme
Shakti, that is, the inner Shakti (*kundalini*). This holds true for many
terms used by tantric texts to describe tantric women—such as
dombi (washerwoman) or other low-caste epithets—and this has
led to the belief that lower-caste women were used in tantric rites
for illicit purposes. But such an understanding of these terms does
not take into account the 'subtle' or 'supreme' content of the texts,
and interprets them only at the gross level.

When lower-caste women were involved—and the specific term
was not being used in a metaphorical sense—they were likely to be
sadhikas themselves, since tantric initiation was available to all.
Indeed, it was far more likely that lower-caste women would be
involved in a non-orthodox sect because they would be under far
fewer social restrictions and were likely to be economically independent through a trade. In any case, whatever the background
of the *sadhika,* the honor that was her due did not change. The
Kulacudamani Nigama prescribes the exact procedures for the
worship of the *shakti*s which mirrors the actual ritual worship

(*puja*) of the Goddess, and it states that they should be viewed as the *Matrikas*, each seen as an aspect of the Mother herself. All rules of class and position are cast aside in the *puja* and the 'elder may bow down to the younger, one of superior caste to one of inferior caste, for the *shakti*s [who are being worshiped] are each and all manifestations of the Mother' (III.22-26).

'*Sa Ham*—I Am She': The Self-understanding of Enlightened Women

We have seen how the presence of female divinity has been foundational for the fulfillment of the highest religious aspirations of Hindu women and for the emergence of female spiritual adepts with religious autonomy and self-agency. We have noted that in sects and philosophical schools that have not emphasized—or, indeed, have devalued—the feminine principle, Hindu women have been effectively denied access to experiential realization of the self as divine. Traditions influenced by tantric theology—where the identification of the human woman with the Universal Goddess is most explicit—have traditionally offered women the maximum opportunity for the fulfillment of their spiritual potential. Yet the existence of female masters, lineage holders, and tantric adepts, although referred to repeatedly by tantric texts, is still doubted by some.

Nevertheless, the tradition of the *yogini* has lived on and is reflected not only in the lives of tantric adepts, but even in the spiritual self-understanding of female religious leaders of the modern era. From the Bhairavi who initiated Sri Ramakrishna, to twentieth-century women mystics such as Anandamayi Ma, an identification with feminine deity—especially when filtered through a tantric understanding of the feminine principle—has empowered Hindu women and enabled them to break free of the shackles imposed by orthodoxy and orthopraxy.

The 'Theology of Identification'

Contemporary scholarship—including several essays in this volume —has noted that the Hindu perspective on the goddess–woman relationship is quite different from the model that Western feminism hopes to find. Indeed, it is true—as I have attempted to show —that the conventional Great Goddess-worshiping tradition (Shak-

tism) distinguishes clearly between the divine feminine energies of
the Goddess, and the female physicality of the human woman.

The perception of the self as Shakti is based on the *theology of
identification* that is a hallmark of Tantra, but not of conventional
Shaktism. In popular Shaktism, the mode of communion with the
Goddess is of a dualistic nature that entails a relationship of worshiper and worshiped. Textual expertise—foundational to Shakta
worship—is the domain of the brahmin priest. The priest is the
agent of the worshiper and has the ability to translate his or her
requests to the Goddess into the language of ritual; he thus assumes
the agency to mediate the blessings.

Shaktism functions in terms of what I would call a *theology of
reciprocity* which revolves around a reciprocal relationship between
worshiper and Deity. The procurement of various articles necessary
for the ritual invocation of the Goddess, the endowment of gifts for
the use of her priest(s), and the provision of necessary funds for the
proper enactment of her rituals (*pujas*, mantra recitation, sacrificial rites and so forth) are expected to please the Goddess and elicit
general blessings, or specific boons.

In contrast, the tantric ritual performed by the individual worshiper (*sadhaka* or *sadhika*) is designed to evoke a sense of sacred
presence and heighten the awareness of the immanence of Shakti
within one's own mind-body complex. To be sure, tantric ritual is
also used to conjure power and channel it towards particular ends,
but, even here, it is a matter of the evocation of, and identification
with, a divine force that allows for the direction of power towards
a certain aim. All tantric ritual has as its end the empowerment of the
individual through the identification of worshiper and worshiped,
of the phenomenal and the noumenal, rather than the gratification
of a transcendent Deity and the resultant granting of blessings.

The difference in ontological perspectives between the Tantric
and Shakta approaches can be explained as the difference between
a perception of Deity as pure 'Being' in and of itself, immanent in
self and world, and a 'Supreme Being', somehow transcendent and
distinct from self and world. Although major Shakta texts such as
the *Devi Mahatmya* and the *Devi Bhagavata Purana* present an
organic identity between the Devi and the cosmos, Shakta worship—including the Shakta *bhakti* of the modern era—operates in
terms of the conception of Shakti as a Supreme Being, and func-

tions in the mind of the worshiper as the locus of a reciprocal relationship between a finite individual and an infinite power.

As we have seen, a dialectic of identification between self and the Divine is not normative for the Shakta priestly tradition. Nor is it the primary mode of connection in Shakta *bhakti* as initiated by Ramprasad and Ramakrishna, where the relationship is that of Mother and child. But, ultimately, it is the *only* mode of relationship between the human and the divine in the tantric soteriological tradition.

From the viewpoint of scholarship, the conventional priestly tradition continues to be the most visible and accessible form of Shaktism. Here, there is no quarter given to feminist spiritual yearnings. However, we cannot assume that priest-mediated, temple-centered Shaktism is the only form of worship offered to the Great Goddess in the Hindu context. Aside from the tantric tradition, which we have examined, there is (and has been) a vibrant and widespread private worship tradition centered on the Divine Mother. Here, no priestly ordinances rule women's experience of the Goddess. No textual bigotry bars a woman from being empowered by communion with the Divine Mother, no liturgical complexity prevents her from realizing oneness with the Devi. It is interesting to note that the majority of contemporary Hindu women gurus of international status are primarily worshipers of the Great Goddess. Examples of such women gurus who identify with the Great Goddess include Amritananda Mayi, Anandi Ma, Sri Ma of Bengal, Jyotir Ma, and the late Anandamayi Ma. From the plethora of Hindu models of the Supreme Reality, including personal, non-personal, masculine and neuter, these women consciously choose to envision the Great Goddess as the embodiment of the Absolute. Whether intentionally or through the aegis of noetic vision, many of today's women mystics have sought to follow the liberating footsteps of ancient *yoginis* who dared to think themselves divine.

Bibliography

Primary Sources with Translations

Devi Mahatmya
    1991   In *Encountering the Goddess: A Translation of the Devi Mahatmya
                and a Study of its Interpretation* (trans. James Coburn; SUNY Series
                in Hindu Studies; Albany: State University of New York Press).

Karpuradi Stotra
1953   Edited and translated by Arthur Avalon. Sanskrit text with English
              translation. Madras: Ganesh & Co., 2nd edn.
Kulacudamani Nigama
1956   Translated by Arthur Avalon. Madras: Ganesh & Co., reprint.
Kularnava Tantra
1973   Translated by M.P. Pandit. Edited by Sir John Woodroffe. Madras:
              Ganesh & Co., 2nd edn.
Mahanirvana Tantra
1953   Translated by Arthur Avalon. Sanskrit text with English translation.
              Madras: Ganesh & Co., 3rd edn.
Yoga Sutras
1983   In *Yoga Philosophy of Patanjali*. Translated with annotations by
              Swami Hariharananda Aranya. Albany: State University of New York
              Press, rev. edn.
Yoni Tantra
1985   Translated by Lokanath Maharaj. San Francisco: Azoth Publishing.

Secondary Sources

Bhattacharya, Narendra Nath
1974   *History of the Sakta Religion* (New Delhi: Munshiram Manoharlal).
Briggs, George Weston
1982   *Gorakhnath and the Kanphata Yogis* (reprint; Delhi: Motilal Benar-
              sidass).
Brown, C. Mackenzie
1990   *The Triumph of the Goddess* (Albany: State University of New York
              Press).
Coburn, Thomas
1991   *Encountering the Goddess: A Translation of the Devi Mahatmya
              and Study of its Interpretation* (Albany: State University of New York
              Press).
Coward, Harold, Julius J. Lipner and Katherine K. Young
1989   *Hindu Ethics* (New York: State University of New York Press).
DasGupta, Shashi Bhusan
1969   *Obscure Religious Cults as Background of Bengali Literature* (Cal-
              cutta: Firma KLM, 3rd edn).
1982   'Evolution of Mother Worship in India', in Swami Madhavananda and
              Ramesh Chandra Majumdar (eds.), *Great Women of India* (Mayavati
              Pithoragarh, Himalayas: Advaita Ashrama, 2nd edn).
De, Sushil Kumar
1982   'Great Women in Vedic Literature', in Swami Madhavananda and
              Ramesh Chandra Majumdar (eds.), *Great Women of India* (Mayavati
              Pithoragarh, Himalayas: Advaita Ashrama, 2nd edn).
Dyczkowski, Mark S.G.
1988   *The Canon of the Saivagama and the Kubjika Tantras of the West-
              ern Kaula Tradition* (Albany: State University of New York Press).

Ghanananda, Swami, and Sir John Stewart-Wallace
    1979   *Women Saints East and West* (Hollywood: Vedanta Press).
Gupta, Sanjukta
    1991   'Women in the Saiva/Sakta Ethos', in Julie Leslie (ed.), *Roles and Rituals for Hindu Women* (Cranbury, NJ: Fairleigh Dickinson University Press).
McDaniel, June
    1989   *The Madness of the Saints: Ecstatic Religion in Bengal* (Chicago: University of Chicago Press).
Payne, Ernest, A.
    1979   *The Saktas: An Introductory and Comparative Study* (New York and London: Garland Publishing Inc. [1933]).
Pintchman, Tracy
    1994   *The Rise of the Goddess in the Hindu Tradition* (Albany: State University of New York Press).
Rastogi, Navjivan
    1996   *The Krama Tantricism of Kashmir* (Delhi: Motilal Benarsidass [1979]).
Rawson, Philip
    1978   *The Art of Tantra* (London: Oxford University Press).
Sen, Sukumar
    1982   'Great Hindu Women in East India', in Swami Madhavananda and Ramesh Chandra Majumdar (eds.), *Great Women of India* (Mayavati Pithoragarh, Himalayas: Advaita Ashrama, 2nd edn).
Sherma, Rita D.
    1999   'Sacred Immanence', in Lance Nelson (ed.), *Purifying the Body of God: Ecological Concern in Hindu India* (Albany: State University of New York Press).
Woods, J.H.
    1966   *The Yoga System of Patanjali* (Delhi: Motilal Benarsidass).
Woodroffe, J.S.
    1951   *Shakti and Shakta* (Madras: Vedanta Press, 2nd edn).
Young, Katherine
    1987   'Hinduism', in Arvind Sharma (ed.), *Women in World Religions* (Albany: State University of New York Press).

Alfred Collins

Dancing with Prakriti:
The Samkhyan Goddess as Pativrata and Guru

Samkhya is one of the six *darsana*s or 'viewpoints' of orthodox
Brahmanical thought, and forms the theoretical or philosophical
basis of yoga (another *darsana*), the ancient Indian technique of
achieving release from the tangles of life and death (*samsara*)
through meditation and insight. With origins at least as early as the
Upanishads (c. 700 BCE), and the subject of intense speculation in
the *Mahabharata* a few centuries later, the ideas of Samkhya are
ubiquitous in classical Indian thought on cosmology, law, medicine,
esthetics, and philosophy—to name only a few of their instantia-
tions—and were codified at least by the early centuries CE in the
Samkhya Karikas and *Yoga Sutras*. Paradoxically, while Samkhya
understands its central purpose to be a reasoned explanation of
how to escape the round of birth and rebirth, its texts spend most
of their time elaborating a theory of the constitution of the world it
wishes to escape.

Authors from Gopinath Kaviraj to McKim Marriott have noted that
Samkhyan categories are at least implicit (and very frequently explicit) in most texts and practices of Indian culture. Marriott, in fact,
has elaborated or reconstructed on a Samkhyan basis an Indian eth-
nosociology capable of interpreting almost every aspect of life and
culture including, most recently, the 'female family core' (Marriott
1998).

Van Buitenen and others have traced the origins of both parts or
aspects of Samkhya—theory of release and developmental and con-
stitutive theory of the cosmos and society—to the cosmogonic
speculations of the Upanishads where a cosmic giant, a male person sometimes named Purusha or Prajapati, gives rise to the universe by emitting it from his body, often through a self-formulation
or utterance. In one passage, for instance, the sentence 'Here I am!'
(*hantaham*) begins a process that evolves into the world (van Buitenen 1957). The word for 'speech' (*vac*, cognate with English *vocal-
ization*) is in fact personified as the goddess Vac, who appears as

the daughter of the cosmic giant with whom he incestuously generates the world. Having fallen into the process of life, decay and death, the cosmic male seeks a way out, a return to his origins. In Samkhyan cosmological speculations (Upanishads and *Mahabharata*) this takes the form of an effort to turn back the clock, to reverse the process of evolution (*pravritti*) and undo or deny Purusha's relationship with his feminine procreative partner.

Philosophical Samkhya as formulated in the classical texts, especially the *Samkhya Karikas* and *Yoga Sutras*, is a doctrine of renouncers, men who have withdrawn from the world of women and who live, ideally, in forest hermitages where they meditate and practice insight into their true nature—attempting in miniature and internally what Purusha practices on the cosmic plane. We will uncover in this classical, philosophical doctrine of masculine escape a series of paradoxes, the central one being the utter reliance of these males (and their idealized alter ego Purusha) on the very feminine presence they seek to flee. Without the aid of the goddess there can be no release from her world.

The Samkhyan Other

From the perspective of classical Samkhya philosophy, everything we think we do for our own purposes is really done for the sake of another, an Other that paradoxically is our own true self, while the self we think we are and act in the interests of is only a construction of matter and presumption. An Indian sage put it that most of us suffer from a 'slight misunderstanding' about ourselves. Recognizing and overcoming this slight and extremely subtle error is the fundamental aim of the system. Verse 2 of the *Samkhya Karikas* (*SK*) states the goal as *vi-jnana*, 'insight that discriminates' between the true self (*purusha*, literally 'male', an internal, psychological version of the cosmic Purusha) and the multi-leveled, feminine world of psychoid matter called *prakriti*, and claims that *prakriti* functions solely 'for the sake of purusha' (*purushartha*). Although Prakriti is also a frequent name of the Indian 'Great Goddess' (Pintchman 1994), Samkhya would hardly seem in any sense a feminist doctrine since it aims at the male principle's definitive separation or escape from the female into a state of transcendental isolation called *kaivalya* ('aloneness').

It will be fruitful, nevertheless, to undertake a psychological/feminist hermeneutic of Samkhya, seeking beneath the surface of the text for the unacknowledged or unconscious yearnings and ambivalence that animate this long-lived and protean paradigm.

I will attempt to return Purusha and Prakriti to their mythical origins, to treat them as a personal (and properly named) couple rather than simply as abstract metaphysical principles, with the intention of comparing this philosophical dyad to better-known heterosexual pairs in Indian mythology. I will suggest that in both benevolent and aggressive ways Prakriti acts toward Purusha much as goddesses like Parvati, Durga and Kali do toward their divine and demonic male partners, and that the same dynamics are present in epic stories such as those of Nala and Damayanti, Savitri and Satyavan, and the like. To anticipate: the female half of each pair saves the male from falling into narcissism by confronting and seeing through his presumptions. This often necessitates splitting the male into two parts, one of which is killed or devalued so that the other can be redeemed.

Although the Samkhya system claims that Purusha does not 'act' at all, I will try to show that—in the form of a deluded 'stand-in' or double—he does in fact act, becoming engrossed in a misguided effort to assert control over Prakriti. Prakriti's response is to act like an abused and resentful wife. In the end, however, she proves to be a *guru* to her deluded husband, chastising his pretense of mastery and sacrificing herself to teach him who he really is.

In Samkhya, the portion of Prakriti that is organized around our ordinary sense of individual selfhood (the *ahamkara* or assertion of 'I') forms a subtle body (called *linga sarira* or 'sign body') and transmigrates from life to life for the sake of Purusha's enjoyment and eventual liberation into genuine selfhood (*SK* 40-44), which can only be achieved by means of Prakriti's highest faculty, 'insight' (*jnana* or *buddhi*). Although its ultimate aim is Purusha's liberation, the day-to-day life of the ahamkaric subtle body (or the persons it incarnates) consists of a struggle for self-enhancement, pleasure, and the cessation of pain through mastery and possession of parts of Prakriti, which the ahamkaric person lacks. The ahamkaric self is what I have identified as Purusha's stand-in (double). It has or asserts a relative 'masculinity' *vis-à-vis* the remainder of the Prakritic world. When its presumption is successfully imposed, the

world becomes functionally the auspicious—because controlled—
'wife' of this lower male self.

Samkhya's notoriously odd theory of the relationship between
the true and false selves (*purusha* and *ahamkara*) can be approached by way of Heinz Kohut's psychoanalytic self psychology
(1977, 1979), although we will see that it suggests additions to that
theory. For Kohut, the experience of selfhood is always two-sided,
involving both a self (in the narrow sense) and a 'selfobject'. A
selfobject is a significant part of the environment that supports or
detracts from a person's sense of self (which includes such things
as agency vs. powerlessness, pride vs. shame, a sense of orientation
in the social or physical world vs. not fitting in, and so on). The
self–selfobject relationship is pictured by Kohut—and similar ideas
have been developed by Carl Rogers and Jacques Lacan—as one in
which a person's specific self sense is received in the form of an
image 'mirrored' to her or him by others, in the first case typically
by the parents and then by other loved ones (but also—an aspect
neglected by Kohut—by forces hostile to the developing person).
The image is necessarily a partial, distorted or creative—rather than
an objective—reflection of the person's qualities. For example, a
given child could receive an image of himself through his father's
eyes as bright or dull, as a 'good' son or a rival. I have elsewhere
tried to show that the selfobject environment includes internal aspects of the personality as well as parts of the outside world: a
Freudian superego or Jungian shadow or anima are outside the ego
but directly reflect on and affect the ego's sense of its own value,
security, powers and place (Collins 1991a, 1991b, 1992).

Similar to the Samkhyan *linga* body, Kohut posits a relatively
stable self–selfobject nexus consisting of aspects of a person's body
and mind, organized around a certain sense of self—in part mirrored to him or her by the world, in part innate. This structure is
called the *nuclear self*. It is formed as the young child gradually
identifies congruent experiences and the mental and physical facul-
ties that bring them about with its nascent, partly inborn sense of
self. As in Samkhya, there is a lack of awareness that body and mind
are selfobjects, so close is their union with the self.

Most people view themselves primarily as the nuclear self, that
is, as the self half of the self–selfobject complex in which they
actually live, and Kohut himself emphasizes the development and

pathology of an increasingly autonomous nuclear self at the center of a universe of selfobjects. Samkhya, however, reverses perspective and teaches that we egos or nuclear selves are *actually self-objects* and that our real self exists on a higher level. Yoga and Vishnu *bhakti* (devotionalism), for example, agree that the aim and meaning of human life are not found in the human person and her or his everyday identity and experiences: they lie in the inner Purusha and Vishnu respectively. Meditation and worship are ways in which humans act as selfobjects to the divine. On a lower plane, Indian social and political thought often locates the selfhood of a human group, family or community outside most of the individuals who comprise it: typically in a king or other fatherly or quasi-royal person.

Selves (that is, full persons) on all levels are represented in Indian thought predominantly as older males and, as with Prakriti, females (and younger males) tend to surround and support them. This is so in social as well as in philosophical and religious thought. Paul Mus asserts that the structure or pattern of the Hindu self 'has always been pre-eminently sociological: the commanding image is that of the head and center of a closely-knit community' (1962: 605). Similarly, Inden and Nicholas (1977) note that the joint family in Bengal is centered on an elder 'seed male' (named *karta* or 'doer'), a patriarch who is understood in effect as the family's self. The rest of the family, from this perspective, are his supportive adjuncts or selfobjects.

There is, therefore, a fundamental contradiction at the heart of senior male identity: the favored image of selfhood is that of a central or dominant male, yet males seeking this status for themselves directly violate the Samkhyan maxim of *purushartha*, the claim that we are not primary selves at all but only adjuncts of a higher self 'for the sake of whom' we really live.

At whatever level, it is highly dangerous to claim to be a self, yet human existence—especially masculine existence, and to an even greater degree kingly and patriarchal existence—is always touched by grandiosity, deluded in claiming too much individual selfhood and seeking to have this confirmed by others. Most Indian demons are male, and typically their demonhood consists in narcissism, the overweening claim to authority (kingship) over and recognition from the world, especially the social world. Female demons are found in Indian mythology, of course, but like Krishna's murderous wet-nurse Putana who seeks to destroy the divine child with poisonous breast milk, their evil usually does not lie in grandiosity—exaggerated claims of personal power or entitlement—but rather in being bad selfobjects, forces that destroy male selves or render them impotent.

Prakriti as Goddess and Wife

Wives are understood in orthodox, Sanskritic Indian culture for the most part as supportive partners to their husbands—that is, as selfobjects rather than as full selves in their own right. The selfobject nature of the 'good' Indian wife is specified by the frequent description of her as *pativrata*, 'devoted to her lord/husband'. Self-effacement and glorification of the husband—to the point of treating the husband as a 'god'—are not only textual but have been recorded in Indian society by many ethnographers. From this perspective, wives are valued in terms of the benefits and harm they do to their husbands' selves rather than by any claim of their own to independent status.

In what follows, I will look for traces of the *pativrata* idea in philosophical Samkhya. The guiding question, as the title of this paper suggests, will be 'Is Prakriti a *pativrata*?' I will show that in some ways she is indeed like a *pativrata*, an auspicious Hindu wife who gives pleasure to Purusha's ahamkaric double. In another way, however, Samkhya views the goddess as liberator of the male self, Purusha, by taking onto herself and 'seeing through' (*jnana, vijnana*) each male person's blinkered view of himself. Here she is clearly *not* a *pativrata* in the usual sense because she attacks her 'husband's' self image rather than fitting in with and glorifying it.

The central, but only implicit, intention of Samkhya is to reconcile these two, apparently incompatible, sides of Prakriti, which are identified in the text as her functions of 'pleasuring' (root *bhuj-*) Purusha and of releasing him (root *muc-*) from his ahamkaric bondage (*SK* 37). This reconciliation is possible because, as selfobject to Purusha, Prakriti apparently *gives* him the delusive message that he is the limited, self-centered (ahamkaric) person he thinks himself to be. As the giver of the message, Prakriti can change it. She begins this process by making Purusha's stand-in suffer: she causes his environment not to fit (not to 'match', in

McKim Marriott's terms) his egotistical presumptions. As *SK* 1 puts it, it is the experience of the 'threefold suffering' (*duhkhatraya*) that leads to the spiritual quest for a way out—which will be found in the liberating discrimination of the prakritic universe from Purusha. I argue, however, that Samkhyan enlightenment is implicitly more than the isolated—even schizoid—state of affairs it appears, and that Prakriti and Purusha at moments approach a union quite similar to the ambiguous conjunction of Shiva and Parvati, Vishnu and Lakshmi, and so on. Prakriti contains the same internal opposition as these other goddesses: she seems at times—when she gives pleasure—a nurturing 'Goddess of the breast' and at other times—when she is Purusha's liberator and the ahamkaric self's destroyer—resembles a destructive 'Goddess of the tooth' (see O'Flaherty 1980 for these categories). Like these goddesses, her story aims to reconcile and integrate the opposites.

A closer look at Prakriti's role in Samkhya will be helpful. At the beginning of the *Samkhya Karikas* we read, 'because of the torment of the threefold suffering (*duhkhatraya*) [there arises] the desire to know the means of removing it' (*SK* 1). This threefold affliction is glossed by the commentators as that coming from within (such as psychomoral anxieties), coming to one from the ordinary environment (such an injury), and originating in the divine or celestial realm (such as the malefic influence of the planet Saturn). It later becomes apparent that all three forms of suffering involve the mistaken determination by the inner organ of insight, *buddhi*, that Purusha is a self attacked and distorted in his sense of his own reality by bad, destructive selfobjects.

In the beginning, the primordial Prakriti (also termed *pradhana*) is in a condition of equilibrium, the *avyakta* or undifferentiated state. Prakriti's three material constituents, the *guna*s, are stimulated by the presence of Purusha, begin to move or act, and evolve into a cosmos. The evolution is actually a devolution: while the highest constituent, *sattva* (a state of full, secure being or selfhood) prevails at first, there follows an increasing dominance of *rajas* (struggle) and finally *tamas* (state of depression or darkness). As in the Puranic (and Greek) cosmological theory of the four successively declining 'ages' (*yugas*), better states are followed by worse. Fullness of being (*sattva*) is followed by struggle (*rajas*) and finally by dejection and lethargy (*tamas*): the 'full catastrophe' of the *duhkha-*

traya. Viewed from the perspective of a Purusha identified with the *ahamkara*-self and acting in his own self-interest—the core mistake—a state of complacent relaxation in himself is followed by a desperate struggle to define himself and eliminate experiences he does not want to have. This struggle fails and he is left oppressed by the sense that he is nothing but gross, suffering matter. In Kohutian terms, *sattva* is a blissful, though unstable and temporary, state of deep self–selfobject congruency: the world suits us and life is good. Brahma's heaven is an Indian example of a purely sattvic place. *Rajas* is a state of self–selfobject discord where the self violently struggles to subdue an increasingly recalcitrant selfobject world and hold onto or restore *sattva*. Human life is primarily rajasic. But the struggle is doomed to failure because of the error of self-claiming at its heart, and *tamas* supervenes. *Tamas* is a state of complete self–selfobject disjunction, which Marriott calls 'unmatching'. The life of plants and lower animals is held to be maximally tamasic.

With recognition of his suffering (*duhkhatraya*), Purusha 'hits bottom'—to borrow a phrase from the recovery movement—and can begin to let go of his struggles, especially the tamasic sense of exhaustion from the never-ending attempt to construct an impossible selfhood. At this point the process reverses (goes from *pravritti* [evolution] to *nivritti* [involution], to use common Sanskrit terms). Prakriti now asserts her higher nature as a selfobject who knows herself *as* selfobject, and begins the therapeutic process of working 'for the sake of Purusha' (*purushartha*), like a good wife striving to give him pleasant (good selfobject, more sattvic) experiences and also to relieve him of his illusion of exclusive selfhood. Of course it is not Purusha *per se* from whom Prakriti seeks to remove this illusion but Purusha's successively devolving embodiments: 'from Brahma to a blade of grass' (Collins 1991a). She works in inverse order from Purusha's later, grosser, more ignorant, tamasic bodies, through his passionate, warring rajasic bodies, to his more congruent, clear, and self-satisfied sattvic bodies. The aim is to stop Purusha's attempt to find his self by controlling and claiming her.

Prakriti's Dance: Indian Esthetic Theory and *Jnana*

Prakriti the goddess obscures and discriminates. Her highest, original, and final nature is *buddhi*, intelligent discrimination of just what things truly are, and layer by layer she peels away delusion, showing Purusha what he is not. In terms of the second verse of the *Samkhya Karikas*, quoted above, she 'removes' the 'affliction' that she herself brings. This process is a negation of a negation, as the Sanskrit words suggest: the same root *ghat-* is used of Purusha's affliction by the triple suffering and for the act of removing it; an unmistakable reflection of Prakriti's dual role.

Prakriti brings both enjoyment and release to Purusha. The oxymoronic idea of a liberating enjoyment suggests the central concept in much of Indian esthetic theory: *rasa* or 'esthetic bliss'. The deep and authentic enjoyment of great art transcends ego and narcissistic concerns and even gives a 'taste' (the literal meaning of *rasa*) of enlightenment. It can be argued, in fact, that Prakriti liberates Purusha through a quasi-esthetic experience which is imaged in a metaphor at the heart of the *Samkhya Karikas*: Prakriti is like a dancer who dances in order to show Purusha what he is not—and thereby what he is. Implicit here is a different and potentially more authentic sense of what a *pativrata* might be—and the undeveloped germ of gender reciprocity.

Ordinary human emotion disjoints the self and its unity with its world, since it always implies a state of imbalance or unfulfilled potential, a rajasic state or an absence of *sattva*. Abhinavagupta and other Indian esthetic theorists considered that emotional experience was sublimated by art into an essence of itself called *rasa* that points to the self as a whole and has spiritually therapeutic benefits for the patron. Profane emotions tempt Purusha—or his double— to identify with a very narrow, temporary, and ultimately unsatisfying aspect of his experience. They make him more ignorant and their occurrence implies that Prakriti is *not* devoted to his best interests in providing and satisfying them. As an example of this, Mandodari, the wife of Ravana, the demon-king in the *Ramayana*, is not a true *pativrata* when she pumps up the demon's pride by praising his tyrannical prowess.

Why does Prakriti delude Purusha in this way, leading him down the path of self-absorption, conflict, and ultimately the threefold distress before finally cutting through his tamasic darkness and redeeming him? Part of the answer may be that Prakriti is under the influence of the ahamkaric self in whose presumptive glory she participates as a junior partner; she 'identifies with the aggressor' and becomes herself deluded. This cannot be the whole story, however, and Prakriti's actions suggest that she has a second motive, one quite opposed to the first: narcissistic anger and a thirst for vengeance. Prakriti is apparently enraged with Purusha for his failure to recognize *her* wholeness and selfhood and for treating her as merely a receptacle of objects sought by his desires. By glorifying the narcissistic male, Prakriti gives him rope with which to hang himself. As he becomes increasingly demonic, the formerly sweet and self-effacing goddess becomes a warrior wielding a sword of discrimination that cuts off her mate's ahamkaric head. This process is clear in the widespread stories where the goddess Durga kills the Buffalo Demon (and in the Ramayana, where Ravana's determination to make the hero Rama's wife Sita his own is the true cause of his destruction). Samkhya, like many of the stories with which we will compare it, tries to sugar-coat the pill and show Prakriti, in the end at least, as all-good. We must open the system to other Goddess materials to foreground the dark side—dark from the *ahamkara*'s viewpoint—of Prakriti.

To repeat the essential point: implicitly, for Samkhya, the unity of the male self rests on—is communicated by—a genuine and unforced unity of the selfobject world, which is his 'wife'. This unity is called the sattvic *buddhi* or *jnana bhava* (the psycho-existential state of being where insight is dominant). When faced with an incipiently demonic husband who is not willing to recognize *her* unity and to see himself as a subordinate part of it—a husband who clings to the limited, controlling and narcissistic intentionality of the seven lower ways of being or *bhava*s—Prakriti makes him even more one-sided. A bit like the witch in 'Hansel and Gretel', when the stand-in Purusha's ego has grown fat enough, Prakriti cuts it down.

Let us consider the situation from the viewpoint of the personality, body and mind—the embodied ahamkaric self—of an ignorant man in whom wisdom (*jnana*) is arising. Only through his acknowledgment and surrender to the truth that 'I am a selfobject and so am not really "I" at all' can this man's *true* self be realized. In effect, male 'I' acknowledges that 'I' am made of, and so am subordinate to, Prakriti. Because the selfobject function has been identified so strongly as feminine in Indian culture, enlightenment for a man connotes a sex change: the male self being enlightened is as if 'feminine' with respect to the insightful (buddhic) Prakriti who enlightens him. If, however, the stand-in refuses to surrender, his struggle with the higher Prakriti—the goddess as *jnana*—becomes a battle that this limited Purusha must lose.

Significantly, this loss is imagined in other genres as a *sexual* defeat. For example, in several versions of the killing of the Buffalo Demon (*mahishasura*) by the goddess, the struggle is explicitly sexual. In the *Skanda Purana*, the demon is represented as puffed up with *ahamkara* (ego) as he pretends to be the god whom the goddess is striving to win for her husband by practicing austerities in the forest. (This masquerade is a common theme found also in the story of Nala discussed below.) The goddess taunts the Buffalo Demon, 'If you are mighty, then show me your own might. Demonstrate your true womanish nature' (O'Flaherty 1975: 246). The goddess's superior 'masculinity' *vis-à-vis* the demon is clearly imaged in her favorite animal mounts, the 'royal' tiger and lion, which she rides into battle against him.

The sex-role or implied gender reversal points toward a higher unity of Prakriti and Purusha. Prakriti reflects Purusha's selfhood to him and so becomes more like him. She does this in a negative way, through saying and dancing the message, 'I am not, nothing is mine, not I' (*nasmi na me naham, SK* 64). Nevertheless, Prakriti does become like Purusha and even indistinguishable from him: through *jnana* and spiritual practices she becomes unified and unmixed (*eka, kevala*) and gains a 'purity' (*shuddhi, vishuddhi*) equal to Purusha's (*Yoga Sutra* 3.55, *SK* 64). To repeat: Prakriti's role as *purushartha* is to negate herself—including especially Purusha's double who is one part of herself—and so reveal Purusha as he really is. Having denied herself, however, Prakriti receives herself back as a unity paradoxically indistinguishable from Purusha. At this point the ahamkaric stand-in is gone, or has become a devotee of the divine couple, Purusha/Prakriti.

Nala and Damayanti as Ego and Goddess

The story of Nala and Damayanti in the *Mahabharata* is one of the most popular and charming love stories in Indian literature but, as Hiltebeitel (1993) shows, it also touches a fundamental philosophical and psychological nerve. Like other similar stories (for instance, those of Shakuntala and Duhshanta, and Savitri and Satyavan) this is a tale in which a wife saves her husband by recognizing him after he has forgotten his true nature (self). We recognize the same theme from the 'myth' of Prakriti and Purusha.

To summarize the tale: the princess Damayanti chooses her husband in the anomalous ritual of *svayamvara* ('self choice'). Unlike the usual process of an arranged marriage where their families match bride and groom, Damayanti is given freedom to make her own choice. She successfully chooses a mortal king, Nala, although her beauty has attracted a number of Vedic gods and demons who attempt to disguise themselves as duplicates of Nala. From narcissistic rage at being rejected, and in order to gain access to Damayanti, the demon Kali possesses Nala, entering his body and mind, and leads him to ruin. Hiltebeitel shows—and I will simply refer to his demonstration—that Damayanti triumphs over the demon and redeems Nala because she thinks only and constantly of Nala's real self, again discriminating between the true Nala and false images of him. The golden swan that brought Nala and Damayanti together in the first place had assured Nala that 'she will never think of any man (*purusha*) but you'. Nala, as Hiltebeitel points out, is another word for 'man' (it is a variant of *nara*, 'man'), so Nala is the equivalent of Purusha. Damayanti lives, like Prakriti, *purushartha*, or, in her case, *nalartha*, 'for Nala's sake'. Nala himself, however, loses awareness of his true nature when entered by Kali. The Kali-possessed Nala is a close literary parallel to *ahamkara*-possessed Purusha. Nothing goes well for him because he is only masquerading as a self, trying to force the issue as all demons—and ordinary humans—do. Thus the dice disfavor this Nala and he loses almost everything, prefiguring the dice match in which Yudhishthira will lose the Pandavas' kingdom. Nala has no willing selfobjects because he is not really a self. The selfobjects—like Damayanti—love the real Nala, not the man possessed whom I will call 'Kali-Nala'. King Nala's subjects remain devoted to the real Nala but, Kali-possessed, he cannot recognize them. In terms of Samkhya, Kali-Nala—and this is the typical condition of all men in the Kali yuga—is tamasic, deluded and dejected, disjointed and unmatched with his world, ironically because he is part of it yet claims a privileged separateness and entitlement to ownership of the whole, in particular of Damayanti. He experiences the full *duhkhatraya*.

In Kohut's language, Kali is in a state of acute self-pathology. Kohut shows that such disorders of the self always imply a defensive effort to uphold one of two delusive fantasies: claiming either *to do completely without selfobjects* or *to assume sovereign control of the selfobject world*. The philosopher Ramanuja defines egotistical life as the demonic claim to be one's own cause (*Gitabhasya* 4.1-3) and have no use even for God, an extreme example of the first strategy. Nala falls into an inverted form of this delusion: self-hatred. He sends Damayanti away, ostensibly for her own good, claiming to spare her his wretched condition. But this is only *ahamkara* again, Nala's identification with Kali's claim not to need Damayanti if he cannot control and possess her.

The goddess triumphs here as in the story of the Buffalo Demon. Damayanti curses Kali who is inwardly burned by snake venom, and finally Kali-Nala's tamasic disconnectedness shows its true nature: Kali is revealed to be *different from Nala*, who now sees the demon's suffering but no longer identifies with it. *Ahamkara*'s claim to be the Purusha self has been burned away from the real Purusha by Prakriti's discriminating *buddhi*, after which both the goddess and a chastened *ahamkara* point directly to the reality of the self, in our story the true Nala. In this paradoxical realization the man Nala (the *ahamkara*-centered subtle body or *linga sharira*) gains humility in recognizing that he does not know himself; he sees, instead, that *the self knows him* (Hiltebeitel) and that it is first Damayanti—the best part of his lower self or subtle body, in fact his *buddhi*—who first recognizes this and shows it to him. Damayanti as *pativrata* is also her husband's guru. She shows Nala's self to be Purusha.

Implications for Indian Thought

Samkhya's attitude toward the goddess is highly ambivalent. Prakriti is understood on different levels as irrelevant to Purusha, as the source of his suffering, and as the means of alleviating it. Purusha's suffering is most often identified as the result of a demonic, *ahamkara*-possessed way of life that Indian thought has often sought to blame on women or a female principle (Prakriti in Samkhya, *maya* in some forms of Vedanta). Like Adam's futile plea in Genesis, 'the woman made me do it', India recognizes that men are ahamkaric, but finds women responsible for making them so.

The idealized woman, on the contrary, is on the one hand the *pativrata*, the wife whose devotion to her husband creates for him a world attuned to his needs (she brings him enjoyment, *bhuj-*), but also the guru/woman who dissolves his *ahamkara* by showing him that what he most deeply wants is not the limited pleasures intended by his 'fruit seeking' desires (as the *Bhagavad Gita* expresses it) but a world experienced as a cohesive and authentic *whole* and containing as one element of this unity the 'self' he had thought he was. By destroying the one-sidedness of *ahamkara*-centered persons, the higher Prakriti shows Purusha his true world, the only one that brings him real satisfaction, through the taste of himself as *rasa*, in a unified, complete, non-grasping self-acceptance. But Samkhya, like Indian culture and society more generally, was unable to hold this insight. At the very moment of Prakriti's triumph, as she takes on the role of guru to the man lost in the illusion of control (*ajnana*), she becomes otiose. The individual Purusha in fantasy renounces his teacher, the goddess Prakriti, and levitates to an onanistic cubicle of self-satisfaction in the never-never land of isolation called *kaivalya*.

Why are there many Purushas in the Samkhyan model—one for each person, apparently—rather than only one as we might expect given the unity of the enlightened Prakriti? This fact has always been something of a puzzle to Samkhya scholars although most have been content to pass it off as the innocent result of an overriding concern for individual salvation in the system. I suggest, however, that in positing one Purusha for every person (that is, every *man*) Samkhya exhibits another symptom of the same failure that led to isolating Purusha in his ultimate 'aloneness'. *Ahamkara* returns as soon as it is defeated, perhaps chastened and purified but unwilling as always to renounce its presumption of individual mastery.

What we miss in Samkhya is Purusha's acknowledgment of *self in Prakriti* and willingness to be *her* selfobject, her affirming environment, her devotee; a state of affairs for which we could coin the Sanskrit term *prakrityartha*, 'for Prakriti's sake'. The ahamkaric self virtually sees this possibility—is forced to see it—at the moment when he is 'feminine' with respect to Prakriti: the moment when the *buddhi* sees through the putatively 'male' *ahamkara*, when the Goddess cuts off the Buffalo Demon's head, and when Damayanti defeats the demon Kali. Perhaps because of the violence of this

moment, it cannot be held and the male fantasizes himself reconstituted *sans* female selfobject in individual isolation: *kaivalya*.
Although the text does not express the idea fully, the esthetic *rasa*
model present in the *Samkhya Karikas* implies a less traumatic,
more integral, version of the same dethroning of the male ego.

Viewing the relationship between Purusha and his 'double' a little differently, as a type of male–male rivalry, we recognize the
ahamkaric male laying claim to the male Purusha's rightful selfhood
and needing to be put in his subordinate place. This struggle can
occur between 'father' and 'son', with the ahamkaric self in the role
of bad, presumptuous and grandiose son, allowing a reinterpretation along self-psychological lines of the 'oedipal' struggles identified by Goldman (1978) in stories of gurus vs. disciples, Brahmins
vs. kings, and so on.

From the viewpoint of this paper, however, the ahamkaric
Purusha pretender is more likely a bad, tyrannical *father* figure
needing to be chastised or killed, and so redeemed, by his son. It is
significant, however, that in the *Mahabharata* and elsewhere (for
instance the endless god/demon, *deva/asura* conflict in the Vedas
that underlies the *Mahabharata*) male/male conflict is never finally
resolved because no male (or his heirs) is willing to remain eternally in the subordinate, selfobject position. This is one reason that
the goddess is so crucial a figure in Indian thought.

Conclusions

Samkhya both depreciates and idealizes the goddess Prakriti, while
at the same time it attacks the presumption of masculine authority
yet readmits this male ego through the back door of Purusha's escape into individuated isolation. Prakriti is profoundly patriarchal in
nay-saying herself and living for the male's sake, yet she is militantly
feminist in afflicting her ahamkaric 'husbands' with the triple suffering and cutting through their presumptions. Prakriti shows a
subtler and more ambivalent *pativrata* than we are used to, one
who is neither doormat to her husband's sense of entitlement nor,
in the end, attacker of his true self. Prakriti, and Hindu goddesses in
general, represent an epitome of selfobjecthood but also penulti-
mate selfhood; as such, they represent the highest authentic state
attainable by embodied beings such as humans and are models for

men as well as women. Only the passive god transcends the goddess, and any who presume to claim *his* selfhood in the name of a particular person are in danger of losing their heads to lion-mounted Durga's discriminating sword.

Bibliography

Buitenen, Johannes A.B. van
1957   'Studies in Samkhya (II)', *Journal of the American Oriental Society*
            77: 15-25.

Collins, Alfred
1991a   'From Brahma to a Blade of Grass: Towards an Indian Self Psychology', *Journal of Indian Philosophy* 19: 143-89.
1991b   'For Purusa's Sake: Psychoanalytic Self Psychology and the Metaphysics of Selfhood in Indian Thought, Part I', *Mankind Quarterly* 32: 19-42.
1992   'For Purusa's Sake: Psychoanalytic Self Psychology and the Metaphysics of Selfhood in Indian Thought, Parts II and III', *Mankind Quarterly* 32: 177-201.

Goldman, Robert P.
1978   'Fathers, Sons, and Gurus: Oedipal Conflict in the Sanskrit Epics', *Journal of Indian Philosophy* 6: 325-92.

Hiltebeitel, Alf
1993   'Nala's Possession'. Presentation at the Annual South Asia Conference, University of Wisconsin-Madison. Forthcoming as Chapter 6 of *Rethinking the Mahabharata: A Reader's Guide to the Education of Yudhisthira* (Chicago: University of Chicago Press).

Inden, Ronald, and Ralph Nicholas
1977   *Kinship in Bengali Culture* (Chicago: University of Chicago Press).

Kohut, Heinz
1977   *The Analysis of the Self* (New York: International Universities Press).
1979   *The Restoration of the Self* (New York: International Universities Press).

Larson, Gerald J.
1969   *Classical Samkhya* (Delhi: Motilal Banarsidass).

Marriott, McKim
1998   'The Female Family Core Explored Ethnosociologically', *Contributions to Indian Sociology* (NS) 32: 280-304.

Masson, Jeffrey L., and B. Patwardhan
1985   *Santarasa and Abhinavagupta's Theory of Esthetics* (Baroda: Bhandarkar Oriental Research Institute).

Mus, Paul
1962   'Du Nouveau sur RV X.90?', in E. Bender (ed.), *Indological Studies in Honor of W. Norman Brown* (Philadelphia: American Oriental Society).

O'Flaherty, Wendy Doniger
    1975   *Hindu Myths* (London: Penguin Books).
    1980   *Women, Androgynes and Other Mythical Beasts* (Chicago: University of Chicago Press).
Pintchman, Tracy
    1994   'Creation and the Great Goddess in the Puranas', *Purana* 35.2: 146-70.

Lindsey Harlan

Battles, Brides, and Sacrifice: Rajput Kuldevis in Rajasthan

Like members of many other castes in Rajasthan and elsewhere in India, Rajputs worship tutelary goddesses or *kuldevis*, who protect members of a lineage from harm.[1] Rajput men and women understand these *kuldevis* as guardians who have helped protégés for many generations and contributed to the health and welfare of family members. This essay will reflect on and streamline material on *kuldevi* worship I have considered elsewhere, and update those reflections in light of ongoing work.[2] It thus examines the different constructions of goddess protection emerging from the stories related by Rajputs about their *kuldevis*.[3] There are two sorts of *kuldevi* narratives that Rajput men and women generally tell.[4] The first reflects primarily, though not exclusively, the experience of men, whose identity and traditional caste duty are martial. The second reflects primarily, though not exclusively, the experience of

---

1. A *kuldevi* usually protects an extensive kinship unit known as a *kul*, but sometimes a *shakh*, a smaller unit or 'branch' of a *kul*. I am grateful for permission to present material and arguments made previously in Harlan (1992) (©1991, The Regents of the University of California). For detailed explanation of *kul* and related kinship units, and for further information on *kuldevis* in general, see *ibid*: 26-33. The term 'Rajput', literally 'son of a prince', refers to members of the martial caste that before 1947 ruled the vast majority of kingdoms in the area that today constitutes the state of Rajasthan, literally, 'Land of the Kings'.

2. *Kuldevi* narratives are considered more extensively in Harlan (1992: 52-111). My work on heroic traditions appears in Harlan forthcoming a and forthcoming c.

3. For a stimulating treatment of different types of narratives frames, see Handelman (1999).

4. These are not indigenous genres but rather categories reflecting recurrent themes and motifs. The categories resemble those (*puram* [public] and *akam* [domestic]) drawn up by Ramanujan (1986).

women, whose foremost concern is to protect husbands and families.[5] Let us examine these in turn.

Stories Way Back When:
'Historical' Accounts and Rajput Politics

Before independence, most of the kingdoms that later joined together to form the state of Rajasthan were ruled by Rajputs, whom other Rajputs, in one way or another, served. Throughout the history of these kingdoms Rajputs led and manned armies defending and expanding their territories. Today Rajput men continue to abound in the ranks of army and police forces, but some have taken up other professions, ranging from truck driving to farming and commerce. Whatever profession, if any, contemporary Rajput men have chosen to pursue, their identity continues to be informed by various Rajput traditional practices, including *kuldevi* worship. Many of these practices reflect the history of Rajput martial endeavor.

The majority of *kuldevi* narratives that Rajput men tell are overwhelmingly concerned with the foundations of Rajput lines and with the roles *kuldevi*s have played in protecting Rajput geopolitical interests. Wives, who are relatively unconcerned with these matters, often characterize such *kuldevi* accounts as *itihasik*, a term literally meaning 'historical' but which, given the appearances of goddesses in human events (especially battles) we might wish to translate as 'mythical', that is, revealing supernatural or transcendent truth. In such stories a goddess manifests herself to a great warrior at a critical point in history, often just before he is about to wage war. Her appearance inspires this warrior to persevere and succeed in battle, while also influencing the battle's outcome directly: by manipulating events. Typically she hovers above the battlefield as a kite, signaling her support but also demonstrating her lust for blood. She will consume the entrails of those slaughtered. In many such accounts, success in battle will enable the warrior to found a kingdom, which will also mean the establishment of a new 'branch' (generally a *kul*) of the family (cf. Harlan 1992: 26-33). The kinship unit's identity will thus be effected and forever informed by

---

5. On the danger of presuming a male or female voice in narratives and of essentializing Rajput kinship units, see Harlan (1992: 26-33). On female voices, see Doniger (1998: 128-35). See also the preface in Raheja and Gold (1994).

the securing of land, which is divinely sanctioned by a supportive, if hungry, goddess. Later, the *kuldevi* may appear (again, usually in a fierce theriomorphic form) to descendants facing military crises and help them to prosper politically.

When I asked women about *kuldevi* origins and martial engagement, many referred me to men in their family. Nevertheless, many women do know and are able to tell the *itihasik* stories that they consider to be better known and related by their husbands (cf. Harlan 1992: 26-33).[6] Listening to *itihasik* stories, whether told by men or by women, and collecting accounts printed by men in books or inscribed on monuments, I quickly realized that these stories subdivide into two categories, which suggest divergent constructions of *kuldevi* motivation. One category comprises narratives treating lineage establishment and the conquest of territory. In such stories *kuldevi*s appear to men in crisis and help them found a kingdom and dynasty. The other category is constituted by stories that may well involve military conflict, but focus primarily on weddings and dowry, concerns located squarely within the household. Explicitly martial or not, these stories are rife with political implications in that marriage is frequently tied up with negotiations of status and the securing or surrendering of property. Sometimes challenging or substituting for conquest accounts, they make up a minority of the *itihasik* stories and reflect women's experience of marrying into a patrilineal conjugal family as well as such a family's recognition, and at times fear, that wives bring with them unfamiliar traditions, which can destabilize and alter their own way of doing things (*riti-rivaj*).

The *itihasik* categories are well illustrated in the following two accounts of Naganechaji, the *kuldevi* for Rathaur Rajputs, whose principal kingdom was Marwar, that is to say, the area around Jodhpur. The first narrative, which exemplifies the first subdivision, was recounted to me by a prominent Rajput nobleman:

> Naganechaji came with our ancestors when they journeyed from Idar [in Gujarat]. While they were fighting for Nagor, Naganechaji became their *kuldevi*. At Nagana they built a temple for her. She was called Naganechaji—Nagana plus *ish*, 'deity'. She appeared to Cundaji Rathaur, who had prayed to her because he was losing a battle.

---

6.   Women's versions are typically sparsely detailed in comparison with the variants men tell.

She manifested herself as a snake and from then on was always with him.[7] Because of this the Rathaurs were able to conquer Marwar.

Here we have the dominant scenario rehearsed with efficiency. There is a battle march, an appearance blessing the mission, and the inevitable conquest. In a second story of Naganechaji, one delivered by a man but which points toward the experiences and desires of women, a woman's natal household goddess persistently insinuates herself into her conjugal family, the powerful Sisodiya family ruling Mewar, that is, the area around Udaipur.[8]

The story goes that when a Rathaur princess arrived in Mewar to marry the king (Maharana), she found that Naganechaji had hopped into one of the baskets filled with dowry items and arrived with her as a stowaway. Once discovered, the *kuldevi* was sent back by the bride's new family to Marwar, but somehow the goddess made it back to the princess in Mewar. A series of stealthy arrivals and prompt dispatches ensued. Finally, exasperated, the Sisodya family acceded to the goddess's desire and installed her in their family shrine.

Curious about this story, I secured permission to visit the royal family's familial shrine in the Udaipur City Palace. There the Brahmin priest in charge confirmed his knowledge of the story and took out for my inspection an image of Naganechaji, which, he said, remains in a chest except on designated holidays, Bhadva Sudi Satam and Magh Sudi Satam. These holidays are known throughout North India as auspicious days on which women perform *vrats*, vows of fasting that are intended to promote familial health and prosperity.[9]

In this account, no kingdom is conquered, but rather, a bride manages to bring along her protecting deity. Hence, the story has it, a tradition of veneration is transported from father's to husband's house. The insinuation of a natal *kuldevi* into the conjugal family's shrine is represented as a hard fought victory: the *kuldevi* makes numerous circuits before securing her place in the household. Although not usurping the position of the conjugal family's *kuldevi*,

7.   Naganechaji also appears in various contexts as a kite.
8.   For reflection on the preservation of women's ties to natal families in the context of goddess veneration, see Tambs-Lyche (1997: 73-84); Sax (1991: 71-126).
9.   For specific information on these holidays, I thank Mary McGee.

the goddess demands and receives royal recognition. She is incorporated into the family temple, but carefully confined to veneration on days that are of particular importance to women. The limitation calendrically contextualizes the *kuldevi* while subordinating her to Ban Mata, the Sisodiya *kuldevi* venerated by the royal family.

In these two Naganechaji accounts, the conquest of a kingdom by force and the arrival of a *kuldevi* by dowry are not connected. They refer to two separate events, a conquest and a marriage unconnected with that conquest. At times, however, such events coincide, conjoin, or even collide, as they do in a story of Ban Mata's arrival in Mewar. In one variant I received from a Sisodiya Rajput woman, but most elements of which are also well known to other Sisodiya women and men, the Sisodiya monarch ruling Mewar conquers Gujarat and demands a Gujarati princess in marriage. (This demand for the losing king's daughter is a common concomitant of conquest in much of Rajasthani history.) As it turns out, the princess had always wanted to marry the Mewar monarch and had already sent him a love letter. Her *kuldevi* helps her marry him by having him conquer her father's territory. The goddess goes to Chittor (the Sisodiya capital before Udaipur) as a pendant around the princess's neck. She then replaces Kalika Mata, whose imposing temple is to be seen amidst the ruins at Chittor, as the Sisodiya *kuldevi*. Today Ban Mata continues to be patronized at a separate temple in Chittor.

Another instance in which conquest and marriage motifs come together is the arrival of Shila Mata of Jaipur. In the previous story Ban Mata manages to displace Kalika Mata, but Shila Mata never usurps the position of Jamvai Mata, the official *kuldevi* for the Kachwaha Rajputs ruling Jaipur. Rather, Jamvai Mata retains her status but Shila Mata substitutes for her on Navratri, the premier holiday devoted to goddess worship. The reason: Jamvai Mata, whose theriomorphic form is a docile cow, is a vegetarian and cannot receive the blood offerings that are given *kuldevi*s during this festival. An odd Rajput *kuldevi* indeed, Jamvai Mata needs a stand-in to consume the blood of a sacrificial goat (or, years ago, a buffalo, for whom the goat has now become an expedient and inexpensive substitute).

As a result of this goddess substitution and of the prominence and patronage of Shila Mata's temple at the magnificent and bustling fort of Amber (Jamvai Mata's tiny temple rests on a remote ridge near the Rajgarh Dam) many people, including quite a few Kachwahas, think of her as the Kachwaha *kuldevi*. Thus Jamvai Mata's position continues to be contested in a way that illustrates the perceived power of brides to influence the religious life of their conjugal families. Like the famous Sisodiya princess and poet saint Mirabai, who defied the *kuldevi* tradition of her husband's family (and ultimately ran away, legend has it, to worship Krishna, beloved by her since childhood), some women, *kuldevi* narratives suggest, have resisted the *kuldevi* worship of their husbands' homes. Importing *kuldevi* traditions to marital domains, Rajput wives demonstrate this kind of subversion.

The two variants of Shila Mata's arrival story I provide here are displayed on one of the gates of the fortress near Shila Mata's temple. The first inscription holds that in the sixteenth century Maharaja Man Singh was fighting King Kedar in East Bengal. Frustrated in his efforts, he prayed to the goddess Kali, who granted him victory in return for his promise to retrieve a stone image of her from the bottom of the sea. After his conquest, he located the image and brought it to Amber, where it was then worshipped as Shila Mata, 'Stone Goddess'.

Contrasting with this conquest account, a second variant illustrates the bridal or dowry scenario. It holds that when King Kedar was beaten, he married his daughter to Man Singh. During the wedding festivities, Kedar presented to Man Singh an icon of the goddess Jessoresvari, who became known as Shila Devi. (Like the surrender of brides, the handing over of religious icons is a well-known element of defeat.) In this variant, princess and goddess are delivered through a wedding that commences the Kachwaha's possession of its fearsome, blood-drinking goddess, who, in the first variant, is explicitly homologized to the pan-Indian goddess Kali.

Taken together, these variants reflect the experience of warriors who fight for kings as well as of women who marry husbands and try to protect them (along with other members of their husbands' families), by performing various forms of devotion, including *vrats*. The scenarios reflect the history of martial conquest and marriage, which may give a bride a new family, but not necessarily or even usually estrange her from her natal family along with the traditions she learned as a child. The arrival of a bride into the family may be necessitated by the conquest of her father, or it may be arranged in accord with the principle of hypergamy, which theoretically at least demonstrates the relative superiority of bride-takers. In either case it represents an ingestion of other traditions and perspectives that may seem or be subversive.[10]

The same holds true for the arrival of a new *kuldevi*, who also shows the conqueror's strength but can challenge its status in that she comes from an inferior background. The question may be asked in the case of *kuldevis* coming through conquest, 'Who has conquered whom?' The adoption of Shila Mata would seem to emphasize the peculiarity of Jamvai Mata, who is held to have tribal origins. And in the case of all *kuldevis* coming with brides, adoption through marriage supports the premise of hypergamy (commonly referred to as *anuloma* marriage, or marriage that accords with the way in which hair naturally falls) but also defeats it in that it demonstrates that women can prevail over husbands (the unnatural, 'hair-raising' situation that *anuloma* marriage is supposed to prevent). A *kuldevi* who comes with a woman then becomes emblematic of the family and makes various demands on the family, including and especially sacrifice, in order to be satisfied.

So closely, in fact, does the situation of the *kuldevi* who comes to a king parallel the situation of a bride who comes to a family, that the *kuldevi* is actually represented in certain contexts as the king's spouse. She is, after all, his *shakti*, his 'power', and Shakti is an epithet of the goddess who empowers him in battle.[11] The convergence of these notions is shown poignantly in the case of the coming of the goddess Shakti Ma to Jhala Rajputs in Gujarat. I have encountered two versions of this coming. According to one known to some Jhala Rajputs from Dhrangadhra in north-west Saurashtra, Gujarat, the hero Harpal, who had fled Sindh after his relatives were slain fighting Hamir Sumra, encounters this goddess in a cremation ground and prepares a feast for her, in which he offers her his own leg. Having dined on his flesh, the goddess then restores his health and wholeness, before enabling him to found a dynasty.[12]

10. For detailed analysis of the dangers of prestations, including and especially *kanydan*, the 'gift of a virgin', in marriage ritual, see Raheja (1988).

11. On this point in the context of the stories of the *kuldevis* Khodiyar and Shakti De, see Tambs-Lyche (1997: 42).

12. The myth is found in M.N.M. (author) (1896: 515-13), and was also re-

According to a version of this story related by Tambs-Lyche, Harpal encounters a young woman who had jumped into a well while possessed by a ghost (*bhut*). Harpal tries to figure out a way to rid her of the ghost and while doing so walks through a cremation ground, where he sees this young woman. He asks her twice for water but she will not respond. Annoyed, he 'pulls her skirt' and laughing, 'she grows "as high as the sky"'. Harpal then beats her feet. Eventually she reveals herself to be Shakti Mata, a goddess who has come to earth to find a husband. She decides to marry Harpal on the condition that no one know her divine identity. She then drives out the ghost and gives Harpal a boon: he can have all the villages on whose gates he can tie a garland in one night. With the help of goddess and ghost, he garlands two thousand, five hundred of which he gives to the Solanki Rajputs he has been serving, before going off to found a dynasty at Patdi (Tambs-Lyche draws here on Maynes 1921: 25-27).

Thus in the case of this Shakti, bride and queen turn out to be not simply allied: they are one in the same female, who is won through marriage, but whose conquest reveals her power over, as well as identification with, her husband's kingdom. She will be responsible for and credited with its fortunes, including and especially its victories. Like human *pativrata*s (women who, being wives, have sworn an oath of devotion to their husbands), *kuldevi*s such as Shakti Mata are accountable for the fates of their men and kingdoms. The price for female protection is, evidently, high. Men must be prepared to sacrifice themselves to sate the avid female appetite.

However great the risk attending the conquest of goddess and/or wife may be perceived to be, it is certain that men's attempts at conquest (or defense, for that matter) also risk the security and identity of *pativrata*s, who have devoted themselves to their husbands' longevity. It may be tempting to read the two variants of the Shila Mata story, as well as other 'twinned' accounts, as setting forth complementary ideals, that is to say, as representing the duty (*dharma*) of Rajput men (fighting in battle) and women (marrying and protecting husbands). Yet the ultimate or ideal *dharma*s of

cited to me by Jayasingh Jhala, while he was an anthropology doctoral student at Harvard in 1984.

Rajput men and women conflict. The perfected Rajput warrior should die in battle, not in bed, whereas the perfected married woman, by preserving her chastity and performing religious devotions to *kuldevi*s and other deities, should protect her husband's life so that he lives to a ripe old age, or at least outlives her. Thus the warrior who sacrifices goats for his goddess on Navratri is ultimately prepared for and even devoted to offering his own life as a sacrifice to his goddess, whereas the wife who performs religious devotions such as *vrats* for the benefit of her husband in effect attempts to thwart her husband's ambition to achieve death in battle and so earn entry to the delightful warrior heaven where heroes enjoy myriad pleasures, including music, intoxicants, and the attentions of comely nymphs. From the *patrivrata*'s perspective, a husband's realization of perfection, however laudable, implicitly indicts her and signifies imperfection of her *dharma* as protectrix. At this point, the ambiguous nature of the potentially menacing in-marrying bride is revisited.

A solution to this conflict of duties lies in the *sati* or 'good woman' ideal, which exonerates a woman from failure to protect her husband's life and effects a temporal warp whereby she 'goes with' him (becomes a *sahagamini)* on his pyre. I have reflected on this drastic solution at length elsewhere and do not wish to rehash those thoughts here (see Harlan 1992: 112-81; 1994; 1996; forthcoming d). Suffice it to say that on the one hand, *sati* sacrifice is seen to free a wife of condemnation from failure to protect, but, on the other hand, the existence of the ideal, and the extreme form of expiation or justification it involves, does not in any way excuse women from trying to preserve their husbands from becoming heroes who offer their heads to their goddesses' gaping maws. Unlike hero stories, *itihasik kuldevi* stories tell of times in which husbands live to fight another day and of their fortunate acquisition of goddesses, who will help them to achieve their worldly ambitions.

The second category of story, the non-*itihasik* sort that overwhelmingly, but not exclusively, reflects the experience and concerns of women, demonstrates the attempts of *pativrata*s to protect husbands (as well as husbands' families) from death, as well as to engender health and happiness.

Stories Whenever or Here and Now:
Recalling Miracles and Female Powers

Most of these domestic accounts relate appearances by *kuldevi*s to family members, typically to women but occasionally to men, during times when household members need something from the *kuldevi* less grand than a new kingdom or the devastation of some menacing enemy army. Instead, the household stories relate incidents occurring in the indeterminate past, that is, a past devoid of historical markers, or located within recent memory. Common are stories about *kuldevi* manifestations in dreams or visions, which are followed by miraculous cures from disease or the receipt of other forms of good fortune. The appearances that women recount are not of fierce theriomorphic *kuldevi*s frequenting the battlefield as birds of prey, snakes, lions, flies and the like, but of auspicious and radiant *pativrata*s who help women perform their duties as *pativrata*s. These notably feminine anthropomorphic *kuldevi*s help women do their job of protecting familial health and welfare.

A vivid example of such an account is found in the following story narrated by a Rajput noblewoman, who was married into a prominent Udaipur family:

> Kuldevi [Ban Mata] appeared to me once. She had a *lota* [vessel] of water, which she gave to me. It was during the war [with Pakistan, 1965] and my husband was in the army. He had been shot. The doctors operated on him. I was there. Kuldevi came to me in order to give me the *lota* of water for my husband to drink. She also gave me a rose and told me to put one of its petals in my husband's mouth. At first I thought that Kuldevi was just my sister, but then I realized who she was.
>
> I knew that the doctor had said that my husband should not drink water, so I was afraid to give him any. Then the nurse—she was a Catholic sister—saw Kuldevi (just as I saw her). Kuldevi was wearing a beautiful red Rajput dress with fine gold beadwork. After a time Kuldevi walked away. I asked the nurse where she had gone. The nurse said, 'Maybe she's in the waiting room.' I went to look for Kuldevi but she had disappeared. I went downstairs and asked the sentry if he had seen a woman leave. He said, 'It's 1:00 A.M. and visiting hours ended at 11:00 P.M. Of course nobody came out the door.' She had vanished.
>
> As I said, I was afraid to give my husband the water. I thought the doctor would be angry because he had said that my husband should not drink or eat anything. So I didn't give my husband the water and

the rose. Instead, I fell asleep. Kuldevi came to me in a dream—this time she came in a dream and not before my eyes—and she said, 'You must give him the water and rose petals.' So I awoke and gave them to him.

The next morning the doctor came to me and said, 'Congratulations, your husband will recover.' He recuperated right away.

Two aspects of this account bear special notice. First, the *kuldevi*'s form is explicitly represented as a woman wearing a 'beautiful red Rajput dress with fine gold beadwork'. The dress's red color, which is worn by brides, as well as its gold ornamentation connote auspiciousness and suggest the *kuldevi*'s power to convey auspicious consequences, such as and especially the recuperation of a seriously injured soldier. The *kuldevi* appears as a *pativrata* to a *pativrata* whose province parallels her own.

Second, although the account refers to a past, it is a personal past, one without generational depth. The account is a first-hand, eye-witness narrative relating the power of a *kuldevi*, and also of the wife who petitions her, to protect a husband, even one who offers his life in battle. From a wife's perspective, we should not be surprised to learn, the husband's recuperation may well be preferable to any martial death, however meritorious and valiant. In general, a living husband is simply better than a dead hero.[13] Thus from this woman's testimony we see the softer side of the *kuldevi*, whom, incidentally, the narrator specifically referred to as looking like a *suhagin* (a wife with the good fortune to have a living husband, that is, a *pativrata*) when she appeared to the narrator on a different occasion.

In the context of noting the *kuldevi*'s power to protect husbands for women, let us observe that the account makes a double claim about female knowledge and power. To begin with, there is the claim that the *pativrata* can—and here does—bring her husband back from the brink of death through her power as a *pativrata* devoted to her goddess. The wife knows best what she and the rest of the family require from the husband, whatever his military career

---

13. Women rehearse this ideology with predictable regularity. Women, of course, may feel conflicted or hostile toward their husbands (some or all of the time), but generally or abstractly speaking, the advantages of having a living husband are considered great.

may require of him and however fulfilling his identification with the *dharma* of career (and caste) may be. Furthermore, like the *kuldevi*, whose power she mediates when (presumably fearing controversion of the male doctor's orders) she reluctantly but surely gives her husband water along with the rose petal, this wife shows that female knowledge is superior to men's.

In this regard I am reminded of the *vrat* many Rajasthani women perform for the goddess Dashamata.[14] For this *vrat*, women tell ten stories, the first of which is about the heroine Damayanti, who is married to a terribly foolish king Nala. When Nala orders her to abandon her *vrat* because the string it requires her to wear around her neck strikes him as ugly, she reluctantly but dutifully obeys. As a result she and her husband are plunged into dire misfortune until the time for Dashamata *vrat* comes around once again and presents an opportunity for Damayanti to tie a new string on her neck and reap the goddess's protection. In one variant of this story I recorded, before a reversal of the couple's bad fortune can occur, Damayanti must tell Nala the name of his family's *kuldevi*, whom Nala has apparently forgotten. As this well-known *vrat* suggests, women and the goddesses they worship are often represented as ultimately knowing best when it comes to matters of survival, success, and good fortune.

Conviction of the efficacy of female power and of the superiority of women's knowledge is also forcefully illustrated in the following foundation account, which was told by another Rajput woman. Returning momentarily to the realm of foundation accounts allows us to see clearly that although *itihasik* accounts are perceived as primarily the province of men, they may be deployed to express perceptions of women's experience—even when they are concerned mostly, if not wholly, with war. Examining one more war story will illustrate the way in which women, whose prayers are answered by miracles recorded in domestic accounts, may be represented as claiming or possessing higher wisdom and power in a context identified as overwhelmingly male. In this account a wife leads a *kuldevi* to protect her husband instead of claiming his life as sacrifice and granting a heroic death:

14. For more detailed reflection on the Nala–Damayanti story in Rajasthan, see Gold and Harlan (1999); Harlan (forthcoming b).

The Kachwaha family is an offshoot of Kush [one of the sons of Rama in the *Ramayana*]. From Ayodhya it moved to Rahitasgarh, then to Nimarana, Dausa, Ramgarh, Amber, and Jaipur. Dhola married a princess of Marwar, Maru. He'd married her at Pushkar below the age of five. His parents had met there [to get them married]. His mother noticed the stars were bad, so she didn't disclose to Dhola that he had been married. [Later, when he found out about his marriage], he marched to Marwar.

[At that time] a Meena [tribal] chief ruled Ramgarh. [Dhola said] 'Let me fetch my wife and on return I'll fight [him].' He returned and fought at Ramgarh. Dhola's army was killed and he was wounded. Maru wept and prayed to her *kuldevi*. She appeared [to Maru] as an old lady and said that a cow would come and give milk on its own [spontaneously, without being milked].

Maru told Dhola to sprinkle some [of the cow's] milk on himself. He did this [and recovered].

So...she [Kuldevi] was called Jamvai: Jamvai Ramgarh was the original name of that place.

Many readers will recognize this story to be not just some *kuldevi* story, but a radically brief version of the story of the hero Dhola, whose adventures with his beloved wife Maru are related in a well-known Rajasthani oral epic.[15] Like the hospital account above, the *suhagin* knows and does what the *kuldevi* wants, with felicitous results.

This story's *kuldevi*, Jamvai Mata, is, let us recall, rather an 'odd bird': she is a vegetarian deity, whose alter ego, Shila Mata, receives Navratri offerings, which are generally given *kuldevi*s. Here she appears in two forms. The first is an elderly lady, who, it goes without saying, is *pativrata*. Otherwise she would have been explicitly represented as a widow, an unlikely designation for a *kuldevi* indeed. It is apt that this *kuldevi*, unlike other anthropomorphic *kuldevi*s, is elderly: she is emblematic of an older woman with a living husband, which is what the *pativrata* Maru is attempting to be in securing her *kuldevi*'s aid. Maru here mediates between the *kuldevi* and Nala. Like the wife in the domestic account above, she is responsible for seeing to it that Nala gets his medicine, and so she implements the *kuldevi*'s cure. The divine and human *pativrata*s work in tandem to step in when men are weak and needful.

15. This variant is at odds in various ways with variants collected by Susan S. Wadley, who is preparing a book-length manuscript on the topic.

The second form in which the *kuldevi* appears is a cow. Here, as elsewhere, Jamvai Mata's bovine form serves to mediate the fierce theriomorphic forms found in foundation accounts and the gentle forms populating domestic accounts. Jamvai Mata may be a beast, but she is the very beast signifying nurturance in Indian iconography. Instead of drinking blood, this *kuldevi* dispenses life-giving milk.

Contemplating this goddess's theriomorphic form in the context of this story and more generally, two thoughts occur. First, although this story does not explicitly state that this appearance by Jamvai Mata is her first appearance to the Kachwahas, other Kachwaha foundation accounts do make it clear that Jamvai Mata was taken from the Meenas by the Kachwahas. As we know, it is common for *kuldevi*s to come to kings through conquest. In Jamvai Mata's case, it is usually held that she wanted to come to the Kachwahas because the Meenas were not vegetarian. To take up with Rajputs for this reason is strikingly strange: Rajputs, who seldom take up vegetarianism, often distinguish themselves from Brahmins and various lower castes by pointing out that they can and do eat meat. Moreover, Rajputs sometimes explicitly liken themselves to tribal peoples such as Bhils and Mers because of their background as martial meat-eaters!

Nevertheless, according to Kachwaha foundation accounts, Rajputs do take her in and take her away from those lowly meat-eating tribals. The change in dietary habits subtly but surely represents a purging of low-caste associations and the acquisition of an image that is more in line with Brahmanical views than Rajput ones. Without the change, elevation would be difficult to signify. This goddess's bovine iconography would be in line with such a move: Brahmins and cows are commonly spoken of in one breath. They are both pure and, like women, in need of protection by Rajput men. In fact, safeguarding Brahmins and cows is often the rationale Rajputs give for martial aggression. In short, ironically, bovine iconography comes to elevate this goddess and render her Rajput. Whether or not this 'herbiforization' actually explains how this goddess gained her bovine form, cow imagery conveys elevation and so defends her Kachwaha protégés against detractors, who might find her origins too base. It would seem such a defense has at times been necessary. Reading the turn-of-the-century diary of

the Rathaur nobleman Amar Singh, I came across a passage in which
the diarist ribs a Kachwaha nobleman for having a *kuldevi* of such
shameful provenance.[16]

If the bovine iconography conveys respectability for this appropriated *kuldevi*, it also, as has been shown, renders her a problematic *kuldevi*, at least in the martial context in which *kuldevi*s are
often constructed. It should hardly be surprising to learn that when
I first asked the woman who narrated the Jamvai Mata story the
name of her conjugal family's *kuldevi*, she responded 'Shila Devi'
and volunteered the information that her family worships this 'Stone
Goddess' on Navratri. Only later, when I asked about Jamvai Mata,
did she say that Jamvai Mata is officially the Kachwaha *kuldevi*.

In any case, in this story, in which a wife saves her husband's life,
the *kuldevi* is allied with the wife and her desire to save her husband's life.[17] Both are complicit in nurturing him back to health.
Thus the story shows that the blood-lusting *kuldevi* of the battlefield may also, paradoxically, be represented as complicit with the
human *pativrata* who, although worshiping the goddess as a divine
pativrata, would deprive the goddess of her husband's flesh. The
kuldevi, inevitably imaged in both theriomorphic and anthropomorphic forms, is thus not identifiable with only one form or the
other. Rather, she is ultimately a solitary presence viewed from
diverging—and sometimes, as in this story, converging—perspectives. Like the human-flesh-eating, cremation-ground-haunting giant-
ess Shakti, who eats, regurgitates, then marries her hero prey,
*kuldevi*s are shape-shifting solitary presences with alternating loyal-
ties, apparent through their differently positioned and often conflicted petitioners. In the case of wives, who overwhelmingly tell
domestic stories, *kuldevi*s are imaged as anthropomorphic divinities sharing more in common with the milk-splashing Jamvai Mata

16. For reflections on this account, see Harlan (forthcoming a). A greatly
abridged version of this diary is being prepared by Rudolph, Rudolph and
Singh (forthcoming).

17. Nowhere in this story is the man's desire revealed. In no Rajput story I
have collected is a man represented as desiring life to the point of trying to
outwit or escape death. Fighting, the warrior desires to win his battles and
winning means persevering and living on, but at all points the warrior is depicted as unafraid of death and willing to sacrifice himself as a blood sacrifice
or *balidan*.

than with the ravenous bird or beast forms that the other *kuldevi*s assume.

In this context it should be observed that the imaging of the martial *kuldevi* as nurturing presence occurs also among Jains, many of whom claim descent from Rajput families and all of whom belong to a religious tradition championing non-violence (*ahimsa*) and vegetarianism. Having contemplated the fluid iconographies of Rajput *kuldevi*s, Lawrence Babb has observed that some Jains who claim to have descended from converted Rajputs continue to worship *kuldevi*s, but 'defang' them, much as Rajput domestic stories appear to do.[18] These Jains conceptualize such goddesses as upholding values that may well be at odds with the martial ethos and they may metaphorically transvalue the martial, as the use of the term 'conqueror' (*jina*) does when used to refer to non-violent Jain heroes conquering attachment and so achieving spiritual perfection. Characterizing Jain transformations of martial Rajput *kuldevi*s, Babb says:

> ...we must note, finally, that in a sense the Jain version of the Rajput lineage goddess is not really 'transformed' at all, because even the Rajput lineage goddess has a 'Jain' side to her character—that is, these is a side to her character of which Jains can approve. We see this in the distinction between the Rajput lineage goddess in her martial and *pativrata* forms—the lineage goddess of the *mardana* (men's quarters) versus the lineage goddess of the *zanana* (women's quarters) respectively. The Rajput lineage goddess does indeed possess an unwarrior-like form, which is her domestic manifestation (Babb 1996: 160).

Hence, the verbal iconization of *kuldevi*s in women's domestic narratives (an iconization reflective of motifs in some dowry-related foundation stories as well) resembles (and perhaps provides precedent for) the representation of 'defanged' Jain *kuldevi*s.

In the Rajput context, human and divine *pativrata*s literally touch one another: like the Sisodiya princess who imports Ban Mata, other

---

18. The use of the term 'defanging' is not intended to argue for the historical priority of foundation accounts but rather to indicate the perception of foundation accounts as instituting household worship, which includes recitation of household accounts. I borrow it from Babb, who takes from Michael Meister. See Babb (1996: 147-48), and Meister (1993).

Rajput wives bear images of their guardian *kuldevi*s on pendants signifying divine presence and protection. Wearing *kuldevi*s around their necks, Rajput women, then, have goddesses who are 'on their side', or rather, supportive of the principle of preserving men rather than eating them. These anthropomorphic *kuldevi* representations contrast markedly with the theriomorphic forms that frequently appear on Rajput coats of arms and other insignia.[19]

And yet, pendant iconography gives us pause. Typically these pendants depict a goddess as one of seven *kuldevi*s, who are implicitly or sometimes explicitly homologized to Sanskritic mythology's Saptamatrikas, or 'Seven Mothers'. These 'mothers' are often rendered elsewhere as the demure consorts of prominent Indian deities. They are also, however, construed as *shakti*s, fierce presences frequenting battlegrounds. Moreover, in many *kuldevi* pendants the seven *kuldevi*s are escorted by the diminutive guardian deity Bheruji (in Sanskrit, Bhairava), a manifestation of the pan-Indian god Shiva and a god of war. Keeping company with Bheruji suggests these goddesses' potential ferocity and even their capacity for decapitating men. In some traditions, it should be noted, a goddess is responsible for beheading Bhairava when he desires her too fervently.[20] Lust leaves him headless, though his sacrifice also renders him a true devotee. Thus *kuldevi* imaging suggests an alliance that may threaten, as well as uphold, the principle of protecting husbands.

So, it turns out, women's *kuldevi*s are not properly viewed as different goddesses from men's. The domestic *pativrata* goddesses women worship are also the death-dealing goddesses that make, and eat, heroes. This conclusion prompts one further reflection on these protean divinities and their female protégés. Rajput women may tell stories of helpful goddesses appearing as *pativrata*s and they may celebrate the life-affirming miracles to which their domestic stories attest, but the same women who narrate stories of *kuldevi* blessings also love to share stories about noble heroines who encourage, even ruthlessly demand, that their husbands sacrifice

19. The homology may suggest further ambiguity: in Indian mythology, the seven mothers are not simply docile protectors; like their guardian Bheruji (in Sanskrit literature, a personification of Shiva's anger), the seven mothers can be irascible.

20. An accessible essay on this theme is Erndl (1989).

themselves in battle.[21] Best known of these stories is that of Hadi
Rani, who slices off her head to encourage her reluctant, love-sick
husband to offer up his life in the sacrifice of battle. Such stories
focus not on women's duty to protect husbands' lives, but on wom-
en's duty to support men's duty to fight and to fortify men's willingness to die in battle. These heroic women, it should be noted,
tend to end up dead. Many become *sati*s, a course which evidently
discounts their failure to protect their men's lives. The women who
are represented as demanding that men attain martial glory, then,
might be thought allied with the goddess of the battlefield (and
the *shakti*, Saptamatrika goddess). It is fitting, therefore, that like
Hadi Rani, whose head accompanies her husband into battle, these
women tend to leave the household, to enter the grounds on which
either battle or cremation takes place. Their return to their domestic station in life is signified by their deaths, especially if they die
dramatically, as *sati*s.

This return is also evident, however, in the case of non-heroic
*sati*s, whose status as *pativrata*s is implicitly challenged by their
husbands' deaths. The case that comes to mind most readily is that
of the lovely Krishna, whose marriage to the famous Rajput folk
hero Kalaji was interrupted by the Mewar king's summons of Kalaji
to Chittor, then under assault by the Moghul emperor, Akbar. This
cultic hero is worshipped in various shrines throughout Rajasthan,
the most prominent of which are at Chittor, where his head is said
to have been severed, and Rundela, where his body fell after a pro-
tracted period of headless, vengeful fighting. The Rajputs in Rundela, who claim descent from the Kalaji's family, worship him at the
cultic shrine to which pilgrims from all caste backgrounds come.
Although there are significant differences between the cultic worship of heroes by people from various caste backgrounds and the
worship Rajputs perform for their heroic ancestors at home, in this
case the traditions coincide, with Rajputs leading cultic services of
their deceased ancestor in the Rundela Kalaji temple.

According to Kalaji's story, after Kalaji sacrificed his head at
Chittor, he fought his way through the countryside to meet his
beloved Krishna, who had heeded omens of his death and come
running to meet him. Reunited with her, Kalaji finally found peace:

21. The 'unholy' alliance and lore is explored at length in Harlan (forthcoming a); for further reflections, see Harlan (1992: 182-204).

his body fell to the ground. In versions I have collected, Krishna is said to have made her body a sacrifice on the pyre she built to cremate his body. In a printed account composed by a Brahmin devotee, by the grace of the goddess—who earlier had received Kalaji's head on a platter—the hero's head was borne on the breeze to Rundela so Kalaji could die a whole and perfect sacrifice. Also in this version, with which the Rajput officiant at Rundela is acquainted, Krishna is said to have cut her own body into twenty-four bits, all but one of which she offered as ablations on his fire. The last had to be offered for her by her trusted maidservant, who lived to tell the tale.[22] Although this detail was not mentioned in the Rajput officiant's account, when he finished narrating his version, he took me to see the memorial for Kalaji's *sati*, to whom he referred as 'Shakti', an epithet that, we have seen, unites goddess and human *pativrata* power. This shared conceptualization is patent in the confluence of female personae in Kalaji's sacrifice. If Kalaji gives his head to his goddess, he brings his body back to his wife. This parallel converges in the variant in which the *kuldevi* who has received Kalaji's head then sends it on to Krishna, who, having received it, then reoffers it in Kalaji's cremation fire before making a sacrifice of her own body and head.

This story also demonstrates clearly the doubly sacrificial nature of *sati* sacrifice. If, as the work of various authors has suggested, *sati* immolation represents a sacrifice of women to men—to the ancestors or 'fathers', including the ancestor her husband becomes—it also, in the Rajput case at least, suggests that a woman's sacrifice is, in some sense, a sacrifice for the goddess, who demands male victims.[23] Krishna's case helps illuminate the premise that like the Rajput king who sacrifices to his goddess and is sacrificed to his goddess, the woman is a sacrificer and a victim, but also, from yet another point of view, a female who, having enabled her husband to do his self-sacrificial duty as protector, then receives his

22. This variant, which was composed by Shil Sharma, is discussed at length in Sharma n.d.

23. On *sati* immolation as sacrifice to and for men, see Harlan (1992: 130-31), and also Hiltebeitel (1999: 71), who, following Weinberger-Thomas, discusses *sati* immolation as an offering to male ancestors. See also Weinberger-Thomas (1996; 1999).

lifeless remains.[24] Imaged from this perspective, then, the demure domestic female is ultimately also a consumer. Like the divine *kulde-vi* protector, her protection comes at a high price: the sacrifice of men in battle.

Bibliography

Babb, Lawrence A.
1996   *Absent Lord: Ascetics and Kings in a Jain Ritual Culture* (Berkeley: University of California Press).

Doniger, Wendy
1998   *The Implied Spider: Politics and Theology in Myth* (New York: Columbia University Press).

Erndl, Kathleen
1989   'Rapist or Bodyguard: Demon or Devotee/Images of Bhairo in the Mythology and Cult of Vaisno Devi', in Alf Hiltebeitel (ed.), *Criminal Gods and Demon Devotees: Essays on the Guardians of Popular Hinduism* (Syracuse: State University of New York Press): 239-50.

Gold, Ann Grodzins
forthcoming   'Damayanti's String: Epic Threads in Women's Ritual Stories', in Susan Wadley and Joyce Flueckiger (eds.), *Nala and Damayanti*.

Gold, Ann Grodzins, and Lindsey Harlan
1999   'Raja Nal's Mistake: Epic Themes in Rajasthani Women's Ritual Narratives', in Jawaharlal Handoo (ed.), *Folklore in Modern India* (Mysore: Central Institute of Indian Languages): 151-62.

Handelman, Don
1999   'Postlude: Towards the Braiding of a Frame', May 1999 Conference at the Hebrew University of Jerusalem titled 'On Framing: Narrative, Metaphysic, Perception'.

Harlan, Lindsey
1992   *Religion and Rajput Women: The Ethic of Protection in Contemporary Narratives* (Berkley: University of California Press).
1994   'Perfection and Devotion: Sati Tradition in Rajasthan', in John Stratton Hawley (ed.), *Sati, The Blessing and the Curse: The Burning of Wives in India* (New York: Oxford University Press): 79-99.
1995   'Women's Songs for Auspicious Occasions', in *Religions of India in Practice* (Princeton: Princeton University Press): 269-80.
1996   'The Story of Godavari', in John Stratton Hawley and Donna Wulff (eds.), *Devi: Goddesses of India* (Berkeley: University of California Press): 227-49.
1997   'Tale of a Headless Horseman: Kalaji Rathor', paper presented at the Annual Conference on South Asia, University of Wisconsin, Madison.

24. This receipt receives copious elaboration in Rajput lore. See Harlan (forthcoming a).

1999	'On Being Framed: Heroic Narratives in Rajasthan', paper delivered at the Conference on Narrative Framing, Academy of Sciences and Humanities, Jerusalem.
forthcoming a	*The Goddesses' Henchmen: Gender and Virility in Heroic Narratives*. Book manuscript in progress.
forthcoming b	'Nala and Damayanti's Reversals of Fortune: Reflections on When a Woman Should Know Better', in Susan Wadley and Joyce Flueckiger (eds.), *Nala and Damayanti*.
forthcoming c	'Heroes Alone and Heroes at Home: Gender and Intertextuality in Two Narratives', in Julia Leslie (ed.), *Gender Constructs in Indian Religion and Society* (Delhi: Oxford University Press).
forthcoming d	'Truth and Sacrifice: Sati Immolation in India', in Margaret Cormack (ed.), *Sacrificing the Self: Perspectives on Martyrdom* (Atlanta: Scholars Press).

Hiltebeitel, Alf

1999	'Fathers of the Bride, Fathers of Sati: Myths, Rites, and Scholarly Practices', *Thamyris* 6.1: 65-94.

M.M.N.

1896	The *Hind Rajasthan*. Bansda, India: privately published as a tribute to H.H. Kmaha Raol Shri Pratapsingh Gulabsinghji.

Maynes, H.

1921	*History of the Dhrangadhra State* (Calcutta: Thacker, Spink & Co.).

Meister, Michael.

1993	'Sweetmeats or Corpses: Community, Conversion, and Sacred Places', paper presented at the workshop on Jains in Indian History and Culture, Amherst College.

Raheja, Gloria

1988	*The Poison in the Gift* (Chicago: University of Chicago Press).

Raheja, Gloria, and Ann Gold

1994	*Listen to the Heron's Words: Reimagining Gender and Kinship in North India* (University of California Press).

Ramanujan, A.K.

1986	'Two Realms of Kannada Folklore', in Stuart H. Blackburn and A.K. Ramanujan (eds.), *Another Harmony: New Essays on the Folklore of India* (Berkeley: University of California Press).

Rudolph, Susanne Hoeber, and Lloyd Rudolph, with Monah Singh of Kanota

forthcoming	*Reversing the Gaze: The Amar Singh Diary as Narrative of Imperial India* (Boulder: Westview Press).

Sax, William

1991	*Mountain Goddess: Gender and Politics in a Himalayan Pilgrimage* (New York: Oxford University Press.

Sharma, Shil

n.d.	*Karmavir Kalla* (Udaipur: Kamdhaj Kalla Rathor Sahitya Prakashan Samiti).

Tambs-Lyche, Harold

1997	*Power, Profit and Poetry: Traditional Society in Kathiawar, Western India* (New Delhi: Manohar).

Weinberger-Thomas, Catherine
    1996   *Cendres d'immortalité: la cremation des veuves en Inde* (Paris:
                    Editions du Seuil). Translated as *Ashes of Immortality: Widow
                    Burning in India* (trans. Jeffrey Mehlman and David Gordon White;
                    Chicago: University of Chicago Press, 1999).

Kathleen M. Erndl

Is Shakti Empowering for Women? Reflections on Feminism and the Hindu Goddess

The study of the Hindu Goddess has been a consuming passion of mine for many years. It is, I hope, no longer unfashionable for historians of religion to admit an affective connection to their fields of study. I have long felt that scholars of religion (and perhaps scholars in general) fall into two camps: those who study what they like and those who study what they do not like. Or, to put it more elegantly, and to borrow the terminology of Paul Ricoeur (1970), there are those who engage in a 'hermeneutic of recovery' and those who engage in a 'hermeneutic of suspicion'. As far as the study of the Hindu Goddess is concerned, I would unabashedly place myself in the former category, though of course, like all scholars, I engage in both kinds of hermeneutic. Nevertheless, though I personally as a feminist find the idea of female power or *shakti* extremely attractive, I have in the past, especially in my published works (Erndl 1993), hesitated to posit any direct correlation between *shakti* and feminism in the Hindu or Indian context. I did not want to be accused of 'misrepresenting' Hinduism or imposing my own cultural biases on another culture. I now wonder, however, whether I had unwittingly accepted a deeply held assumption of Western scholarship, that in Hinduism women are universally subjugated and that feminism, however it might be defined, is an artifact of the West. I remember that at my PhD dissertation defense (in 1987), one of my committee members asked if there were Indian equivalents to the Western feminist spirituality movements which focus on Goddess imagery and worship. As I recall, I replied that I thought women's movements in India tended to be more concerned with economic issues, following a more socialist-feminist agenda and informed by a dialectical materialist ideology, borrowed from the West, which is extremely suspicious and critical of anything religious. From an Indian feminist point of view, I surmised, *shakti* and the Goddess, as part of the Hindu religious system, would be viewed as contributing to the oppression of women. My committee members seemed satisfied by this answer, but I was not. First of all, what did I really know about what 'Indian feminists' thought or if there were anything which could be called the Indian feminist position? Secondly, what did I know about how *shakti* impacted on Hindu women's lives? Since then, I have tried to explore these questions more deeply. I have conducted fieldwork which focuses specifically on Hindu women's experience of the Goddess (Erndl 1997 and forthcoming). I have become more aware of the diversity and complexity of the rapidly changing women's movement in India (R. Kumar 1993; Liddle and Joshi 1986; Berry 1994; the magazine *Manushi: A Journal of Women and Society*). And I have become somewhat familiar with evolving critiques by Indian women thinkers of Western scholarship, feminism, and colonialist discourse (Mohanty 1991; Shiva 1989; Chakravarti 1989; N. Kumar 1994; Narayan 1989).

My current thinking is that there are definite connections between *shakti* and Hindu women's lives and between *shakti* and feminist movements in India. However, I must point out that *shakti* is a fluid and multivalent concept which is found in many different contexts and can be used, even manipulated, for many different purposes. I am not making any *a priori* claims. It is not inevitable that wherever *shakti* or the Goddess is found there will be positive implications for women; indeed, examples of the opposite can be found. The purpose of this essay is empirical rather than programmatic, that is, to suggest some ways in which *shakti* has been empowering for Hindu women and has been consciously embraced in contemporary Indian women's movements.

There are those who would claim that feminism is a Western ideology and that any feminist or women-oriented political movements in India must therefore be a result of 'Westernization', and are thus not 'authentically' Indian. To answer that claim, I quote two passages from Liddle and Joshi's study, *Daughters of Independence: Gender, Caste and Class in India* (1986). The opening words of the book are as follows:

> The women's movement has a long history in India. Much longer than the 'second wave' movement, or even the 'first wave' of earlier this century. The Shakti cults go back centuries, and the concept of Shakti—the female power principle—was recognized thousands of years ago. In this form the women's movement represents, not

merely an oppositional force fueled by anger, a rather negative approach to oppression, but the development of a distinctive female culture, a positive creative force inspiring men and women alike (Liddle and Joshi 1986: 5).

I find it interesting and significant that a study which uses an empirically oriented, social science methodology and focuses on the social construction of caste, class, and gender should begin by invoking such nebulous and empirically unverifiable concepts as *shakti* and 'women's power'. But *shakti* is so ubiquitous and appears in so many contexts that it cannot be ignored. Liddle and Joshi show that while the subordination of women is real enough, it varies according to caste, class, and other factors; it is not monolithic. In their conclusion, they argue that the British championed the cause of women in order to 'maintain colonialism and to demonstrate national superiority' (Liddle and Joshi 1986: 239). They further write:

> A similar process occurs today whereby Indian women are portrayed in the West as abjectly submissive, without any reference to the contrary images and realities of female power. The notion that women's liberation is Western inspired is a further mystification of women's history in India, serving to emphasise the Indian form of male domination over the Western forms and perpetuating the myth of Western superiority in gender relations... Ideologically, cultural imperialism has introduced the notion of female inferiority which had no part in Indian culture, where female power and its containment was stressed (Liddle and Joshi 1986: 240).

It is not difficult to find examples in so-called 'traditional' Hindu religious life which attest to the positive impact of *shakti* and goddesses on women's religious lives. There is evidence to suggest that Shakta traditions tend to be more inclusive of women as practitioners and more accepting of women as leaders or gurus than do Vaishnava or Shaiva traditions. The work of Lisa Hallstrom (1999) suggests that the prominence of the woman saint Anandamayi Ma must be viewed against the backdrop of her Shakta-influenced Bengali milieu and, more specifically, the Shakta affiliation of her husband's family. Sanjukta Gupta (1991: 209) has observed that Shakta women saints have more religious freedom and higher status than Vaishnava women saints. June McDaniel, in her study of Bengali ecstatics, was able to find many Shakta holy women, but was less successful when it came to Vaishnava holy women (1989: 231, 315). In Tantric circles, women gurus are also fairly commonplace. A famous example is the Tantric holy woman called the Bhairavi who was for a time Ramakrishna's guru (Kripal 1995: 117-30). The fact that holy women or women gurus can exist at all in male-dominated Hindu society is due to the divine model of femaleness which the Goddess provides. Several Indian scholars have argued that Shaktism, with its theology and ritual which place a high valuation on female embodiment, is in fact essentially feminist (Patel 1994; Khanna 1999). One of these, Tantric scholar Madhu Khanna, has established a Tantra Foundation in Delhi whose aim is not only to preserve Tantric traditions but to promote Tantra as relevant to the lives of contemporary women. Khanna has been heard to proclaim the motto, 'Tantra is a dharma for women!' (personal communication 1996, 1997).

Women gurus and holy women generally are called Mataji (respected Mother), which is also the most common name of the Goddess. The holy woman identifies herself with the Goddess and is so identified by others. I have written elsewhere of such Matajis, including a recent essay (Erndl 1997) describing the transformation of a Kangra village woman Tara Devi from a near invalid into a Goddess-possessed healer with a home temple and a large clientele. In that essay, I suggested that Tara Devi's identification with the Goddess was empowering for her and for other women in her village. I also suggested that because of the prominence of Goddess worship in Kangra and the cultural acceptance of women as her legitimate vehicle, Tara Devi had tapped into a traditional source of power for women. Tara Devi had to work within the constraints of her marriage to live her life dedicated to serving the Goddess, but other Matajis operate more independently, rejecting marriage, often at the behest of the Goddess herself. Such women are self-supporting through their healing and ritual activities and are often well respected and sought after in their communities (Erndl 1993: 113-34; forthcoming). Divine possession by the Goddess is one of the few culturally accepted forms of avoiding marriage in traditional Indian society, which allows few avenues of self-expression for women outside marriage. However, while Matajis are viewed in their communities as extraordinary women to whom the normal rules do not apply, they do exercise influence concerning women's roles. For example, Passu Mataji, a woman healer living in a village near Dharmsala in Kangra District, Himachal Pradesh, is very active in the local Mahila Mandal (Women's Organization) and supports educational, social, and economic opportunities for women. More radically, while respecting the status of the householder and stressing interdependence and an ethic of caring among men, women, and children in the family, she believes that marriage is not necessarily a sacred duty for women. She told me that women should think long and hard before agreeing to marriage and that no one should be forced into marriage against her will (Erndl forthcoming). Such ideas she attributes to the influence of the Goddess in her life, for she is illiterate and has had virtually no exposure to Western ideas.

The concept of *shakti* is, of course, also widespread among Hindus generally, even those who are not specifically Shakta in their sectarian orientation, and is connected with life-giving female properties. Frédérique Marglin (1985a, 1985b) has argued that in Hindu culture female power is the power of life and death, a power which encompasses both auspicious and inauspicious aspects but is exclusively neither one nor the other. She further argues that the auspiciousness/inauspiciousness principle, that is, *shakti*, is profoundly nonhierarchical, presenting a different 'axis of value' (1985a: 40) than the hierarchical purity/impurity principle. While in general agreeing with Marglin, I would add that though *shakti* is a nonhierarchical value associated with women, and is openly acknowledged as such, even in Hindu hegemonic discourse, at the same time the Hindu patriarchal impulse to subordinate women is rooted in the acknowledgment that women are powerful. To support my claim, I quote two famous verses from Manu, which for me sum up Hindu hegemonic discourse on women:

> In the home where women are worshiped, there the gods shower blessings. In the home where women are not worshiped, even virtuous deeds go unrewarded (*Laws of Manu*, III, 56).

> By a girl, by a young woman, or even by an aged one, nothing must be done independently, even in her own house. In childhood a female must be subject to her father, in youth to her husband, when her lord is dead to her sons; a woman must never be independent (*Laws of Manu*, V, 147-48).

The first verse glorifies women, celebrating their auspiciousness and life-giving powers, and instructs men to keep the women in the family happy. The second verse, on the other hand, prescribes women's dependence upon male protectors. These two verses, however, are not at all contradictory. They recognize women's power and pro-pose to control it for patriarchal purposes. These verses, however, do not necessarily portray what women are or were, but rather are representative of the highly influential and hegemonic ideology of the Brahmanical Sanskritic tradition, for which Manu is the most famous spokesperson.

One might say, then, that the task for Hindu feminists, on an ideological level, is to rescue *shakti* from its patriarchal prison. In using this metaphor I am reminded of a well-known book by Gail Omvedt on Indian women's movements entitled *We Will Smash This Prison!* (1980). The metaphor, however, should not be taken to imply that *shakti* is locked up so tightly that it cannot get out or has never before got out. The security of this prison is not as tight as its wardens would hope or like to believe. The *shakti* has seeped out underneath the doors and between the bars on numerous occa-sions. Furthermore, Hindu patriarchy is not monolithic or unchang-ing. The walls and bars, to continue the metaphor, are constantly being torn down and reconfigured. Some examples of that 'seep-age' I have given above. Many others can be found in various folk, vernacular, and heterodox traditions; that is, those traditions which are at some remove from the Sanskritic Brahmanical traditions (Berreman 1993). Writing of the Indian women's movement in the 1980s, social historian Radha Kumar says:

> If the interest in traditionalism led some to create images for femi-nists, others were more interested in defining ways in which ordi-nary, or unexceptional, women used the spaces which were tradi-tionally accorded them to negotiate with their husbands, families, communities, and so on. Special attention was now paid, for exam-ple, to the way in which women simulated possession by the devi (goddess), particularly at times of pregnancy, in order to wrest con-cessions...Though this tactic was more commonly espoused by preg-nant women to get special food during their pregnancy, accounts began to circulate of women who simulated possession in order to reform alcoholic husbands, or get money for household expenses, and this began to be recommended as a means of gaining some degree of power (R. Kumar 1993: 145-46).

There are those who would argue that *shakti*-related phenomena such as Goddess possession and women gurus are safety valves which ultimately function to preserve the patriarchal system. The idea that women (and other disadvantaged people) engage in religious practices and experience spiritual empowerment as a kind of consolation prize for losing status in the 'real world' (a version of what has been called the 'deprivation theory') has been advanced by such scholars as I.M. Lewis (1971) and critiqued by Susan Starr Sered (1994) among others. I would respond that that depends on whose point of view one is speaking from and also on how much importance and legitimacy one gives to religious experience and spiritual phenomena as significant in their own right and not as merely indices of social, economic, and political status. But I postpone any detailed consideration of that question to a later time.

Instead, I will devote the remainder of this essay to some examples of contemporary Indian feminist activists, artists, and writers who have embraced *shakti* or the Goddess as both spiritually and socially liberating for women. I believe, however, that they are doing something different than contemporary Western feminists who are reviving Goddess imagery and worship (for example Christ 1979). Unlike the Western religious traditions in which female divine imagery has been obscured for centuries and has only recently been rediscovered by feminist theologians (or thealogians), Hinduism has had popular, pervasive, and longstanding Goddess traditions for many centuries. *Shakti* is part of the mainstream; it is not at all radical or shocking for a Hindu to say that God is a woman or to talk about women being powerful.

Some Indian feminists realize this, and are promoting *shakti* and Goddess images to generate a feminist consciousness among a broad base of women, especially more traditional women for whom powerful religious images carry more weight than do political rhetoric and dialectical materialist analyses. I do not mean to imply that these Indian feminists are cynically exploiting religious images and ideas for their own ends. Rather, I think that many Indian feminists are expanding their own visions of feminism to include a spiritual dimension and are finding powerful resources within their own traditions.

One example of such a feminist is Abha Bhaiya, director of the Delhi-based women's development resource center, Jagori. Raised in a conservative Rajasthani Hindu family, Bhaiya had for a time turned away from religion as her feminist consciousness developed. More recently, however, she has become interested in spirituality,

traveling throughout the countryside visiting Goddess temples and
holy women in a quest for positive female images both for her personal spiritual fulfillment and to integrate into her activist work
with women (personal communication 1997). Thus, her feminism
is one which is not alienated from the spiritual pulse of the grass-
roots level.

As a general observation, I have noticed that the Indian women's
journal *Manushi* has in recent years included many more articles
on goddesses, women *bhakti* saints, and other Indian cultural resources than in the first few years since its inception in 1979, when
the journal tended to employ a more strictly socialist-feminist approach which ignored or denigrated religious and other traditional
cultural forms. I think this is part of a general trend in Indian wom-
en's movements to shift away from reliance on purely Western ana-
lytical modes such as dialectical materialism, to embrace Indian cultural resources, and to include women who have a religious outlook.
It is also significant that the most prolific press publishing books on
Indian women is called Kali for Women, after the Hindu Goddess
Kali. Hindu philosopher Lina Gupta has said, 'It is in the goddess
Kali that I find the inherent power of women made explicit' (1991:
20). She has urged contemporary Hindu women to identify with
Kali in her most liberating aspects, going beyond the 'patriarchal
view of the goddess, and woman, as untamed and unsubjugated
and therefore in need of control' (1991: 37).

Bharata Natyam dancer, graphic artist and activist Chandralekha
is known for her feminist appropriation of the Kali image, 'from
whom all traces of manic bloodlust had been removed, though she
continued to wield weapons of destruction, chosen by Chandralekha to represent the different religious communities of India'
(R. Kumar 1993: 145). In an interview in 1983 with Manjulika Dube
of *The Book Review*, Chandralekha said, 'We need to...understand
Shakti...as an energy within ourselves which generates the power
to act... We have to use our ears and eyes and see the creative
energies in us... Personally, I believe this energy is directly related
to the Shakti cults which are still very strong in our culture. I feel it
in my own body and consciousness' (quoted in Liddle and Joshi
1986: 5).

Taking a somewhat different approach, ecofeminist Vandana Shiva
(1989) has argued that gender subordination and patriarchy have

intensified in India through what she calls 'maldevelopment' and advocates a return to values and practices associated with Prakriti, the feminine principle. Lesbian-feminist poet Suniti Namjoshi has evoked stories and images of Hindu goddesses in her writings (1989). Writer Giti Thadani (1996) has gone so far as to locate evidence of a positive lesbian identity in ancient myths and images of goddesses and other female figures, which she argues was later obscured by Brahminical hegemony and the legacy of colonialism. Whether or not such assertions are historically valid is not at issue here. Rather, I wish to point out that it is significant that an Indian lesbian-feminist has chosen to embrace and recover elements of 'her' tradition, rather than reject it wholesale.

Another artist-activist who has incorporated Goddess images into her work is Sheba Chhachhi. Based in Delhi, Chhachhi is both a professional photographer and a creator of multi-media installations. Her photos documenting the women's movement have been widely credited (R. Kumar 1993) and exhibited internationally. But she sees her 'real work' as putting together a series of exhibits, most recently Wild Mothers I and II. The Wild Mothers series was inspired by a pilgrimage Chhachhi made to Kamakhya, the temple in Assam where the *yoni* or female organ of the Goddess is enshrined and where female and male ascetics perform Tantric practices in caves on the hillsides. These installations, bringing together historical and contemporary representations using poetry, song, narrative, photography, sculpture, and painting, are multi-media excursions into the lives of Khepis, Matajis, and Yoginis, women 'who dare to define themselves in relation to the metaphysical rather than the social' (Chhachhi 1993: 150). Chhachhi sees such women as dangerous in that, while living in a patriarchal culture, they interrogate and subvert the assumptions underlying women's subordination (Chhachhi 1993: 151). She is, however, keenly aware of the potential for religious images, including those of female power and divinity, to be manipulated by fundamentalist ideologies and sees her work as countering such tendencies. Although much of her work is informed by Hindu Goddess images, she is interested in all spirituality which transcends the boundaries of institutional religions and thus includes in her exhibit images from Islam, Buddhism, and Sikhism as well. When I asked her how her interest in the Goddess was viewed within the feminist community, she said

'In the beginning I was quite alone. Now, for the past five or six years, I have more company' (personal communication 1996).

One of the challenges which Indian feminists face is to generate among women a sense of identity and common cause with other women as women across caste, class, regional, linguistic, religious, and kinship lines. This identity is not a given; it must be constructed, and for Indian feminists, there are compelling political reasons to do so. *Shakti* is the female creative power which cuts across other identity boundaries and is thus effectively used to generate community among women. I was particularly interested to hear of the organizing strategies employed in Mahila Mandals, women's organizations, in Kangra villages not far from my own fieldwork site in Kangra. Anthropologist Kim Berry, who has been conducting a study of Mahila Mandals in Kangra, presented a paper (Berry 1994) in which she reported that Sutra, a development group, holds camps for women in Mahila Mandals. At these camps, women share stories of their common sorrows and joys (*dukh-sukh*), see slides of 'pre-Aryan goddesses', discuss the reclaiming of menstruation and reproductive powers, and shout slogans such as 'Jay Mahila Shakti' (Victory to Women's Power). Berry observed women at these camps dancing with their long hair flying loose and with their *cunnis* (long headscarves) discarded. The Mahila Mandals have mobilized for such actions as demanding the building of schools, the provision of water supplies for their villages, and the closure of alcohol shops. They believe they can accomplish these goals, because, as one woman was heard to say, 'Women's *shakti* is very great; it can shake not only the DC [District Commissioner] but the PM [Prime Minister]'.

In this essay, I have focused on the positive aspects of the question, 'Is *shakti* empowering for women?' I acknowledge and even caution that the answer to such a question can only be context specific. The context in which I speak is as a feminist and scholar of Hinduism in the post-colonial era who is sympathetic to both Indian feminist movements and to traditions of the divine feminine. Not surprisingly, I look for spaces in which the two come together and reinforce, even enrich, each other. While not excluding the possibility of other interpretations, I see ample scope for feminists to embrace the concept of *shakti*, should they choose to do so. Thus, from where I stand now, in answering the question, 'Is *shakti* empowering for women?', I would prefer to reply with a qualified 'yes' than with a qualified 'no'.

Bibliography

Berreman, Gerald D.
1993   'Sanskritization and Female Oppression in India', in Barbara Diane Miller (ed.), *Sex and Gender Hierarchies* (Cambridge: Cambridge University Press): 366-92.

Berry, Kim
1994   'Spaces of Imagination: Mahila Mandals (Village Women's Organizations) in District Kangra, Himachal Pradesh, India', paper presented at the 23rd Annual Conference on South Asia, Madison, Wisconsin.

Chakravarti, Uma
1989   'Whatever Happened to the Vedic Dasi? Orientalism, Nationalism, and a Script for the Past', in Kumkum Sangari and Sudesh Vaid (eds.), *Recasting Women: Essays in Colonial History* (New Delhi: Kali for Women): 27-87.

Chhachhi, Sheba
1993   'Wild Mothers: Khepis and Matajis', in Sunil Gupta (ed.), *Disrupted Borders: An Intervention in Definitions of Boundaries* (London: Rivers Oram Press).

Christ, Carol P.
1979   'Why Women Need the Goddess: Phenomenological, Psychological, and Political Reflections', in Carol P. Christ and Judith Plaskow (eds.), *Womanspirit Rising: A Feminist Reader in Religion* (San Francisco: Harper & Row): 273-87.

Erndl, Kathleen M.
1993   *Victory to the Mother: The Hindu Goddess of Northwest India in Myth, Ritual, and Symbol* (New York: Oxford University Press).
1997   'The Goddess and Women's Power: A Hindu Case Study', in Karen L. King (ed.), *Women and Goddess Traditions in Antiquity and Today* (Studies in Antiquity and Christianity; Minneapolis: Fortress Press): 17-38.
forthcoming   *Playing with the Mother: Women, Goddess Possession, and Power in Kangra Hinduism.*

Gupta, Lina
1991   'Kali, the Savior', in Paula M. Cooey, William R. Eakin and Jay B. McDaniel (eds.), *After Patriarchy: Feminist Transformations of the World Religions* (Maryknoll, NY: Orbis Books): 15-38.

Gupta, Sanjukta
1991   'Women in the Saiva/Sakta Ethos', in Julia Leslie (ed.), *Roles and Rituals for Hindu Women* (Rutherford, NJ: Fairleigh Dickenson University Press): 193-210.

Hallstrom, Lisa Lassell
1999   *Mother of Bliss: Anandamayi Ma, 1896-1982* (New York: Oxford University Press).

Khanna, Madhu
 1999 'The Goddess–Women Equation in Sakta Tantras', in Mandakranta Bose (ed.), *Faces of the Feminine in Ancient, Medieval, and Modern India* (New York: Oxford University Press).

Kripal, Jeffrey J.
 1995 *Kali's Child: The Mystical and the Erotic in the Life and Teachings of Ramakrishna* (Chicago: University of Chicago Press).

Kumar, Radha
 1993 *The History of Doing: An Illustrated Account of Movements for Women's Rights and Feminism in India 1800-1990* (New Delhi: Kali for Women; London: Verso).

Kumar, Nita (ed.)
 1994 *Women as Subjects: South Asian Histories* (Charlottesville: University of Virginia Press).

Lewis, I.M.
 1971 *Ecstatic Religion: An Anthropological Study of Spirit Possession and Shamanism* (Harmondsworth: Penguin Books).

Liddle, Joanna, and Rama Joshi
 1986 *Daughters of Independence: Gender, Caste and Class in India* (New Brunswick: Rutgers University Press).

McDaniel, June
 1989 *The Madness of the Saints: Ecstatic Religion in Bengal* (Chicago: University of Chicago Press).

Marglin, Frédérique Apfel
 1985a 'Female Sexuality in the Hindu World', in Clarissa W. Atkinson, Constance H. Buchanan and Margaret R. Miles (eds.), *Immaculate and Powerful: The Female in Sacred Image and Social Reality* (Boston: Beacon Press): 39-59.
 1985b *Wives of the God-King: The Rituals of the Devadasis of Puri* (Oxford: Oxford University Press).

Mohanty, Chandra Talpade
 1991 'Under Western Eyes: Feminist Scholarship and Colonial Discourses', in Chandra Talpade Mohanty, Ann Russo and Lourdes Torres (eds.), *Third World Women and the Politics of Feminism* (Bloomington: Indiana University Press): 51-80.

Namjoshi, Suniti
 1989 *Because of India: Selected Poems and Fables* (London: Onlywomen Press).

Narayan, Uma
 1989 'The Project of Feminist Epistemology: Perspectives from a Nonwestern Feminist', in Alison M. Jaggar and Susan R. Bordo (eds.), *Gender/Body/Knowledge: Feminist Reconstructions of Being and Knowing* (New Brunswick: Rutgers University Press): 256-69.

Omvedt, Gail
 1980 *We Will Smash This Prison: Indian Women in Struggle* (London: Zed Press).

Patel, Kartikeya C.
 1994 'Women, Earth, and the Goddess: A Shakta-Hindu Interpretation',

Hypatia 9.4: 69-87.
Raheja, Gloria Goodwin and Ann Grodzins Gold
    1994   *Listen to the Heron's Words: Reimagining Gender and Kinship in*
                North India (Berkeley: University of California Press).
Ricoeur, Paul
    1970   *Freud and Philosophy* (trans. Denis Savage; New Haven: Yale University Press).
Sered, Susan Starr
    1994   *Priestess, Mother, Sacred Sister: Religions Dominated by Women*
                (New York and Oxford: Oxford University Press).
Shiva, Vandana
    1989   *Staying Alive: Women, Ecology and Development* (New Delhi: Kali
                for Women; London: Zed Books).
Thadani, Giti
    1996   *Sakhiyani: Lesbian Desire in Ancient and Modern India* (London:
                Cassell).

Rita M. Gross

Is the Goddess a Feminist?

Is the Goddess a feminist? Well, that's a good question. In my view, the only possible answer is 'It depends'. I want to suggest that it depends on two things. It depends on how the term 'feminist' is defined. And it depends on who the Goddess's devotees are.

Depending on how the term 'feminist' is defined, various Hindu and Buddhist goddesses could be shown to be either feminists or non-feminists in their traditional manifestations. But, in the long run, if the goddesses' devotees are feminists, then the goddesses will either come to be seen as feminists or will be abandoned by their feminist devotees. And if the goddesses' devotees are anti-feminist or non-feminist, then the goddesses will not be feminists, whatever their appearance to outsiders.

Thus, the answer to this question lies, not in the imagery and mythology of the Goddess per se, but in a complex and subtle inter-action between the Goddess and her devotees. I make these corre-lations between goddesses and devotees because, as historians of religions, we know that, in the long run, gods and goddesses are created by devotees, though, in the short run, any individual is formed in part by the images of gods and goddesses she imbibes from her culture. As historians of religion, we know that divine im-agery is not arbitrarily given by something outside human cultural creativity and we know that divine imagery always bears some rela-tionship to human culture, though that relationship is not as simple as the direct mirroring some expect. Nevertheless, despite my em-phasis on definitions, answering this question is not merely a mat-ter of clever definitions. Important issues are at stake in the question of whether or not the Goddess is a feminist.

Definitions of feminism, it seems to me, turn on the point that, according to feminism, women are human beings in their own right. This contrasts with androcentric scholarship and patriarchal social forms, in which males are the only genuinely human sub-jects. In patriarchal societies, women are controlled by men and, at least theoretically, do not have self-determination. In androcentric scholarship, women are classified, analyzed, and, in general talked *about* as if they had no consciousness, no sense of self, and no ability to name reality. Thus, despite the many varieties of feminism and the many arguments within feminist theory, I am suggesting that feminism focuses on the *humanity* of women and searches for that which promotes and recognizes their humanity, though there is significant disagreement over what women need or want as human beings. Nevertheless, to focus on women's humanity, rather than to legislate *for* them and to theorize *about* them, is a massive conceptual leap from the way most of us were taught to think about women by our cultures and by our academic mentors. We were taught to gather information about women, to analyze and theorize about them, as if women were no more human than the phenomenal world or the deities.

Since Hindu society is at least nominally patriarchal and since much Hindu religious thought is androcentric, it would seem, at least superficially, that Hindu goddesses have not done a good job of promoting the humanity of Hindu women. This could mean that the goddesses are not feminists, but are the creation of patriarchal males, and serve their needs. Some would even argue that the goddesses function to help maintain patriarchy by feeding women divine images of either decent goddesses who are submissively married or frighteningly out-of-control unmarried goddesses. The message would be clear: since independence makes females bloodthirsty and dangerous, women will imitate Sita rather than Kali. Some Christian feminists who do not regard re-imaging the divine as feminine as the central agenda for Christian feminism often make this assertion about ancient Near Eastern goddesses and regard with skepticism the notion that there is any real correlation between goddesses and women's well-being. Certainly, looked at superficially, the evidence presented by world religions does not present a strong case that the goddesses have been very good feminists.

On the other hand, some Western feminists, myself included, have been attracted to some Hindu goddesses as providing intensely liberating symbols. The traditional imagery of the Indian goddesses, abstracted from the Hindu social context and considered in the context of what some Western feminists want, seems compelling, provocative, and inspiring. Their ferocity is not at all frightening but is a model for our own strength and autonomy; many other dimensions of the symbolism of Hindu goddesses are also provocative and inspiring. I have long claimed that Western feminists could learn a great deal about the Goddess from contemplating her various Indian forms (Gross 1978). For us, the Hindu Goddess is a feminist because she promotes our humanity in powerful ways.

But how can the same goddesses serve patriarchy in one case and promote women's humanity in another case? Obviously everything depends on what the devotees make of the Goddess, on how the devotees interpret her myths and images. The Goddess herself is neither feminist nor non-feminist, since she does not exist as an independent autonomous entity, but only in relationship with those who know her, revere her, and follow her bidding—as they understand it.

Since the Goddess is neither feminist nor non-feminist apart from her devotees, it is most effective not to ask the question of whether or not the Goddess is a feminist in the abstract, but to look into specific situations. Therefore, I will focus on two separate arenas. First, we must ask whether the Goddess really is such a patron of patriarchy in the Hindu context as is often superficially claimed. Second, we will investigate what is going on when Western feminists use the Hindu goddesses as a model for their feminist reflections.

It is intriguing to ask to what extent the Hindu goddesses have actually served the interests of patriarchy in India. Perhaps they have served instead, or additionally, to affirm the humanity of women but in ways that Western feminists are ill prepared to notice or appreciate. Western feminists tend to evaluate women's status and well-being in terms of women's autonomy and self-determination. They tend to look at law, politics, and economics as the factors that determine how well off women are. But in societies in which individualism is less pronounced and much less valued, very few people, male or female, have much autonomy. And the Hindu goddesses have given Hindu women neither autonomy nor the legal, economic, or political status that most Western women find essential.

But Hindu goddesses can promote the humanity of Hindu women by providing the psychological well-being that positive female imagery brings. Against some Western feminists, I have long argued that the first function of goddesses is not to provide equal rights or high status, but to provide psychological comfort, and that nothing is more basic to psychological comfort than the presence of positive female imagery at the heart of a valued symbol system. The sheer contrast between Hindu polytheism, with its numerous goddesses, and Western monotheism, with its long struggle to exterminate the Goddess, is overwhelming. What could possibly be a clearer indicator of the humanity of women than the visual presence of numerous divine females in a variety of roles and poses? And what can more effectively undercut the humanity of women than to regard femaleness as unworthy to symbolize the sacred? I always remember the question and the comment of a Hindu friend who, on our strolls through the Delhi suburb in which she lived, asked me things she didn't understand about America. 'Is it really true that there people don't regard God as female?' 'Yes', I replied. Her quick response was 'What does that say about what they think of women?'

In this way, even a goddess like Sita, who certainly would not be the *ishta* (chosen deity) of any Western feminist, may well promote the humanity of Hindu women by providing a relevant and comforting model of wifehood. It is not difficult to imagine or to understand that the life of a Hindu wife would be even bleaker without the example of her divine counterpart and role model. The fact that Western feminists do not approve of the way in which Sita promotes women's humanity does not mean that Sita has been a negative factor for Hindu women. Rather, given their life situation, Hindu women are probably better off with than they would be without Sita, just as the Moroccan women Fatima Mernissi writes about are better off with than without their refuge in the saints' sanctuaries (Mernissi 1989: 112-21). Or to use an example closer to home, even though most Western feminists do not find Mary an acceptable female image, nevertheless, Mary has been comforting to women who had few other solaces in their lives. In our zeal to promote the kind of human life we Western feminists value, we should not overlook or deny the ways in which things we do not want for ourselves can comfort women whose lives are very different from our own.

In addition, some Hindu goddesses provide something that is unavailable in the West's repertoire of images—strong-willed, creative, and powerful females who are auspicious and beneficent.

For, clearly, it was a misperception on the part of earlier Western scholars of Hinduism to see the strong goddesses as feared, negative entities; this is not the dominant Hindu response to them, though in some contexts they are feared. Furthermore, these images are appreciated by men as well as by women. Because both men and women are used to and comfortable with divine images of female strength and power, powerful women should be less frightening than they are to Westerners. It is worth noting that no American woman could possibly attain the political position of Indira Gandhi, no matter whose relative she might be. Though powerful Hindu women may, at present, be few and far between, nevertheless, they are not without divine counterparts, who should make them more acceptable and familiar. In some instances the goddesses clearly promote the humanity of women by encouraging men's approval of strong, empowered females. I was once quite struck by a male guide telling, with great enthusiasm, the story of a virgin goddess of South India who had killed her would-be rapist. He clearly identified with the female and had no sympathy for the violent male.

In this context, one may well question the pervasiveness of patriarchy in Hinduism. Hindu society is patriarchal, at least in what it tells itself and what it says about itself when asked. Though the preference for males and male control is clearly real in many instances, nevertheless, Hindu communities yield interesting results when they are analyzed in terms of the distinction between *authority*, which is held by men, and *power*, which both men and women wield.[1] Some Hindu patriarchy may be what anthropologists call 'mythical male dominance',[2] rather than the literal male dominance the Laws of Manu prescribe. Studies such as those done by Susan

---

1.   This distinction, which has been made by some anthropologists, is very useful. Authority, which is men's prerogative, is the right to command and to be obeyed. Power is the ability to influence how things happen, even though one does not the formal authority to determine what is done. Women often have considerable power in patriarchal societies, even though they have little or no authority.

2.   In a situation of 'mythical male dominance', both men and women *say* that men control society. But when the society is observed, women actually have considerable influence, though that influence is not acknowledged openly by either men or women.

Wadley (Wadley 1989: 72-81) indicate that women do what they can to take control of situations that are important to them, often with a goddess as their patron.

These are some possible ways in which Hindu goddesses may promote the humanity of Hindu female devotees who are not especially feminist by Western definitions. In addition, in the present and future, the Hindu devotees of these Hindu goddesses may well become more frequently and more overtly feminist, though in Hindu not Western terms. Then the Hindu goddesses will easily and naturally become feminists, though some, such as Kali and Durga, seem more attuned to the role than others, such as Sita and Lakshmi. Because deity is so naturally seen as female in Hinduism, feminist interpretations of Hinduism would, in fact, be less revolutionary than are feminist interpretations of monotheism. And some Hindus who are also familiar with Western feminist theology are beginning to write of a Hindu Goddess who is overtly a feminist (Gupta 1991: 15-38). Expansions and elaborations of such discussions will be intensely interesting, and some of us are very curious to see what will be forthcoming. Such discussions, however, simply cannot be done by outsiders, no matter how knowledgeable and sympathetic we may be.

Nevertheless, the goddesses of Hinduism and Buddhism can have meaning to Western feminists; even more than that, as I claimed earlier in this article and have claimed repeatedly, Western feminists who are interested in Goddess theology would be well advised to study carefully the imagery, symbolism, and mythology of Hindu and Buddhist goddesses. After all, they represent the largest extant collection of living goddesses anywhere on the planet. By virtue of that fact alone, they should be used as theological resources in the contemporary rediscovery of the Goddess, to quote the title of my own work on the subject (Gross 1978), as resources for our own religious thinking. This complex practice brings up at least two critical questions. The first concerns the relationship between the images of Hindu goddesses in Western feminist reflections about them and the images of Hindu goddesses found in Hindu culture. The second concerns the politics and theology of using seemingly foreign images as a resource for one's own thinking and reflections.

The process that occurs when a Western feminist is inspired to make certain suggestions about Goddess theology on the basis of her knowledge of Hindu or Buddhist goddesses is a kind of translation project. Clearly, it does not involve the literal translation of a text from one language to another. Nevertheless, translation is involved in that meaning is transferred from one context to another. A cultural commentator, familiar with both Hindu goddesses and Western theological contexts, suggests that the symbolism, imagery, or mythology familiar to Hindu goddesses might help us think through certain issues, problems, or lacks in Western religious discourse. Or, put another way, the cultural commentator, familiar with both contexts, might be inspired by specific symbolisms found in connection with Hindu or Buddhist goddesses to construct or intuit certain interpretations that would be helpful to Western religions.

However, clearly, such discussions are *not* about the meanings the Goddess has had in traditional Hindu contexts, but about how her imagery, contemplated in a certain way, can empower and inspire us in our quest for the Goddess. She is now the Goddess whom we envision, owing something to her Hindu models, but she is not the Hindu Goddess. Non-Hindus cannot worship the Hindu Goddess, but only their version of the Goddess, who owes something, perhaps a great deal, to her Hindu prototype, but who is, nevertheless, distinct. Some people have missed this subtlety in critiquing my work, and have assumed that I was talking about Hindu goddesses as perceived by Hindus. On the basis of that misperception, they have critiqued my comments about Hindu goddesses as inaccurate. Others have claimed that since Hindu women do not seem to experience the kind of liberation I am seeking, the Goddess does not provide it and I have misunderstood the Hindu goddesses. But I have been quite clear in stating that I am discussing Hindu goddesses as a *resource* in the contemporary rediscovery of the Goddess, *not* the Hindu Goddess.

To some, the entire practice of using materials from another culture as resources with which to think is rather suspect. Such suspicion travels in two directions. On the one hand, many from Western religions simply dismiss non-Western religions as having no theological relevance to them. Such people may be willing, at best, to study non-Western religions as information. But they cannot imagine taking such religious ideas or images seriously into

their own thinking, whether because of attitudes of cultural superiority or because they feel that it is just too much work to learn
the non-Western religion well enough to be able to use it as a theological resource. I remember well the incredulous hostility that
sometimes occurred when I showed slides of Hindu goddesses to
Jewish audiences while I discussed the theological meanings these
images might suggest for female God-language in a Jewish context
(Gross 1983).

On the other hand, in an era of growing post-colonial sensibilities, there are pressures from the opposite direction. Some would
contend that it is improper for Westerners to be inspired by images
from the religion of a formerly colonized people and to translate
them into their own repertoire of theological images. As frequently
as not, this argument comes from a certain kind of Western liberal
who is using the argument in an attempt to garner a certain kind of
political-academic capital against other scholars.

This complex issue cannot be fully discussed in this context, due
to lack of space, but I have written about it quite extensively recently in a number of contexts (Gross 1996: 103-34, 244-47; Gross
1998). In brief, it seems to me that both versions of the argument
against cross-cultural inspiration for religious thinking depend on a
false notion of cultures as hermetically sealed units isolated from
one another and developing internally, without significant influence
from 'outside', wherever that might be. If such has ever been the
case, it certainly is not the case now in a global village linked by
multifarious webs of communication. Cultures and religions are
influencing each other willy-nilly, so there should be no problem
with self-conscious, deliberate, and educated mutual transformations. Furthermore, as I have long argued, nothing so stimulates
one's religious imagination as deep, thorough, long-standing, well-
trained immersion in another religious context. Finally, the kind of
borrowing that is objectionable is the kind of superficial shopping
in the great spiritual supermarket that characterizes some more
commercial cross-cultural translations. That such shopping occurs
should not be used to condemn the translations of serious religious
thinkers who put in years-long apprenticeships before they begin
to attempt to suggest in what senses the Hindu Goddess might be a
resource in the contemporary rediscovery of the Goddess.

Bibliography

Gross, Rita M.

1978   'Hindu Female Deities as a Resource in the Contemporary Rediscovery
            of the Goddess', *Journal of the American Academy of Religion* 47.3:
            269-91.

1983   'Steps Toward Feminine Imagery of Deity in Jewish Theology', in
            Susannah Heschel (ed.), *On Being a Jewish Feminist: A Reader*
            (New York: Schocken Books): 234-47.

1996   *Feminism and Religion: An Introduction* (Boston: Beacon Press).

1998   'Why Me?: Reflections of a Wisconsin Farm Girl Who Became a Jew-
            ish Theologian When She Grew Up', in Rita M. Gross, *Soaring and
            Settling: Buddhist Perspectives on Contemporary Social and
            Religious Issues* (New York: Continuum): 19-33.

Gupta, Lina

1991   'Kali, the Savior', in P.M. Cooey, W.R. Eakin, and J.B. McDaniel (eds.),
            After Patriarchy: Feminist Reconstructions of the World's Religions
            (Maryknoll, NY: Orbis Books): 15-38.

Mernissi, Fatima

1989   'Women, Saints, and Sanctuaries in Morocco', in Nancy Auer Falk and
            Rita M. Gross (eds.), *Unspoken Worlds: Women's Religious Lives*
            (Belmont, CA: Wadsworth): 112-21.

Wadley, Susan S.

1989   'Hindu Women's Family and Household Rites in a North Indian Vil-
            lage', in Nancy Auer Falk and Rita M. Gross (eds.), *Unspoken Worlds:
            Women's Religious Lives* (Belmont, CA: Wadsworth): 72-81.

Alf Hiltebeitel

Draupadi's Question

A surprising thing is observable in scholarly work on Indian classical and folk epics: their goddesses, and their heroines' divinity, we are told, are not part of the original stories. Goddesses are one thing, and scholars who have favored the notion that epics begin as heroic tales about 'real men' have not treated them that much differently from male deities: both have been viewed as afterthoughts in the 'epic process', mythologizations of the historical kernel, latecomers to the presumed epic amalgam. The only difference, and this has been said of Indian religion more generally, is that goddesses are supposed to come a little later into the epic mix than gods. They are presumed to be the very last thing an epic would *really* or *originally* be about. But what about heroines and their associations with divinity? If goddesses do not belong to authentic epic, then a heroine's links with divinity need not be seriously considered at all.[1] Yet India's classical epics and many of its folk epics have central places for heroines who are understood to have some kind of divinity. Draupadi, the heroine of the *Mahabharata*, for instance, is from birth dark like the goddess Earth and an embodiment of Shri, the goddess of Prosperity. And indeed, Draupadi is worshiped as a form of the Great Goddess by certain communities in Tamilnadu, south India (see Hiltebeitel 1988, 1991). In studying her cult along with the classical epic, I have, over the years, wanted to insist that the scholarly pattern of occluding the goddess, which I have tried to show is textually untenable for the epic precisely because of the way it portrays the heroine,[2] has also taken the form of 'another' scholarly occlusion of the feminine, which one may take as implying that of women.

Here, however, under the title 'Draupadi's Question', I would like to take the matter of the heroine not in the direction of the god-

---

1. See my criticism (Hiltebeitel 1999: 37-43) of Blackburn's views of 'epic development', of which these comments are an extension.
2. On the textual issues, see Hiltebeitel (1980; 1981; forthcoming, ch. 7).

dess, but in the direction of real flesh-and-blood historical women, both those for whom a heroine—whatever her divinity—might have 'spoken' in the time of the epic's composition and as its text unfolds in history,[3] and for whom she might still speak today. I would like to engage these issues initially as they are at play in both the epic text itself and in modern scholarship on the epic, and then look at what has become of this question in an instance of contemporary fiction. Between goddesses and flesh-and-blood historical women, what a heroine questions can be of interest in thinking about whether the goddess is a feminist.

The scene is the epic dice match between the rivaling Pandava and Kaurava cousins. Having bet all his wealth and brothers, Yudhishthira is prodded into losing himself and then Draupadi, his wife, who is also the wife of his four brothers. The wager lost, Duryodhana orders that Draupadi be brought to the Kauravas as the slave of her new masters, and Draupadi asks her question to the messenger, refuses to come with him, and challenges him to ask it in the gambling hall, which he does. Says the messenger, ' "As the owner of whom did you lose us?" So queries Draupadi. "Whom did you lose first, yourself or me?" ' Here, and for the rest of the scene, 'Yudhishthira did not stir, as though he had lost consciousness' (*Mbh* 2.60.9).

It is the insolubility of the question, and the impasses it opens, that provoke the two violent scenes of Draupadi's violation, her hair-pulling and disrobing. The latter, the very last straw, is ordered by the threefold response of the usually noble Kaurava ally Karna, who, unbeknownst to himself and almost everyone at this point in the story, is the Pandavas' oldest brother. Karna says: (1) Yudhishthira could bet Draupadi because she is 'included within his total property' (61.31); (2) he may have been prodded, but he bet her audibly and uncontestedly; and (3) 'One husband per wife is ordained by the gods...; she, who submits to many, is for certain a whore...strip her' (61.38). Textual contestation is especially rich here. How was she protected by inexhaustible sarees? In reducing its 'reconstituted' text, the Poona Critical Edition makes it an

---

3.   For a comparable approach to 'questions' raised by heroines in the putatively 'male world' of Western epics, see Suzuki (1989). I view the *Mahabharata* as from about 200 BCE.

unexplained wonder.[4] In possibly the oldest interpolation, they come from the 'concealed' dharma. Cynthia Leenerts, one of my recent graduate students who has written on the Sanskrit epics and twentieth-century Indian fiction (1997), proposes that Draupadi's own *dharma* as a devoted wife protects and vindicates her. The Critical Edition editor Franklin Edgerton thinks 'cosmic justice' is 'apparently implied' (1944: xxix). Or was it the story everybody knows, including Draupadi and Krishna *later* in the Critical Edition (5.58.21; 80.26), that Draupadi prayed to Krishna?

We cannot follow the full debate over Draupadi's question, the insults, and the terrible vows of revenge.[5] It is overtly a question of *dharma* in the men's gambling hall or *sabha* as a courtroom. Dire omens finally interrupt and prompt the Kauravas' blind father to offer Draupadi boons that allow her to choose Yudhishthira's freedom, and Karna recognizes that she has been the Pandavas' salvation (*shanti*) and their boat to shore (64.1-3) by asking a question that now hangs unresolved over the entire epic.

How then does Draupadi's question relate to our book's question? For the epic poets, Draupadi is asking a woman's question, if not *the* woman's question. Other heroines in the *Mahabharata*—Damayanti, Sita, Amba—also raise it in varied forms: Is it really you who is doing this to me? We see what subjugates Draupadi in the men's hall in the sarcastic words of Karna: 'There are three who own no property: a slave, a student, and a woman are not independent (*asvatantra*). You are the wife of a slave, his wealth, dear, without a lord, the wealth of a slave, and a slave (yourself)'. It is the *dharma* that subjugates Draupadi: these words echo a famous verse in the *Laws of Manu* that describes women as 'never independent' (*asvatantra*). Yet her appeal to the *dharma* is also what saves the Pandavas and, in some sense, herself. As we have seen, Draupadi is also the incarnation of a goddess. Is she a feminist? Granting definitional, historical, and intercultural cautions, if we say yes, we have our best support from a speech she begins as follows: 'These Kurus stand here in the hall, lords of their daughters and daughters-in-law,

4.   Thus Edgerton (1944: xxiv): 'No prayer by Draupadi; no explanation of the miraculous replacement of one garment by another; no mention of Krishna or any superhuman agency.'

5.   See especially Mehendale (1986), and my response in Hiltebeitel (forthcoming, ch. 7).

all considering even my word—answer this question of mine the proper way' (61.45). She speaks about, and perhaps for, *women as a class*, and challenges the men to consider a question that questions their lordship over and 'ownership' of women in contexts of patriarchy. But we also have reasons to say no. Draupadi is a literary figure, not a woman. The Dead Indian Sanskritizing Males (DISMs) who wrote the epic have made her a 'voice' for what is at best their sympathetic understanding of a woman's question. And what a strange image and voice! Let us look at the moment that she is wagered and lost.

Shakuni, Yudhishthira's deceitful opponent at dicing, addresses Yudhishthira with the probing verse: 'There is surely your dear lady (*priya devi*), one throw unwon. Stake Dark (*Krishnaa*) Panchali. Win yourself back by her.' The first meaning of *devi* is of course 'goddess', which would be an overtranslation but hardly an overestimation of the lady. More than this, *devi* is the goddess as 'she who plays' (Biardeau 1985: 17), and Panchali is a name for Draupadi that is used with heightened frequency in this scene (Biardeau 1985: 11, 13-14), meaning 'the puppet'. As Yudhishthira sets to wager her, he speaks from what feels like a revery: 'She is not too short or too tall, not too black or too red—I play you with her...' Doll-like, iconic, she is bet and lost, and Yudhishthira will say nothing until her question wins him his freedom. Later, Draupadi will say we are all puppets, our strings pulled by the Creator—to which Yudhishthira will reply that she is eloquent with passion, but heretical. As Panchali, Draupadi is thus the doll or puppet who speaks, who even recognizes herself as such; as *devi*, she is the lady who plays who is also played. She raises the feminist questions of a Barbie doll—which can, of course, be interesting.

It is clear that in all this talk about betting oneself, Draupadi's question is a philosophical one about the nature of Self. As a philosophical question, it is compounded by legal issues of *proper*ty, *own*ership, and slavery in the hierarchical context of patriarchal marriage, and symbolized around the figure of the ultimate lord, master and owner, the king, in relation to the subjecthood and objecthood of the queen, his wife. These themes are in the Sanskrit, as are those of possession of Self vs. possession by the madness of dicing, and, I submit, the theme of love and abandonment, of love tested to, and maybe past, the breaking point—love between

six people in one and the same marriage! Listen to what Yudhishthira says when he bets himself just before he wagers Draupadi:
'I am left, so beloved of all my brothers. Won, we shall do work for
you when the self is itself a deluge' (*upaplave*; 58.27). Slipping into
his loving revery when he bets the 'dear lady' whom all five brothers hold dear, Yudhishthira descends into silence once he has lost
her. Here we see Draupadi's question from a new angle. Yudhishthira's loss of self *appears*—it is only described so by others—
to be a loss of consciousness. Is it the higher Self that is ultimately
at stake in Draupadi's question?

Here we seem to be in an agonistic multi-dialogical situation that
reverberates with Upanishadic scenes in which fathers and sons,
gurus and disciples, and, in a few memorable passages, especially
men and women churn the oppositional languages of rivalry and
status to release the saving knowledge of the Self that is one. Gargi,
whose questions to Yajnavalkya are like arrows; Yajnavalkya to
Maitreyi, renouncing the world and saying goodbye forever to his
dearer-than-ever 'knowledge-discoursing' (*brahmavadini*) wife:
'Not for love of the husband is a husband dear, but for love of the
atman…; not for love of the wife…'

But in the *Mahabharata*, the language of such questions and
answers has been compounded by the terminologies of Samkhya,
Yoga, and bhakti. Here Al Collins has been immensely helpful in
revealing how a sovereign self, male (*purusha*), replicates itself in
other selves through a 'scale of forms' that 'presents a problem for
male identity formation' (1994: 3-4). Man (and, for that matter,
woman), as mind-ego-intellect, is feminine matter, *prakriti*, living—
ultimately unconsciously—'for the sake of *purusha*', of 'man' as
conscious self or soul. As Collins says, 'The problem is not limited
to kings' who top this 'scale of forms', 'but is universal: it is highly
dangerous to claim to be a self' (1994: 4). How beautifully this describes Yudhishthira's predicament; no wonder he is silent.

But what about Draupadi? In a context where the feminine is
unconscious matter, can this be a feminist question and the ques-
tioner be feminist? Madeleine Biardeau, also insistent that a Samkhya
problematic underlies *Mahabharata* portrayals of heroines, gives
us our best route to a negative answer. For her, the heroine-god-
dess represents *prakriti* as unconscious matter, blind ignorance
given to 'obstinancy'; matter that unknowingly yet somehow in-

errantly works on behalf of *purusha* through 'blind initiatives'; heroines whose ignorance is unknowing in particular about *dharma* (1984: 263). There is more to this than I can go into, but I think it is one-sided. Biardeau says nothing about ignorance when it is a question of the heroine's ingenuity in posing questions that are riddles that prompt the hero's anagnorisis and draw him out of his concealment, riddles about the intimacies and pains of love, riddles that are a lifeline allowing him *and her* to use their wits and to 'play', or as David Shulman puts it, 'fight for time' (n.d.: 1). Draupadi certainly knows enough about *dharma* to question it. It is not just her obstinancy that makes her persist. As another of my recent graduate students, Lena Taneja, says, Draupadi never seems to doubt for a moment that she is truly free. It is perhaps her sense of this freedom that keeps her sticking to the question that will also free her husbands.

I cannot trace the *Mahabharata*'s tale of love (and other things) between Draupadi and Yudhishthira any further here. Suffice it to say that from the dice match on, there is no humanly happy ending. But even on the level of Samkhya ultimates, there are strange goings-on for epic love stories to activate. Here again Collins is eye-opening, showing that there are ways in which *prakriti* as *buddhi* (the 'intellect' or 'faculty of awareness') becomes 'indistinguishable from purusha' (1994: 21-22). It is worth asking whether Draupadi's sense of her freedom might be a reflection of what James Larson and Ram Shankar Bhattacharya call the intuitive capacity of the *buddhi* for freedom—the capacity 'finally of discriminating the presence of contentless consciousness' (1987: 82-83). 'Pure contentless consciousness' as witnessing 'passive presence' (1987: 77-81) is, however, probably not that attractive a mate, so it is not surprising that *prakriti*, as Collins says, makes a very ambivalent feminist.

So Draupadi too must be an ambivalent feminist. Perhaps the most we can say is that her question is one that an interculturally sensitive feminism might find interesting, and that it is not surprising that Indian feminists sometimes find it worth writing and thinking about. I refer especially to Mahasveta Devi's Bengali short story 'Draupadi' and Gayatri Spivak's translation and discussions of it (1988).

Draupadi is Comrade Dopdi Mejhen, a Santal tribal woman who has participated in Naxalite resistance to landlord oppression, survived a police raid, escaped to the forest, and joined book-educated young 'gentlemen' revolutionaries, for whom she is a courier between forest and village. She is being hunted down by army Intelligence and its half-breed Santali informers. Mahasweta Devi's story keeps us on course; she writes: 'Government procedure being as incomprehensible as the Male Principle in Samkhya philosophy', the hunt for Dopdi is first led by a captain whose diabetes was inflamed when he did not find her and her husband in the body count after the raid. He soon turns the case over to Senanayak, 'the elderly Bengali specialist in combat and extreme-Left politics', who 'respects the opposition', hoping to write eventually about his '*theory*' that '*In order to destroy the enemy, become one*' (Spivak 1988: 199).[6] He has much in common with the passive witnessing incomprehensible male principle. Mahasweta Devi satirizes this principle as analogous to Archimedes' fulcrum point: 'one of the tribal specialists runs in with a joy as naked and transparent as Archimedes' and says, "Get up, sir! I have discovered the meaning of that 'hende rambra' stuff. It's Mundari *language*" ' (p. 190).

Dopdi's husband Dulna is killed in ambush. She 'loved Dulna more than her blood. No doubt it is she who is saving the fugitives now', says a narrative reminder of Draupadi. When Dopdi is captured, she is officially Sanskritized to Draupadi for Senanayak, who questions her for about an hour, breaks for his dinner, and orders her gang rape: 'Make her. *Do the needful*' (1988: 195). In the morning, rather than wash and wear the white cloth that has been kept aside for her to appear in before Senanayak, Draupadi 'stands up. She pours the water down on the ground. Tears her piece of cloth with her teeth. Seeing such strange behavior, the guard says, She's gone crazy, and runs for orders.' Senanayak comes and, at the end, is terrified: 'What is this? He is about to bark. Draupadi comes closer. Stands with her hand on her hip, laughs and says, The object of your search, Dopdi Mejhen. You asked them to make me up, don't you want to see how they made me?' He sees her raped nakedness—'Where are her clothes? Won't put them on, *sir*. Tearing them.' He receives her defiant questions, spoken as her lips bleed. She 'shakes with an indomitable laughter that Senanayak simply cannot understand... What's the use of clothes? You can strip me, but how can you clothe me again? Are you a man?' She spits blood

6.   Spivak italicizes the Bengali usages of English words in her translation.

on his shirt, and says, 'there isn't a man here that I should be ashamed. I will not let you put my cloth on me. What more can you do? Come on. *Counter* me—come on, *counter* me—? Draupadi pushes Senanayak with her two mangled breasts, and for the first time Senanayak is afraid to stand before an unarmed *target*, terribly afraid' (1988: 196).

So Dopdi has three, four questions, but the last one is really left hanging. What more he can do to her is an unpleasant matter to contemplate. This Senanayak can do a lot. There is little doubt that he will kill her. His fear might not even prevent what Dopdi's comrades call her 'next stage': interrogation? torture? There are no suppressed husbands and descending deities left. This is not that story. And this story does not go on (and on...). We know that Senanayak cannot clothe her either as a man or a god. He is neither. And we know that Dopdi has no fear before him.

Spivak writes, 'It is when [Dopdi] crosses the sexual differential into the field of what could *only happen to a woman* that she emerges as the most powerful "subject", who, still using the language of sexual "honor", can derisively call herself "the object of your search" ' (1988: 184). 'She is the only one who uses the word "counter" '—as in ' "killed by police in an encounter", the code description for death by police torture. Dopdi does not understand English, but she understands this formula... What is it to "use" a language "correctly" without "knowing" it?' (186).

Let us remember Draupadi's class-action appeal for daughters and daughters-in-law. It calls into question two kinds of male lordship: that of kinship and family, and that of the *dharmic* politics of kingship in the *sabha* or men's hall. Dopdi Mejhen is captured because she is caught between two kinds of loyalty—one, the tribal community of Santals; the other, the comradeship of the gentlemen revolutionaries. Here Spivak can return us to the questions of territoriality, the occlusion of women, and the 'scale of forms' that allows patriarchal patterns to replicate themselves from one political situation *and* scholarly situation to another:

> The figure of the exchanged woman still produces the cohesive unity of a 'clan', even as what emerges is a 'king'... [T]hrough all the heterogeneous examples of territoriality and the communal mode of power, the figure of the woman, moving from clan to clan, and family to family as daughter/sister and wife/mother, syntaxes patriarchal

continuity even as she is herself drained of proper identity (1988: 219-20).

If Sheldon Pollock can question whether there is a 'deep Orientalism' in classical Sanskrit sources, perhaps Draupadi can be a deep feminist. If not, she has thought up a good question, one that seems to have been good for feminists to think with. I can say no more than 'seems', revive Yudhishthira's silence, and thank Spivak for one last question, and the answer she gives it: 'can men theorize feminism, can whites theorize racism, can the bourgeois theorize revolution and so on. It is when *only* the former theorize that the situation is politically intolerable' (1988: 253).

Bibliography

Agarwal, Purshottam
    1995   'Surat Savarkar and Draupadi: Legitimising Rape as a Political Weapon', in Tanika Sakar and Urvashi Butalia (eds.), *Women and the Hindu Right: A Collection of Essays* (New Delhi: Kali for Women).
Biardeau, Madeleine
    1984   'Nala et Damayanti. Héros épiques. Part 1', *Indo-Iranian Journal* 27: 247-74.
    1985   'Nala et Damayanti. Héros épiques. Part 2', *Indo-Iranian Journal* 28: 1-34.
Blackburn, Stuart H.
    1989   'Patterns of Development for Indian Oral Epics', in S.H. Blackburn, Peter J. Claus, Joyce B. Flueckiger and Susan S. Wadley (eds.), *Oral Epics of India* (Berkeley: University of California Press): 15-32.
Collins, Alfred
    1999   'Dancing with Prahriti', Paper delivered at the Annual Meeting of the American Academy of Religion, revised for this volume.
Devi, Mahasweta
    1988   'Draupadi' (trans. with Foreword by Gayatri Chakravorty Spivak). In Spivak 1988: 179-96.
Edgerton, Franklin
    1944   *Sabhaparvan. Introduction and Apparatus*, in V.S. Sukthankar *et al.* (eds.), *Mahabharata: Critical Edition* (24 vols. with *Harivamsa*; Poona: Bhandarkar Oriental Research Institute, 1933-70): II.
Hiltebeitel, Alf
    1980   'Draupadi's Garments', *Indo-Iranian Journal* 22: 97-112.
    1981   'Draupadi's Hair', *Purusartha* 5: 179-214.
    1988   *The Cult of Draupadi*. I. *Mythologies, From Gingee to Kuruksetra* (Chicago: University of Chicago Press).
    1991   *The Cult of Draupadi*. II. *On Hindu Ritual and the Goddess* (Chicago: University of Chicago Press).

1999   *Rethinking India's Oral and Classical Epics: Draupadi among Rajputs, Muslims, and Dalits* (Chicago: University of Chicago Press).

forthcoming *Rethinking the Mahabharata: A Readers' Guide to the Education of Yudhisthira* (Chicago: University of Chicago Press).

Larson, Gerald James, and Ram Shankar Bhattacharya

1987   *Encyclopedia of Indian Philosophies: Samkhya. A Dualist Tradition in Indian Philosophy* (Princeton: Princeton University Press).

Leenerts, Cynthia

1997   'Epic Transformations: Reinscriptions of Sita and Draupadi in Twentieth-Century Indian Literature' (PhD dissertation; Washington, DC: The George Washington University).

Mehendale, M.A.

1986   'Draupadi's Question', *Journal of the Oriental Institute of Baroda* 35: 179-94.

Pollock, Sheldon I.

1994   'Deep Orientalism? Notes on Sanskrit and Power Beyond the Raj', in Carol A. Breckenridge and Peter van der Veer (ed.), *Orientalism and the Postcolonial Predicament* (Delhi: Oxford University Press).

Shulman, David

n.d.   'The Yaksha's Question' (Manuscript. Personal communication).

Spivak, Gayatri Chakravorty

1988   *In Other Worlds* (New York: Routledge).

Suzuki, Mihoko

1989   *Metamorphoses of Helen: Authority, Difference, and the Epic* (Ithaca, NY: Cornell University Press).

Cynthia Ann Humes

Is the Devi Mahatmya a Feminist Scripture?

The *Devi Mahatmya*, 'Glorification of the Goddess' (c. sixth century CE), remains one of the most important Sanskrit sources central to Hindu goddess worship today. Millions of people in every
state of modern India have heard of this scripture—known by
various names—even if they have not read it or sponsored its
recitation. For two years, I conducted fieldwork to explore contemporary uses and interpretations of this text. My fieldsite was
Vindhyachal, a north Indian village home to the 'Vindhya dwelling
goddess'. Vindhyavasini is famous in millennia-old sources as the
slayer of two demons named Shumbha and Nishumbha. Today, she
is more commonly remembered for having helped save the god
Visnu's incarnation as the baby Krishna from infanticide at the
hands of a murderous uncle. Vindhyavasini is understood at Vindhyachal in terms very much in accord with the *Devi Mahatmya*—
indeed, her temple officiants deliberately cultivate close associations between the text and this goddess (Humes 1996a). Many
devotees believe that she is simultaneously the formless absolute
reality known as *brahman*; *prakriti* or matter; *adi shakti*, the
original or first power; as well as Krishna's savior. While many goddesses may be married and subordinated by a husband, Vindhyavasini is known today to be ever virgin, who remains independent of all male control. She is Maha Devi: the Great Goddess.

   After several months of research, I noticed that a commonality in
undirected interviews was a persistent emphasis on the great gulf
informants perceived to exist between ordinary women and the
Great Goddess. Often in making this contrast, they denigrated wom-
en's nature, and some used passages from the *Devi Mahatmya* to
support what I felt to be sexist views. While I was familiar with
unfavorable portrayals of women in other scriptures, their
responses still surprised me, especially since I had not detected a
misogynist flavor in the *Devi Mahatmya*. In theory, women are
closely connected with the concept of *shakti*, which is variously
defined. Usually, *shakti* is understood to be a pre-eminently moral

and creative power, possessed primarily by women and/or by individuals of moral purity. I had thus supposed that goddess-worshipers must feel there to be at least some—if not a close—relation between women and the Goddess, yet their insistence on such a distance was adamant. I knew from prior experience in India that married women were sometimes worshiped as Lakshmi—the goddess of wealth—and young girls were honored at certain rites, including *navaratra*, the nine-day fall festival dedicated to the Goddess; indeed, women are often called *devi*, or goddess. So why were my informants insisting on there being such an enormous difference between women and the Great Goddess? Were their comments representative of most Hindus there, or were they anomalies? Accordingly, I resolved to address this issue specifically with a sample of pilgrims. I asked fifty-four males and twenty-five females the question, 'How does the Great Goddess Vindhyavasini compare to ordinary women? What are the differences, and what are the similarities?'

The responses I got to this question were striking. First, there was one very obvious gender difference: male respondents felt more comfortable answering the question. More than 96 per cent of the men attempted to answer the question, but only 60 per cent of the women ventured to comment—even though the subject presumably dealt with their own nature. Second, the majority of respondents—of both genders—held to there being a huge difference between women and the Goddess, confirming the data I had gathered before. Forty out of fifty-one males and nine of the fifteen females who answered the question either said that there was a great difference or that no comparison was even possible. Put simply, they identified the Goddess as a divine being whose power is immeasurably beyond that of human females, and whose nature does not conform to their perceptions of women's nature. For instance, women and the Goddess differ in ways ranging from how they are created and create their ability to create and protect life, levels of spiritual awareness, and even modes of mothering: only four respondents asserted a close similarity between human and divine mothering. Moreover, not a single one of the seventy-nine pilgrims linked women and the Goddess together as similar through the concept of *shakti*. Twelve men, however, *contrasted* them through *shakti*.

My surprise at these answers was due in part to my own pre-
judgements and feminist political sentiments. I had read the *Devi
Mahatmya* and other goddess myths with the belief that, to some
extent, they were magnifications of human beings; portrayals of the
Goddess could thus tell us about Hindu perceptions of women, and
might inspire the reader or listener. In part because Hinduism is
one of the rare religions with a living Goddess tradition which dates
from ancient times, and also because of the power of its passages,
this majestic scripture has captured the attention of a number of
Western feminists. By 'Western', I mean the general directions of
Continental and Anglo-American traditions based on European and
American Protestant Christian thought. A noteworthy segment of
Western feminist religious revisionism relies on Hindu goddesses as
a resource for imaging the divine as feminine, and for many, this
necessitates the close association of goddesses and women. Such
an assumption rests in part on the traditional conflation of male
human dominance and a male god/savior in Judaic and Christian
traditions. Western language and theories of being, too, contributed to my confusion—either you are, or you are not, X; if the
scripture says a portion of the Goddess dwells in women, then
women are divine. But that was not what my informants were
telling me. I soon realized that I had not internalized a central
religious tenet held by most Hindus: the *Devi Mahatmya* is about
Devi, the Great Goddess, not a Great Woman, nor even 'a goddess'.
Further, when I asked reciters direct questions about specific
verses, I came to realize that I had not paid sufficient attention to
the nuances of its language and myths, which can be interpreted to
betray decidedly antifeminist views of human women. Indeed,
rather than being a direct model of women's nature, in important
ways Devi's nature tells us what ordinary women are not.

To ask, 'Is the *Devi Mahatmya* a feminist scripture?' is to ask a
question which preoccupies persons within a specific time, place,
and mindset. The authors never intended to answer all questions
on men's or women's nature. They were interested in religious
goals, not worldly goals, by which I mean they were preoccupied
with what they believed to be the ultimate human concern: enlightenment and salvation from suffering. My goal here is different, and,
in important ways, does not engage the text in the way it was intended. As an historian, I can only discuss the stuff of history, which

does not include true reality or enlightenment itself. I will thus limit myself to worldly phenomena, and explore the scripture's feminist and antifeminist dimensions. By 'feminist' I mean that which offers women worldly liberation, whether that be in terms of freedom from oppressive thought, or oppressive social structures. Despite the fact that the text may have misogynist undertones and has been used to support oppression of women in the past, I believe that its historical uses do not completely vitiate its utility for female worldly empowerment now or in the future, for Hindus and non-Hindus. I base this claim on my observation of Hindu men and women directly engaged with the scripture.

For the purpose of brevity, while I discuss the entire text at certain points, I focus particularly on issues of power and gender in just the third of the text's three myths. I am concerned with what the scripture itself suggests about the Goddess's nature and her relation to other beings: male gods and demons, other goddesses, and humans—especially women. I offer signposts periodically to indicate how my portrayal differs from or resonates with the ways in which others have interpreted the text, that is, scholars of religion, accepted Hindu authorities, and my informants. Throughout my exegesis, I reflect on cross-cultural issues, and cite other scriptures that have set up opposing concepts of the Goddess and gender. I also describe some of the ways the scripture has been used and interpreted which have not been empowering for women as I have defined that, as well as examples of women whose own experiences prove that some Hindus believe the *Devi Mahatmya* to be empowering for them. All applications of the text in their nature are culturally constructed ones. Thus, Western feminists' appropriations of the *Devi Mahatmya* and visions of what it may contribute to what they perceive to be liberation may not be shared by Hindu women. Hindu women's use of the scripture as a means of empowerment may seem antifeminist, a symptom of false consciousness, or internalized oppression to Western feminists. Then again, perhaps false consciousness and internalized oppression are in the eye of the beholder.

Her Story: A Lone Woman and Unwilling Bride

The *Devi Mahatmya*'s thirteen chapters are organized into three edifying episodes or *caritas*, tales of her 'conduct', or 'way'. Each

teaches us that, contrary to what we may have learned before, Devi
is the true cause of the triumph of good over evil. She alone
bestows the wisdom which liberates one from suffering, as well as
granting material prosperity. She accepts with love the sacrifice
and worship that is performed—with or without true understanding (12.10). Thus, although Vishnu is well known in other works to
have defeated the twin demons Madhu and Kaitabha, the first les-
son counters that the 'great deluding' Mahamaya, immanent in all
things as either wisdom or ignorance, is truly responsible for his
victory. The second tale affirms Devi to be a latent luminosity or
power (*tejas*) in beings that when evoked from the gods themselves
assume female form to defeat the shape-shifting Buffalo-demon,
Mahisha. Here, too, earlier myth cycles credit the victory to another
male god: either Shiva or his son Skanda. The third story owes its
origin to popular traditions associated with the ancient regional
goddess, Vindhyavasini. Her defeat of twin demons Shumbha and
Nishumbha in the Vindhyas is mentioned in many earlier Sanskrit
sources which describe her as the 'sister' of Krishna-Gopala. The
Devi Mahatmya recasts the story, however. To ward off criticism
that the Great Goddess is merely a site-specific deity of the expan-
sive Vindhyas—or worse, a consort of a rival sect's dominant male
deity—the authors have changed a number of features in the story.
They locate the battlesite in the Himalayas, graphically show that
she transcends a well-known wedded goddess, and they portray
her literally fighting off potential suitors to boot.

As the third story begins, the gods are in trouble, unable to defeat
a second pair of demon twins, Shumbha and Nishumbha. Remem-
bering her promise to assist them, they trek to the Himalayas to
seek their protectress's intervention. After they laud her as the *maya*
(delusory/magical power) of Vishnu (recalling the first episode of
our scripture and Vindhyavasini's ancient mythic connection with
Krishna-Gopala), Devi chooses yet another way to appear. Parvati—
understood in contemporary literature as Shiva's wife—is bathing
nearby, and on hearing their prayer, asks the gods whom they are
praising, for she sees no goddess there other than herself. Immediately, 'Kausiki' springs forth from Parvati's outer skin or sheath
(*kosha*), and replies that their praise is directed to her, also called
Ambika ('mother'). Parvati is thus unaware of the Great 'Mother'
Goddess latent within and surrounding her, under and inside her

very skin. Devoid of her luminous sheath, Parvati became Kalika, 'the dark one'.

When Shumbha and Nishumbha learn of the beautiful, unclaimed Ambika, they pronounce her to be a valuable jewel. Declaring themselves to be 'enjoyers of jewels', they send forth a messenger to convey to her a marriage proposal: she may choose between them. She has other ideas. She refuses, explaining in 5.69, 'He who conquers me in battle, who overcomes my pride, whose strength (*pratibala*) is comparable to mine in the world, only he will be my husband' (*bharta*, literally, 'bearer', 'supporter', thus 'lord').[1] The messenger scoffs at this woman whom he denounces as 'haughty/ proud' (*avalipta*), saying, 'All the gods, led by Indra [the king of gods], were no match in battle for Shumbha and the others. How can you, a lone woman, go into battle with them?' (5.73) When her suitors learn of this exchange, they assail her as an 'evil woman' (*dushta*) who should be dragged to them by her hair, humiliated, if necessary.

Throughout her battles in this episode, Ambika creates other forms from out of herself. From the flat surface of her forehead whose brows are bent in a frown, Kali, 'whose countenance is terrible', emerges directly. The site of creation is the third eye, as is the luminous force produced from the gods in the buffalo demon story, but here Kali appears from the outer skin between Ambika's eyebrows, just as Ambika appeared from Parvati's outer skin. When Devi, her lion mount, and Kali are surrounded on all sides, *shaktis* or separate female 'powers' emerge from the bodies of a group of seven extremely virile and strong (*ativiryabalanvitah*) male gods. These *shaktis* appear as feminine doubles of their male sources, with the same vehicles, weapons, and ornaments. An eighth *shakti* emerges from the Great Goddess's body.

The goddesses encounter the demon Raktabija, whose name means literally, 'red/blood [*rakta*] seed/semen [*bija*]'. Raktabija has the miraculous ability to regenerate identical forms of himself whenever any drop of his blood 'seeds' the earth. The eight *shaktis* wound him, but since even more demons arise from his blood, hordes of demon duplicates are produced from what seem to be unilaterally fertile blood drops. Laughing at the sight of the gods quaking in fear, Ambika develops a brilliant battle plan: as she stabs

1.   All translations from the Sanskrit are my own.

Raktabija, Kali consumes his spurting blood as well as any demons born from it. Working as a team, the goddesses cause Raktabija to literally dry up and die.

After his brother Nishumbha is subsequently defeated, Shumbha accuses the Goddess of being a conceited hypocrite: she has relied on the strength of other goddesses, yet claims victory alone. She denies being 'aided', declaring a profound truth claim: 'I, alone, exist here in the world; what second, other than I, is there?' The *shakti*s then merge into Devi rather than returning to the male gods, and standing as a lone female, Ambika slays Sumbha. She promises the grateful gods to return in many future incarnations whenever needed.

A Feminist Exegesis of the *Devi Mahatmya*

The creators of the *Devi Mahatmya* envisioned the single, ultimate force of the universe to be fully resident within the phenomenal world. In each episode the Goddess is extolled as *prakriti*, and in the third, she is described as truly within creation: she is one 'who has become everything (11.6)', 'abiding in the qualities of primordial matter, actually consisting of those qualities (11.10)'. To express this divine materialism, they spoke of the Goddess. In this sense, the *Devi Mahatmya*'s gender modeling is continuous with earlier portrayals of immanent goddesses, as well as with the views of prior religious proponents who had successfully characterized matter (*prakriti*) itself and rootedness or immanence within the world in general as 'female'.

Speaking of the divine as immanent and female raised a host of issues with which Western readers can readily identify in the vast majority of their own religious and philosophical works. By the time of our text's composition, matter (*prakriti*) had already come to be opposed to spirit (*purusha*), literally, 'male', 'man'. Centuries before, as these polar principles were gradually adapted and adopted into Hindu orthodoxy, despite impulses toward unity, the material was progressively devalued and *purusha* was exalted as true reality, apart from *prakriti*, and identical with absolute reality (*brahman*). Ancient rituals connected with or modeled on human reproduction reflected these assumptions. Males provide the seed (*bija*, *virya*), the efficient cause, or enduring essence to life; females merely serve as fertile fields, which nourish the seed. The devalued world reflected notions of the female, and vice versa. Women embody sexuality, unconscious reproduction (in their nature as mindless but necessary fields), and the family, all supposed obstacles to liberation. Hence, despite their greater tangibility, the world, *prakriti*, and women came to be linked and understood as less real, and partially responsible for (if not identical with) illusion (*maya*). One must avoid or destroy negative female elements in the quest to free the transcendent spirit/*purusha*, or male. Thus while *brahman*, absolute reality, is a neuter noun, linguistically (and mythically and ritually) the divine spirit or *purusa* within human beings is clearly modeled on the male, just as the male is modeled on divine spirit, and the female on the chaotic material (Humes 1996b).

There are striking parallels between Western and Hindu paradigms of gendered reality. These parallels in paradigms of gendered reality afford a fruitful convergence to their critique, although caution must be maintained to ascertain cultural difference. Hélène Cixous, for instance, gives voice to common objections to 'masculine writing' in the West which segments reality by coupling concepts and terms in pairs of polar opposites, in which one is always privileged over the other. Attributing these dichotomies to the fundamental dichotomous couple, man/woman, she notes that man is consistently associated with all that is active, cultural, light, high, or generally positive, and woman with all that is passive, natural, dark, low, or generally negative. This characterization is remarkably similar to most Hindu philosophical models, save in one important respect: the concepts of activity and power are more complex in their worldview.

The type of passivity that *purusha* exemplifies—beyond the vulgarities of the phenomenal realm—is held to be higher than, or superior to, the type of vigorous activity of *prakriti*. While *prakriti* is feminine or female, and human women exemplify *prakriti* in terms of fertility (and attendant negative features), women are considered incapable of heroic action in battle. Heroic activity and brute strength in men are superior to the passivity and victimhood of women. Thus these dichotomies retain the set of hierarchical values which privilege men's transcendent uninvolvement with the world yet virile power in battle, just as Western models approve of men's transcending the world, yet manifesting virility. To describe the Goddess's intervention in world affairs, that is, her incarnations to fight battles against demons, the *Devi Mahatmya*'s authors insisted that she has heroic power, which was already understood to be a masculine quality.

The scripture's authors clearly view dualistic language as a barrier to expressing their view of reality, which despite its multiplicity is affirmed as one. To transcend the Hindu heritage of opposing phallologocentric structures so similar to those of the West, they employ various strategies. The manner in which they choose to express the Goddess's nature shows that they reject traditional philosophical explanation mired in dualism. I base this conclusion on several factors. First, such exposition is proven insufficient in the frame story introducing the Goddess's deeds. Two men, seeking an answer for their attachment to those who do not return their affection or respect, ask a learned seer why even 'men of knowledge (*jnana*)' are deluded. He responds philosophically, explaining that the Goddess is simultaneously Delusion and Wisdom (*vidya*); it is she who causes both in humans. This does not explain her nature satisfactorily, however, so the seer changes his strategy. As in many other devotional works, he comes closer to describing her by telling stories about her actions. As wisdom itself, she must be experienced by the listener—initially, vicariously through story, but even that proves insufficient, for the two seekers remain deluded. The sage at last implores them to take refuge in her and to meet her directly themselves, rather than to absorb someone else's perceptions, or to deny perception altogether. The seekers succeed in meeting her through dedicated ascetic practice (*tapas*). Their religious program included residing on the bank of a river for three years; fasting periodically and restricting their diet; offering flowers, incense, fire, water, and their own blood; chanting the Devi Sukta; and crafting and concentrating on an earthen image of the Goddess.

It seems to me no coincidence that the Other yet immanent Reality, who embodies and transcends all opposites, is considered best reflected by the Female, who must be experienced and engaged first-hand to be understood. The text's creators posit that matter and spirit are both aspects of a single divine being, who is best understood as female precisely because she is plural, immanent, and active. Perhaps, too, it is *She* because to most (probably male) authors, it is Other, paradoxical, and difficult to understand, qualities long associated with *maya* or illusory power, conceived as feminine, and estranged from the Absolute in many Hindu philosophies. This insistence that the unfathomable Goddess is To-Be-Experienced reminds me of Derrida's recognition of *différance*, the inevitable, meaning-creative gap between the object of perception and our perception of it. This is also in sync with postmodern feminists who posit that woman is consistently conceived as the Other, which has been left—unthematized and silent—in the gap that continually blocks union between language and reality.

To some extent, early Western feminist theory internalized dualistic segmentations of reality. Simone de Beauvoir questioned why women must remain earthbound in immanence and determinism, handicapped by their biology. This was in contrast with men, who can fly off into transcendent realms and zones of freedom. This internalized a belief in the reality of duality, as well as the value-system that posits immanence as disadvantageous and inferior. Embodiedness, Otherness, must be transcended. By contrast, in their critique of dominant, totalizing structures such as language and knowledge, postmodern feminists who follow deconstructionist currents have tended to celebrate that very Otherness—being in the world—that preoccupied de Beauvoir as a fault. The *Devi Mahatmya*'s creators share the postmodern exaltation of embodiedness, divinizing it as does much of the Western feminist spirituality movement. The *Devi Mahatmya*, too, rejects dichotomy or opposition; there is thus an underlying universal essence, within the world, and it truly is plural, multiple, and different, even as it is simultaneously unified in the Being of the Goddess.

Language and myth contribute strongly to socialization and encoding gender roles, just as they reflect both processes. The *Devi Mahatmya*, like many living scriptures, continues to influence and reflect social and gender values. A window into this role is provided by Levi Strauss's theory that every society is regulated by a series of interrelated signs, roles, and rituals; Jacques Lacan has termed this the 'symbolic order'. For a child to function adequately within any society, he or she must internalize the symbolic order through language. As one increasingly submits to society's linguistic rules, the more those rules will be inscribed in the unconscious. The symbolic order regulates society through individuals; so long as individuals speak its language, thereby internalizing its gender and class roles, society will reproduce itself in fairly constant form. This process is dynamic. If individuals transform language, rejecting linguistic rules and substituting new ones, the symbolic order will reflect the changes.

Lacan concluded that women are permanent outsiders to the symbolic order because they are largely unable to internalize the 'law of the fathers'. Hence, the law must be imposed from the outside by men, which results in the squelching and silencing of femininity, because the only words that women are given are masculine words. If one accepts Lacan's theories that the symbolic order can be changed through the contributions of its participants, since women are increasingly sharing in the creation process of the symbolic order, there is good reason to reject Lacan's pessimism and posit a more egalitarian future. Nevertheless, his point remains apt in assessing texts composed under patriarchy.

Postmodernists argue that in the patriarchal symbolic order inherited in the West, the only woman we know is the 'masculine feminine', the phallic feminine, or woman as man sees her. The *Devi Mahatmya* can be similarly criticized for not entirely breaking free from obvious Hindu phallocentric conceptions of women. To assert the superiority of their Goddess, the text's authors reject the view that the Goddess is consistently 'feminine', but maintain she is 'female'. By this I mean that they deny she shares all of the traits which contemporary society had presumed to be characteristic of women's socially defined behavior or their essential nature, but accept her basic nature, her gender, as female.

When describing Devi as warrior, the text makes use of clearly phallic and related masculine imagery. This fact may be interpreted in two ways. On the one hand, one might argue that (1) when the female deity exhibits controlled heroism or strength, traditionally a male function, she is being described as a 'masculinized female', in contrast with lesser goddess incarnations who 'spin out of control' and become destructive from battle and bloodlust, as women are supposedly wont to do (Gupta 1991: 31-32). On the other hand, given that the only words that the authors had available to them were masculine words, one could assert that (2) the ascription of male imagery to the Goddess serves precisely to subvert its dominance. I think the second interpretation is more in keeping with the spirit of the text. Further, this subversion may prove that the divine feminine is beyond gender itself, or actually sublates the masculine. For reasons I will show, I think the theory of sublation fits the evidence best. Yet such bold claims are asserted explicitly only on the transcendent, and not the human, level. The gender-bending of Devi does not necessarily reflect similar freedom for women (or men) from conformity to gendered roles.

Many (if not most) contemporary canonical scriptures paired goddesses with male consorts in a pattern of 'natural' female sub-ordination similar to that which existed in the human realm. In her Glorification, the Goddess eschews all suitors and remains unmarried. Most interpreters explain that Shumbha and Nishumbha's mistake was viewing Devi to be an ordinary woman or lesser goddess. Those who read and recite the text find their error highly amusing. Importantly, not a single informant criticized the assumption that women should be subordinate to men. Rather, time and again, respondents pointed to the impropriety of assuming the Goddess to be conquerable by anyone, male or female. Women are not directly offered in the text an empowered role outside of marriage, family, and subordination. Indeed, the special nature of Devi and her mythical narratives do not make sense unless the patriarchal subjugation of the ordinary human—or even lesser divine—female is assumed.

The authors of our text deliberately revealed a variety of ways by which Devi manifests herself. They took care to portray her as eschewing marriage. She is proven the ultimate power over creation and fertility in the Raktabija episode. Unlike human women, this divine force is entirely self-sufficient and creates by her own power from internal resources as well as manipulating matter out of herself. The authors even put into her mouth the express denial that she depended on any other, and the claim that she alone was real. Thus, while one of the *Devi Mahatmya*'s verses commonly quoted to support women's 'high' status in Hinduism affirms that 'each and every woman' is a 'portion' of the Goddess, the rest of the verse deliberately minimizes their role in creation: 'By you alone as mother has this [world] been filled up' (11.5). This underscores the fact that none of the ways in which Devi creates resembles ordinary human reproductive techniques, whether male or female: she is not a 'mother' in an gynemorphic sense, nor does she 'mother' in the same way. However, although Devi acts in 'masculine' or 'non-feminine' ways, as creatrix and true resident within material, she is nevertheless 'female'. Divine materialism suffused with intelligent power seems to be an essential aspect of the authors' interpretation of her gender, and it preoccupies them throughout. In this way, the *Devi Mahatmya* links women to what will come to be reified as the concept of *shakti*.

To consider in greater detail the relations of women and the Goddess, and to interpret to what extent and manner the *Devi Mahatmya* is feminist or antifeminist, I will first examine one of the most important qualities attributed to Devi that is very rarely attributed to women: virile, heroic power. In the following section, I will consider the type of power which is attributed to women: *stri shakti*, the premiere examples of which do not characterize the unmarried Great Goddess.

Her Power: Feminine Virility

The Goddess's *virya*, or virile heroism, is extolled in each of the three episodes. Moreover, her virility is specifically contrasted with that of male figures as being far greater, and more importantly, ever under her control, even when she is excited from drink or angered in battle. In the first episode, the two 'tremendously virile' (*ativirya*) demons have become 'intoxicated' and 'deluded' by the excess of power (*atibala*) generated in battle, caused by the intervention of the Goddess when she is appealed to by a god (1.71, 73). In the second, a similar contrast is made. Here Devi is actively engaged herself. Both Devi and Mahisha become 'intoxicated and puffed up', he from his 'might and virility' (*balaviryamadoddhatah*), and she from both the glass of wine she dashes down, and 'emotion' (*raga*). The Goddess 'slurs' to Mahisha that he is a deluded fool, and quickly pins him down. She then kicks him so hard that she literally turns him inside out; half of his human torso is projected through the mouth of his buffalo form by the immense force of her foot. Completely surrounding him with her virile power (*devya viryena samvritah*), she wards off any further transformation and decapitates the struggling demon's human head (3.33-39). This mythical structure is repeated in the third *carita* when Devi cuts off the head of yet another 'man of great strength and great virility' (*mahabalo maha virya*) who springs from the heart of the fallen demon, Nishumbha (9.33-34). Since both of these two male demons are tightly connected with self-transformation or self-regeneration, her slicing off their heads while they are trying to recreate themselves in the onslaught of her attacks suggests a form of symbolic castration, and at minimum, her control of male fertility and self-assertion.

An even more obvious female sublation of masculine power occurs when Ambika and Kali conspire to drain the very life-blood out of Raktabija. His blood-seed creates multiforms of himself, but only once they have touched the soil. The earth cannot exercise its own will to override its inherent propensity to create. In our text, Ambika forces the demon to shed his blood-seed unwillingly by piercing him with her lance. Further, unlike other Hindu mythical structures in which female oral ingestion of seed causes impregnation, when Kali swallows the seed, she does not give birth to Raktabija's forms but instead 'dries' him up. This myth thus explicitly refutes a masculine, unilateral creation model in which the female Ultimate is merely an earth womb awaiting male seed. Devi is an active, conscious creatrix, who can spawn multiforms of herself directly in various ways, and inhibit male procreation. Further, latent within her are ferocious goddesses who assume shape at her order. They consume blood and flesh to maximize orderliness in service to the greater good. This passage supports the understanding of varying levels of conscious power of creation within the world. Conscious beings have greater control over fertility than the earth, just as the Goddess and her forms have greater control than other conscious beings.

The Raktabija myth resonates with earlier themes which expressly identify virility and seed, and view semen as an instrument of power that males should attempt to reclaim from women. A mantra from the *Brihad Aranyaka Upanishad* (6.4.4-5) requests: 'Let virility return to me, and energy and strength. Let the fire be put in its right place, on the fire altar.' The ritualist should then take semen/seed with his thumb and fourth finger and rub it between his breasts over his heart, or between his eyebrows. These are precisely the body parts that are the sources of the male warrior from Nishumbha, Kali from the Goddess, and luster or *tejas* from the gods. This concept persists in popular culture which posits that not only do women have more 'inner heat' to begin with, but they also take through intercourse what little quantities men build up. (See, for example, Reynolds 1980: 47.)

The Goddess's battles reveal her to have a lustrous 'feminismo'; effortlessly drawing upon the inexhaustible powers within herself—which may take external forms as goddesses or male troops—she proves she is not the 'lone woman' her opponents assume her to be. Indeed, the gods honor her in feminine but also explicitly masculine terms: 'By you who exist in the form of water, all this universe is filled up, O one of great virility (*ativirya*). You are the power (*sakti*) of Visnu, of boundless virility (*virya*), the seed [or 'semen'; *bija*] of all, the supreme, magical power/illusion (*maya*)' (11.3cd-11.4ab). Verse 11.5 acknowledges women as 'particles' or 'portions' of her, but attributes true creation to the Goddess alone: 'All divisions of wisdom are yours, O Goddess, and each and every woman in the world are parts of you. By you alone as mother has this been filled up; what praise of you can suffice for you who are beyond praise, beyond utterance (*parokti*)?' This linking of virility, *shakti*, seed, and universal motherhood, together with the deliberate de-emphasis of humans' role in creation, underscore that Devi is not merely field or womb, nor a facile combination of the masculine and feminine: her personal nature extends beyond her creation or routinely constructed gender roles.

The *virya* of Devi differs from that of simple male power, reflecting that the authors were moved to situate it within their view of her female gender. In a hymn to the Goddess, the gods marvel at how her *virya* destroys enemies, yet acts as a salvific device; it is simultaneously compassionate. This leads them to wonder (4.21), 'What comparison can there be to your bold acts? Where [else] is there such a lovely form, yet one which strikes such fear among foes?' Thus, the Goddess is female because of her beauty, embodiedness, and creative power, but also because of her wondrous, compassionate use of virile power in service to others. This feminized *virya* of Devi has significant symbolic ramifications: it is a compassionate, righteous, self-controlled power used in service for the good.

The appropriation and transmutation of the masculine word and symbol *virya* by the Goddess is obvious in the original Sanskrit, but obscured in English versions because translators intuitively render the word differently. Sometimes this is to spare the reader repetition, no doubt, but it is also translated differently depending on the gender of the warrior. One could take issue with my insistence on keeping in the foreground the masculine aura of *virya*, arguing that it is a relatively neutral term referring to either creative power, or might in battle. There are reasons why such a view of neutrality is untenable for both meanings.

First, in *puranas* composed several centuries after the *Devi Mahatmya*, *virya* is shown to be an important term which is deliberately portrayed as a creative power specific to the supreme male deity, in contrast with the goddess (Pintchman 1994: 133-34, 152-54). In the *Garuda Purana*, for instance, 'the principle of creative energy is allied more with the power of male virility than with female creative potential' (Pintchman 1994: 153). These subsequent texts depict the goddess as a field, and the male god as the outside agent who 'inserts his *virya* into her', and thus is the efficient cause of creation (Pintchman 1994: 130-31). These later works thus appear to have deliberately reacted to the promotion of the Goddess's superior agency in creation—as well as her appropriation of *virya*—by (re-)asserting masculine-modeled concepts of creation through the contested notion of *virya*.

Second, Kathryn Hansen demonstrates how language and artistic conventions construct together a gendered dichotomy in the Hindu aesthetic symbolic system: men's bodies are the locus of heroism, and women's bodies of eroticism:

> The concept of heroism cannot be glossed without reference to masculinity insofar as viryam is also commonly used with the meaning 'semen.' It appears that Brahminical culture in India constructed the masculine body as the site of virility and metaphorized its notion of heroism from the male organ's capacity for potency and firmness. From the outset, then, heroism or viryam comes bundled as a gendered category (Hansen 1992: 1).

Because of gendered aesthetics, females who wish to represent the heroic mode in the visual and performing arts must step out of a female persona and then impersonate a male (Hansen 1992: 2).

Hansen reports that narrative traditions have celebrated warrior women as agents of heroic action (*virangana*), often likening them to the goddesses Durga or Kali. They share iconographic and moral links; their 'defeat of threatening enemies is comparable to the warring goddesses' punishment of evil demons' (Hansen 1992: 35).

This suggests that at least in narratives, appropriations of masculine heroism by goddess traditions such as our text have succeeded in making human female heroism—that is, acts conducted for others which require demonstrable, purposeful power—at least thinkable or imaginable, if not visible, as in drama. The Goddess's feminine machismo is thus identified as the same kind of moral strength invigorating living heroines, whose examples, although rare, can be a resource for feminist struggle.

Although a full comparison is beyond the scope of this essay, I wish to note that portrayals of the Goddess in the later *Devi Bhagavata* (c. ninth century CE) bear crucial differences from those of the Goddess in the *Devi Mahatmya*. This is particularly so in the specific case of possessing *virya* or heroism in battle. The *Devi Bhagavata* suffuses its retelling of the three major myths of the *Devi Mahatmya* with patriarchal values, as well as the gendered aesthetics described by Hansen above.

Nowhere does the *Devi Mahatmya* actually say negative things about women; instead, it explicitly says that all women are portions of the Goddess (even if the Goddess takes the credit for their fertility). By contrast, in the *Devi Bhagavata*, the Goddess herself is made to expound the negative attributes of *stri svabhava* or 'women's nature' as reckless, foolish, deceitful, cruel, and so on at length. Further, to her opponents, the goddess assumes the form of a stereotypical seductress, whose sexuality has a negative effect on the seduced. Together with an explicit androgyny, this re-fashioning of the Goddess as femme fatale to her enemies, and mother to her devotees, causes significant revisions of the myths. Unlike the *Devi Mahatmya*, in the *Devi Bhagavata*, Mahisha—as well as Shumbha and Nishumbha—have been granted boons from Brahma allowing them only to be slain by a woman. Most remarkable to me is the Goddess's denial of her female nature, and her outright recognition that her virile power in battle is counterintuitive and actually proves her true nature is male.

In the *Devi Bhagavata*, a series of envoys are sent to convince the Goddess to marry Mahisha, but she refuses. She angrily replies,

> 'Think it over what it meant, fool, when you said I have the nature of a woman. I am not a man (*puman*), but I have that nature, having [merely] donned the guise of a woman. Since your master requested death by a woman, he is a fool who knows not the heroic sentiment. Only eunuchs, not heroes, take pleasure in such a death. Thus I have

come to carry out this business, assuming the form of a woman'
(Brown 1990: 104).

Brown comments that this passage suggests that, on the highest
level, she has encompassed and transcended the distinctions of
gender (Brown 1990: 105). Although in the *Devi Mahatmya* the
Goddess is ascribed traits normally considered male—especially
virya, *bija*, and the like—at no point is she herself described as
being anything other than female. Here in the *Devi Bhagavata*,
precisely because she exemplifies the heroic sentiment, the Goddess denies that she has a feminine nature, and insults her opponent's manhood for wishing to die by the hand of a woman. As
with gendered aesthetics in which females who wish to represent
the heroic mode must step out of a female persona and impersonate a male, here the Goddess must reject her female persona,
claiming she is actually a he, who is impersonating a female—in a
sense, a castrated warrior—in order to counteract the curious boon
requested by the 'eunuch' Mahisha.

Observing a longstanding Hindu belief that ultimate reality transcends gender, Brown comments,

> 'In view of such well-established and enduring traditions, it is rather
> remarkable that the *Devi Mahatyma* gives no explicit voice to the
> androgynous character of the Great Goddess... But the sexual im-
> agery and associated symbols used by the *Devi Mahatmya* to
> describe and glorify the Devi are all feminine... She is the supreme
> *prakrti*. But nowhere is she called father, nowhere Purusha' (Brown
> 1990: 216).

The authors of the *Devi Mahatmya* did not somehow forget to
comment on the possible androgyny of the Goddess. I believe they
intentionally portrayed her as female, not androgynous, but they
insisted, too, that she had qualities, which—although characteristi-
cally 'masculine'—did not cause her to lose her femaleness.

Were the *Devi Mahatmya*'s authors to have argued that the Goddess was both a male and a female, Father and Mother, or beyond
both, the hierarchy of sexist values and gender dualism would
continue, which is precisely the case in the *Devi Bhagavata*. In
the *Devi Bhagavata*, the masculine is venerated, the feminine de-
cried. Strong females are truly males in disguise. The female aspect
of the Goddess's androgynous nature is linked to the erotic, *prakriti*
and so on, which—although less negative than in other texts—is

still inferior to the male and conflated with the destructive nature of *maya*. The masculine is linked to the heroic, spiritual, and so on. The *Devi Mahatmya* rejects the gender modeling in the *Devi Bhagavata* includes in which 'both genders must be included in the ultimate if it is truly ultimate' (Brown 1990: 217). That very inclusivity serves in the *Devi Bhagavata* to privilege the less dominant of the pair. Indeed, only by affirming and insisting on the integrity of her female nature does the Devi of our Glorification maintain her own integrity and truly ultimate position in the universal hierarchy. She is not diminished by being (only) female; and she is the Truly Ultimate, resident in all things, and thus imparting her nature to all of reality.

Women's Power: *Stri Shakti*, *Pativrat* and *Saubhagyavati*

Western concepts of 'power' connote the ability to control and dominate. But to many Hindus, while women may embody *shakti*, they do not necessarily control it, nor are they consciously aware of it. *Stri shakti* refers to 'women's power', which is interconnected with and augmented by the 'pure and gentle, but firm and tenacious strength which…women continuously display' (Chitnis 1988: 87). A woman's strength is usually assessed by her ability to tolerate difficulty, which itself is perceived as a type of *tapas* or religious austerity. In this sense, a woman might be 'strong', but she is not necessarily 'powerful'. When respondents differentiated women and the Goddess through the concept of *shakti*, they stressed that the Goddess controls her power, saying outright or implying that women do not, or that hers is far greater. The term *stri* is not merely a genitive modifier designating that *shakti* belongs to women; rather, the compound denotes a specific type of power that is quite different from the power connoted by unmodified word *shakti*. In the English language, if we say someone is a 'power', we mean that person is 'powerful'; he or she has the ability to control and to dominate. This equation of 'power' with 'possessing power' is assumed. When Indologists write on the paradoxical nature of women 'being shakti' yet experiencing hardships that reveal a social powerlessness under South Asian patriarchy, their sense of paradox may be catalyzed by their own cultural assumptions regarding the concept of 'woman's power' and Hindu women's embodiment of a reified notion of 'power'.

There are three phases commonly ascribed to a Hindu woman's life: maiden, wife and mother, and widow or *sati*. Patriarchal sources, perhaps recognizing and fearing 'the force of the creative power present in the divine female', 'created an environment for the feminine to be restricted and restrained' (Gupta 1991: 35). This is shown in the religious ideal of the *pativrat* (one who makes a vow [*vrat*] to her husband [*pati*, literally 'owner' or 'lord']). The concept of *pativrat* fuses devotionalism (*bhakti*) and self-renunciation directed to the husband (*patiyoga*). It encourages women to accept service and devotion to a man as the ultimate religion and duty, rather than being concerned for their own worldly needs. Thus although many models of female *pativrat*s exhibit great intelligence, tenacity, resourcefulness, and so on—for example, Sita or Savitri—exemplars almost always use those qualities in service to their husbands or others, in pursuit of a teleological objective deemed to be a greater concern than worldly upliftment. Myths also portray them as enduring without question harsh treatment from their husbands, and thus serve as models to tolerate any amount of abuse to win one's husband over to an eventually agreeable position. In many groups, because of the vow to remain true to her single husband, a widow was declared unable to remarry. Widows are commonly assumed to have caused the death of their husbands, and hence are inauspicious. A widow's inauspiciousness is compounded by the fact that since she cannot create without a mate, she no longer manifests *shakti*, or creative potential, or at least, acceptable fertility.

Hindu society and its texts unquestionably do exalt human motherhood. The married woman who has children and a living husband is *sumangali*, 'she who is auspicious', also called the *saubhagyavati*—literally, the 'woman with a good womb', whose chastity and devotion to her husband, fruitfulness, and subsequent womanly powers are believed to maintain and enrich the family. The *saubhagyavati* is believed to closely approximate married multiforms of Devi such as Shri-Lakshmi, who in *Devi Mahatmya* 4.4 and 12.37 is the 'good fortune' who grants prosperity in the home, just as the widow is correlated to Alakshmi (misfortune), also described there. Just as the *sumangali* enjoys considerable privilege and prestige, the widow experiences the reverse.

The *Devi Mahatmya* and Women: Realities and Possible Futures

My informants took two major stances when comparing and contrasting women and the Goddess. Either they claimed that only
Devi transcends the essential nature of woman (understood to be a
dependent being, whose nature has at its core considerable faults),
or they asserted that only Devi is free of the socially constituted
gender roles expected of all women—even goddesses. Most interpreted the text to mean that like the goddess, the 'supreme female
woman' can act in powerful 'feminine' ways, even if subordinated
by a husband. This view was exemplified by some women who
have employed the text itself or its mythological heritage in what
they believe to be liberating ways in this life. I did not find women
or men who interpreted the text such that it legitimated a life for
women outside of the normal pattern of heterosexual marriage and
motherhood. In this way, the personhood of women continues to
be defined sociocentrically, embedded in family structures as daughter, wife, sister, mother, and so on.

Hindu visions of women's empowerment differ markedly from
Western secular perceptions of women's empowerment. Even Western feminist spirituality generally promises fulfillment in the world,
and less commonly, beyond it. The concept of *shakti* is rooted
deeply in a spirituality of self-abnegation and asceticism in pursuit
of transcendent goals, although it does promise that the successfully subordinated wife will see great worldly merit from her sacrifices, depending on her past *karma*. Clearly, given these different
assumptions, there are going to be equally strong divergences in
outlook on what a feminist lifestyle entails and what 'empowerment' is.

Suma Chitnis believes that the most important factor contributing to the poor status of women in India is the religious ideal of the
pativrat (1988: 90). *Stri shakti*, the *pativrat* ideal, and fertility are
not generally believed to function as sources of empowerment for
women to use for their own ends. Yet many women found these
ideals to be empowering nevertheless, precisely because they are
not to their own worldly benefit; they are a form of *tapas* or austerity which builds their spiritual power. Thus, they concur that 'A
subordinated woman, an auspicious woman, emerges as the most

powerful female being, and, indeed, in certain circumstances, as a female being more powerful than men, responsible for the well-being, continuity, and prosperity of the lineages and generations she brings together' (Reynolds 1980: 57). Not mere compensatory powers, they are 'grounded in a religious apprehension of reality where self-denial and suffering engendered by subordination yield powers of a religious, as opposed to a physical, sort. Women, then, do not forsake a life of subordination, for to do so is to abandon what is, in essence, a salvific condition' (Reynolds 1980: 57).

A concrete instance of this view is found in the example of a woman who is widely regarded as an exceptional Vindhyavasini devotee, who composes hymns to her and is known to be an authority on the Sanskrit *Devi Mahatmya*. Her adoring husband describes her as his 'guru', and is one of the few instances I have found of a *patnivrat*, or a man devoted to adoring his wife. Many come to her home each week to attend her lectures; most of her audience is women and children, but there are also some men. Mrs Pathak's engagement with the *Devi Mahatmya* is intriguing. Those groups who have tended to use the text—at least in Sanskrit—have been predominantly men and members of privileged groups. Women who do use the text usually do so in vernacular translations (Humes 1998). This means that most non-privileged group members and women do not draw on the text's power as *mantra*. In other words, whereas men and members of privileged groups have functioned as agents who use the text as a device to shape future events and cause change, others—such as women—have primarily used the text to engage the Goddess from a more Bhaktic stance, requesting boons from her in an attitude of strict dependence, and relying on their own devotion's strength as proven by their recitation to impel the goddess. My fieldwork suggests that this gender dichotomy is changing. Women such as Mrs Pathak are engaging with the text more directly as confident agents who hope to co-create a desired future, perhaps doubly invigorated by their internal stores of *shakti*.

Mrs Pathak, whose male relations have recited the text professionally for generations, taught herself recitation after having learned Sanskrit in a secular school. In one lecture, she asserted that just as Parvati is unaware of the Goddess within her (*DM* 5.38-39), so women remain ignorant of that portion of Devi within them. What is the essential nature that ties woman to the Goddess? This can best be understood by experience, specifically, by following the ideal of Parvati. Parvati is a *pativrat*, ever devoted to Siva. Mrs Pathak therefore preaches from the *Shiva Purana* on how a woman should act in this world: remaining devoted to one's own husband, a woman should strive to be a good mother, and through her powers, sustain the welfare of her family. Although having memorized most of the Sanskrit *Devi Mahatmya*, she recognizes male authority over it and defers to pandits for its ritual recitation at public events. The high status she enjoys in her community is directly related to perceptions that she embodies the ideals of *stri shakti*, *pativrat*, and *saubhagyavati*, as well as being the ideal *bhakta* or devotee. Each of these three feminine modes of power glorifies specific female attributes, which are generally considered to be essential to the nature of ideal Hindu womanhood: uncomplaining endurance of all difficulty; adoration of and compliant subordination to one's husband; and fertility. None of these models is likely to appeal to most Western feminists, and few would see them as 'empowering'.

Indeed, Western and Hindu feminist constructs seem to be at odds on many issues. Suma Chitnis holds that feminist anger in the West is in part tied to the hypocrisy of a culture that stresses the value of equality and individual freedom, but nevertheless denies social and legislative equality to women (Chitnis 1988: 83). The concept of 'equality' in Western feminism, Chitnis cautions, does not have much relation to the highly stratified society of India. There, hierarchies abound in terms of not only sex but age, ordinal position, affinal and consanguinal kinship relationships, and, of course, community (birth-group, lineage, learning, wealth, occupation, and relationship with the ruling power) (Chitnis 1988: 83). The notion of radical equality is foreign to the inherited Hindu world-view. The *saubhagyavati* may not wish to give up her status for a more egalitarian vision. Yet because Indians were forced to deal with questions of domination and hierarchy in all their forms when faced with constructing their own legal system from scratch, modern Indian law was drafted in support of equal rights. The problem women face is that they either do not know about, or they are inhibited (either internally or externally) from insisting on, their rights (Chitnis 1988: 89-90).

Consider a second instance of female empowerment which is more in keeping with Western notions of a liberated woman, and perhaps, goddess worship as an ideally 'feminist' faith. Rama Rani Malhotra of Banaras is believed to be a channel of Devi. Her apotheosis from *pativrat* to Mataji, or Mother, was reflected graphically in her shedding of *purdah*. Although *purdah* is meant to connote respect to him, her husband insisted she end the practice, and indeed, began worshiping her. He used to recite the *Devi Mahatmya* in Sanskrit for her since she could not. She now performs it herself in a Punjabi version which she transforms through her *shakti* and connection with the Goddess to the same ritual power level as recitation in Sanskrit. Her advice to women followers fuses Tantric and Bhaktic ritual to the Goddess with traditional female values to change husbands, effect cures, and gain material welfare.

The *Devi Mahatmya* is not a good source for exploring directly the religious practices or the lives of contemporary Hindu women. The Goddess is unlike nearly every woman who might read or hear her story; she is portrayed as an exception. What might be fruitful, however, for imagining possible connections between human women and the Goddess is examining those attributes which make her exceptional and respected. These are: (1) embodiedness, yet transcendence; (2) control over her sexuality and fertility; and (3) power to conquer or subdue evil, to create and support life, and to bestow rewards, with predictable benevolence to all dedicated petitioners.

Even within their patriarchal heritage, none of these attributes is believed to be entirely excluded from standard conceptualizations of Hindu women's nature. There can be far greater correspondence between women and the Goddess of our text, made all the more explicit since the *Devi Mahatmya* is becoming more popular, and greater debate is taking place on gender roles, dominance, and power. Thus:

1. Neither the embodiedness of women nor the materiality of the world need be considered negatively. The elevation of the social role in Hinduism during the last century has shown a willingness to adopt native modes of action on behalf of social welfare and engagement in the world. Many nationalist leaders reinterpreted the *Bhagavad Gita* to support a new interest in *lokasamgraha*, or grasp-

ing the world. Gandhi's 'grasping of truth' or *satyagraha*, for example, is a mode of conjuring power to promote service to the greater good of society specifically drawing on women's model of *shakti*. Further, if *shakti* is in all things, and especially so in women, beauty, transcendence, and purpose can be found within them.

2. In our text, Devi was contrasted with women in part because she was in control of the creative power of her fertility. Greater knowledge and technological advances in contraception and fertility treatments, in addition to increasing acceptance of their use, have minimized this distinction. Changing social customs have also afforded women greater autonomy and control over their own bodies, in some cases, including legal protection far superior to that found in many Western countries. Thus women's reproductive and creative powers may be perceived to resemble the Goddess more closely than the Earth or field, which had no choice but to give birth when sown.

3. The issue of women's agency lies at the crux of female empowerment and feminism in Hinduism. Some south Indian models grant women great autonomy over their *shakti*; hence there are indigenous Hindu paradigms of female self-control over their own power (Daniel 1980; Wadley 1980). Western individualist models do not need to be adopted.

I often heard comments from both women and men that the *pativrat* ideal in itself is not problematic, but in practice, its ability to instill self-respect and fulfillment has been diminished by men's lack of proper respect towards their wives. Indeed, since service is integral to Hindu devotionalism, and the Divine is believed immanent in all, the *pativrat* ideal is not intrinsically demeaning in Hindu theology. The problem is not how we conceive women's power and men's nature, but how we conceive men's power and women's nature. Adopting the imagery of the *Devi Mahatmya*, men should realize the power of the Goddess is within all, and bow down to her in respect. This Mr Pathak and Mr Malhotra have done, seeing the Goddess manifest herself in their wives, whom they serve with dedication and great love. A more reciprocal attitude of devotional service between men and women is a defensible interpretation of proper gender relations in our text. Shumbha and Nishumbha were sorely punished for not respecting the Goddess's wishes; so might women argue the same should hold for themselves.

Rather than adopting masculine ideas of power over things or events, simple *virya*, one can argue that a superior stance would be to adopt an attitude of exalting strength from within, and power with, both models which are deeply connected with Western goddess traditions. Power from within is not a power of control, but one which comes from valuing self, community, and experience. It is the power which can heal and renew, a power which—like the Goddess of our text—exemplifies compassion even when violent, and strives to contribute to an ultimately positive outcome for the greater good. This is in contrast with the outcome in which there must be a loser in a contest of wills.

Still contested is whether this immanent power is something that can develop in situations of improper domination and estrangement. The wifely subordination model is at odds with some egalitarian visions of gender. Many egalitarian models adopt the cultural attitude that greater respect is accorded to those in the position of determining outcomes, and eschew 'separate but equal' arguments limiting women's influence solely based on their gender and culturally mandated heterosexualism. Ideally influence would be shared among equals of both genders. If women so will it, they can turn as groups or individuals to Hindu examples of warring, goddess-like *virangana* heroines, who engaged in battle to overturn oppressive structures. The anger of the goddess can thus be appropriated to support the validity of righteous fury against other perceived injustices. After all, the gods ask her intervention against those who oppress them. Righteous anger and appropriate battle have long been thought to be a useful catalyst by Western feminists who rise up against wrongs.

In our text, Devi works with other goddesses, who have different personalities and strengths, yet ultimately they comprise a whole. Working with other females collectively, recognizing plurality yet a unity, just as the concept of a single *stri dharma* or 'women's duty' does, may also serve as an important unifier women can draw on. The universal motherhood of Devi, too, hints at a greater concern for the commonweal, and a less selfish or parochial approach to world problems. Particularly since certain patriarchal models of the feminine hold much more at stake than others—such as the elevation of the *saubhagyavati* and degradation of the widow—the inculcation of a sense of common feminist concern or struggle while recognizing difference may be seen as an important value in feminism among Hindus. Respect and authority will be natural outgrowths of women's increased power and various contributions to the world.

The *Devi Mahatmya* has been used in service of both antifeminist and feminist approaches. To call it a 'feminist' text is to ignore its use in patriarchy, but to call it 'antifeminist' is to oversimplify its complex vision of the female nature of the Goddess, and its obvious significance for women's quest for meaning. Given its exaltation of the Goddess's powers—of beneficent creation, her close accessibility and immanence, and her compassionate, predictable involvement to set right the affairs of men and gods—powers which are consistently understood as *female*, in contrast with *male*, powers, I find it to be a far greater stretch to emphasize the text's antifeminist than its feminist implications, even if it does reify concepts of the feminine. From what I have observed, I thus believe that the *Devi Mahatmya* is, and can indeed remain, if not increasingly become, a great feminist resource. The *Devi Mahatmya* has been, and can continue to be, drawn on to help reconstruct or reform male-dominated notions of the world and the divine into a more empowering, human-centered vision of possible futures.

Bibliography

Brown, C. Mackenzie
1990   *The Triumph of the Goddess: The Canonical Models and Theological Visions of the Devi Bhagavata* (Albany: State University of New York Press).
Chitnis, Suma
1988   'Feminism: Indian Ethos and Indian Convictions', in Rehana Ghadially (ed.), *Women in Indian Society* (New Delhi: Sage Publications): 81-95.
Daniel, Sheryl B.
1980   'Marriage in Tamil Culure: The Problem of Conflicting Models', in Susan S. Wadley (ed.), *The Powers of Tamil Women* (Delhi: Manohar): 61-91.
Gupta, Lina
1991   'Kali, the Savior', in Paula M. Cooey, William R. Eakin and Jay B. McDaniel (eds.), *After Patriarchy: Feminist Transformations of the World Religions* (Maryknoll, NY: Orbis Books): 15-38.
Hansen, Kathryn
1992   'Heroic Modes of Women in Indian Myth, Ritual, and History: The

Tapasvini and the Virangana', in Arvind Sharma and Katherine K. Young (eds.), *The Annual Review of Women in World Religions*, II (Albany: State University of New York Press): 1-62.

Humes, Cynthia A.

1996a   'Vindhyavasini: Local Yet Great Goddess', in John S. Hawley and Donna M. Wulff (eds.), *Devi: The Goddess in India* (Berkeley: University of California Press): 49-76.

1996b   'Becoming Male: Salvation through Gender Modification in Hindism and Buddhism', in Sabrina Petra Ramet (ed.), *Gender Reversals and Gender Cultures: Anthropological and Historical Perspectives* (London: Routledge Press, 1996): 123-37.

1998   'Great Goddess or Great Woman? Women's Recitation of the Devi Mahatmya', in Karen L. King (ed.), *Women in Goddess Traditions in Antiquity and Today* (Minneapolis: Fortress Press): 39-63.

Pintchman, Tracy

1994   *The Rise of the Goddess in the Hindu Tradition* (Albany: State University of New York Press).

Reynolds, Holly Baker

1980   'The Auspicious Married Woman', in Susan S. Wadley (ed.), The *Powers of Tamil Women* (Delhi: Manohar): 35-60.

Wadley, Susan S.

1980   'The Paradoxical Powers of Tamil Women', in Susan S. Wadley (ed.), *The Powers of Tamil Women* (Delhi: Manohar): 153-70.

Usha Menon and Richard A. Shweder

Power in its Place:
Is the Great Goddess of Hinduism a Feminist?

Feminist discourse has fractured in so many ways these days that
the specific implications of actually being a feminist have become
far from clear. At the very least one can identify three camps of 'feminists', who are separated from each other by deep ideological fault
lines: (1) liberal feminists, who argue that men and women are
essentially alike and equal; (2) ecological feminists and goddess
worshipers who argue that men and women are essentially different and unequal, and that women are superior beings who should
be free to cultivate and take advantage of their femininity independent of men; and (3) deconstructive feminists, who argue that nothing is essentially anything and that everything, including (indeed
especially) 'gender categories', are essentially historical and accidental and should be despised as little more than figments of an
ideologically motivated imagination. Given these very different
kinds of 'feminist' voices any attempt to answer the question 'Is the
Hindu Goddess a Feminist?' must either specify the question further (Is the Hindu Goddess a liberal feminist? Is she an ecological
feminist? Is she a deconstructive feminist?) or else unify the idea of
feminism around some general criterion such as a sense of moral
outrage over the subordination of women by men.

In this essay we are going to argue that the answer to the question 'Is the Hindu Goddess a Feminist?' is 'yes and no, but mostly
no'. On the one hand, in South Asia, there are heterodox, more
specifically 'tantric', discourses about the Great Goddess that might
offer a sliver of encouragement to the view that the Great Goddess
is an ecological feminist, although as we shall see, such an interpretation can be quite hazardous, and is probably misleading. On the
other hand, in the local Oriya community of the temple town of
Bhubaneswar with which we are most familiar, the canonical or
'culturally correct' discourse about the Great Goddess strongly
suggests that the answer to the question is 'no'.

We are going to focus on a local canonical story about the Great Goddess and on the way gender relations are organized in the temple town of Bhubaneswar in Orissa, India. More precisely, we are going to present material on the relations that exist between husbands and wives in this community. We believe that these relations are profoundly influenced by indigenous perceptions about the goddess and the nature of her power, her *shakti*. By examining these relations it is possible to arrive at what could be described as an indigenously valid answer to the question 'Is the Goddess a Feminist?' We shall assume that feminism, in its broadest sense, refers to advocacy of women's rights based on a belief in the equality of the sexes. We shall assume that feminists are those who are aware of and are seeking to end the inequality of men and women (Tuttle 1986). We shall argue that from the point of view of most local men and women in Orissa, the Great Goddess is not a feminist.

Before describing the ways in which gender relations are structured in the temple town of Bhubaneswar, a word or two about this neighborhood. Bhubaneswar, today, consists of two distinct parts: there is the modern city, barely 50 years old, which is the capital of the state of Orissa and the temple town that claims to be at least 900 years old. Life in the temple town revolves around the tenth- to eleventh-century temple dedicated to the Hindu god Shiva, who is represented here as Lingaraj—the Lord of the Phallus. Bhubaneswar is a pilgrimage center of some note although it does not rival Puri, one of Hinduism's four sacred centers that lies about 40 miles to the south. For the most part, households in this neighborhood have hereditary links with the temple, the menfolk performing different services for the deity. While everyone is aware of the world outside (the television being a ubiquitous presence in every household), people continue to adhere to traditional custom and practice in their daily lives: most marriages are arranged, most women remain secluded in family compounds, menstrual taboos are observed, upper caste widows do not remarry or wear colored clothes or ornaments, and untouchability continue to be practiced as far as entering the temple is concerned—except for the day following *Shivaratri* (Shiva's Night, commemorating Shiva's marriage to Parvarti), when everyone is welcome.

Perhaps, the most remarkable feature of worship and rituals in the temple town is its inclusive quality. Although the presiding deity

is Shiva, the worship of Vishnu is explicitly integrated into temple
rituals, and the priests often describe the granite *lingam* as representing both Shiva and Vishnu—Hara and Hari. Devi, the Great
Goddess, also has her special significance in their neighborhood.
Practically every lane has a small shrine dedicated to one or the
other forms of the Goddess—Chandi, Jogeshwari, Parvati—and to
cap it all, there is the Koppali temple where she is represented
with her foot on a supine Shiva and her tongue hanging out.

Is the Great Goddess an Ecological Feminist? An Example of 'Tantric' Discourse

Figure 1 is an iconic representation of the Great Goddess of Hinduism in her manifestation as Kali or Chandi. The icon is well
known among Oriya Hindus in the temple town of Bhubaneswar.
In 1991, Usha Menon conducted interviews with 92 women and
men in that community, asking each person for his or her understanding of the icon. The sample was composed entirely of upper-
caste men and women: 73 of the participants were Brahmans while
the remaining 19 belonged to what are referred to locally as clean
castes. While almost all informants identified the icon correctly as
representing the Goddess in her manifestation as Kali, very few
appeared to recognize its Tantric origins. Of the few who did, one
male informant did offer the following interpretation of the icon
(see Menon and Shweder 1994; Menon and Shweder 1998; Shweder
and Menon forthcoming).

The narrator is a 70-year-old male Brahman, married with two
sons and two daughters. All his life he has been a priest in the
Lingaraj Temple in Bhubaneswar. During the interview he admitted
having attended some Tantric ceremonies, although he claims that
he is not a 'siddha' or a fully initiated worshiper of Kali.

Question (Q.)   Do you recognize this picture?
Answer (A.)   This is the Tantric depiction of Kali. Kali here is
naked. She has thrown Shiva to the ground and is standing on him.
She displays here absolute overwhelming strength. She is in a terrible rage, wearing her garland of skulls and in each arm a weapon of
destruction. Look: in this hand, the *trishul* (trident), in this the
chakra (discus), in this the sword, in this the sickle, in this the

Figure 1: *Kali standing on Shiva*

bow and arrow. This is how Kali is shown in Tantric *pujas*, where the devotee is praying to the goddess for perfect knowledge and awareness. All this kind of worship goes on in the Ramakrishna Mission. The monks there are all Tantrics and they know all about it. Sri Ramakrishna and Swami Vivekananda, both great sages, knew all about such *shakti pujas* and Tantric rites.

Q.   Can you tell me about the story that is associated with this picture?

A.   In all these Tantric *pujas* the goal is to acquire perfect knowledge and ultimate power. The naked devotee worships Mother on a dark moonless night in a cremation ground. The offerings are meat and alcohol. Ordinary people cannot participate in such worship. If they were even to witness it they would go mad. I have attended such worship once, but I am not a true worshiper and I have no special knowledge of Tantric worship.

Q.   How would you describe Kali's expression here?

A.   She is the image of fury.

Q.   You mean she is angry? She is in a rage?

A.   Yes…yes. You must understand that this is how she appears to her devotee. He has to have the strength of mind to withstand her fierceness. She is not mild or tender but cruel and demanding and frightening.

Q.   Do you think that she has put out her tongue in anger?

A.   Yes, she has put out her tongue in anger. Kali is always angry. She is always creating and at the same time destroying life. Here you see her with her foot placed squarely on Shiva's chest. When the time comes for the universe to be destroyed entirely, no one will be spared, not even the gods, whether Vishnu or Shiva. Everyone will be destroyed.

Q.   Some people say that she is feeling deeply ashamed at having stepped on her husband and that is why she has bitten her tongue. You don't agree?

A.   People have different views. People believe whatever makes them feel comfortable and if they like to think that Kali is ashamed, then let them. What I have told you is what the special devotees of Kali believe. They believe that Mother is supreme. Even Brahma, Vishnu and Shiva are her servants.

Q.   Can you tell me why Shiva is lying on the ground?

A.   Kali has thrown him on the ground and she puts her foot on him to make clear that she is supreme.

Q.   So you don't think he is lying on the ground to subdue Kali?

A.   No, that is beyond Shiva's capacity. If Kali becomes calm, it is because she wishes to, not because she is persuaded to do so. Even to her most faithful devotee, Kali's actions sometimes don't make sense. But life itself often doesn't make sense, so what can one say?

Q.   Who would you say is dominant in this picture? Is it Kali or Shiva?

A.   Obviously Kali. But it is also important to realize that while *shakti* [female energy] is absolutely necessary for the creation and evolution of the universe, by itself even *shakti* cannot achieve anything. *Shakti* has to combine with consciousness for the process of creation to take place. And so consciousness as symbolized by Shiva has a unique position. Just as it is only through the union of a man and a woman that a child is conceived, so too, only when *shakti* and *cit* (consciousness) come together does creation occur.

Now this is the kind of Tantric interpretation of the power and superiority of the Great Goddess that excites the imagination of ecological feminists up and down the west coast of the United States. 'Everyone knows about Tantra in Marin County' a female friend from northern California told us as we began to explain to her what Tantra was about in India. These days, in our new age postmodern world, Mother Kali has her bookstores and devotees in lands distant from India, where people are free to see new meanings in her image that may not have their origin in South Asia.

It is worth noting, for example, that even in this heterodox Tantric interpretation of Kali by a Hindu temple priest, the emphasis is on the fundamental or essential difference between female and male (energy versus consciousness) and on their asymmetrical interdependency (in this case with males doing service for the female). This is not an egalitarian story about equal rights. It is not a protest about the subordination of one gender by the other. It is not even a claim for autonomy for females. The Great Goddess is not parthenogenic. She needs men to make the world go round.

More important, this Tantric discourse about her is not canonical in most communities in India. It is certainly not the standard or 'culturally correct' interpretation of the deeper meaning of the icon in the temple town of Bhubaneshwar.

A More Canonical Oriya Story about the Great Goddess

In the temple town today, the most commonly told story of the icon in Figure 1 goes something like this (see Menon and Shweder 1994). To the extent that this local contemporary version is the ideal story for most upper-caste women and men in this neighborhood, we present it as the canonical story of the icon. This particular narrator is a 74-year-old male Brahman, who is a retired businessman and hotel owner.

Q.   Do you recognize this picture?
A.   Kali.
Q.   Can you describe the incident that is portrayed in this picture?
A.   This is about the time when Mahishasura [the buffalo demon] became so powerful that he tortured everyone on earth and heaven; ...he obtained a boon from the gods according to which no man could kill him. All the gods then went to Narayana [Vishnu] and they pondered on ways to destroy Mahishasura; ...each contributed the strength and energy of his consciousness—his '*bindu*' —and from that Durga was created. But when Durga was told she had to kill Mahishasura she said she needed weapons to do so and so all the gods gave her their weapons. Armed thus, Durga went into battle. She fought bravely but she found it impossible to kill the demon; ...he was too strong and clever. You see the gods had forgotten to tell her that the boon Mahishasura had obtained from Brahma was that he could only die at the hands of a naked female. Durga finally became desperate and she appealed to Mangala to suggest some way to kill Mahishasura. Mangala then told her that the only way was to take off her clothes, that the demon would only lose strength when confronted by a naked women. So Durga did as she was advised to. She stripped and within seconds of seeing her, Mahishasura's strength waned and he died under her sword. After killing him a terrible rage entered Durga's mind and she asked herself: 'What kinds of gods are these that give to demons such boons, and apart from that, what kinds of gods are these that they do not have the honesty to tell me the truth before sending me into battle?' She decided that such a world with such gods did not deserve to survive and she took on the form of Kali and went on a mad rampage, devouring every living creature that came in her way. Now the gods were in a terrible quandary. They had all given

her their weapons. They were helpless without any weapons, while she had a weapon in each of her ten arms. How could Kali be checked and who could check her in her mad dance of destruction? Again the gods all gathered, and Narayana decided that only Mahadev [Shiva] could check Kali, and so he advised the gods to appeal to him.

Now Shiva is an ascetic, a yogi who has no interest in what happens in the world. But when all the gods begged him to intervene he agreed to do his best. He went and lay in her path. Kali, absorbed in her dance of destruction, was unaware that Shiva lay in her path, and so she stepped on him all unknowing. When she put her foot on Shiva's chest, she bit her tongue, saying 'Oh! My husband!' There is in Mahadev [Shiva] a '*tejas*', a special quality of his body that penetrated her, that made her look down, that made her see reason. She had been so angry that she had gone beyond reason. But once she recognized him she became calm and still. This is the story about that time.

Q.   How would you describe the expression on her face?
A.   She had been extremely angry but when her foot fell on Mahadev's chest—after all he is her own husband—she bit her tongue and became still. Gradually her anger went down.
Q.   So is there still any anger in her expression?
A.   Oh yes, in her eyes you can still see the light of anger shining.
Q.   And her tongue? What is she feeling when she bites it?
A.   What else but shame [*lajya*—perhaps best translated as 'respectful restraint']? Shame. Because she did something unforgivable she is feeling shame.

Most members of the temple town community, both female and male, tell stories about this icon that are consistent with the above narration (Menon and Shweder 1994). Their stories express the sense of moral outrage experienced by the Great Goddess over the deceit and incompetence of the male gods. But the ultimate message of their stories is that anger (even over exploitation) is destructive of society and nature, and that it is important for the sake of social reproduction for the Great Goddess to exercise respectful restraint and to nurture rather than devour the universe. The story celebrates wifely virtues and presupposes the asymmetrical inter-

dependency of husband and wife. Again it is not an egalitarian story
about equal rights. It is not a protest against the subordination of
one gender by the other. It is a story about the power of women to
create and destroy and to have the proper judgment to choose life
over death. The story reveals much about normal gender relations
in the South Asian cultural world.

Oriya Hindu Women and the Great Goddess

Oriya Hindus of the temple town describe the Great Goddess, Devi,
as embodying *shakti*, for it is her energy and power that keeps the
world going. They state quite explicitly that even the gods have no
shakti of their own and they play on the words *Shiva* and *shava*.
Shiva without *shakti*, they say, is a corpse, a *shava*. According to
the origin story from the *Shiva Purana* that they quote, Shiva accepted Devi the Great Goddess without reservation. That is why he
is immortal, never reborn, unlike Vishnu who recoiled from accepting her completely and is therefore condemned to being incarnated
several times. Whenever Vishnu's *shakti* is depleted, he is reborn
into the world and his *shakti* replenished.

Oriya Hindus of the temple town, both men and women, also say
that human females, like the goddess, simply by being female, embody *shakti*. In ordinary everyday conversations, Oriya women will
say that they embody *adya shakti* (primordial power), *matru
shakti* (mother's power), *stri shakti* (women's power). Both men
and women are liable to say that women have more of the *gunas*
(the three 'qualities' or constituents of the phenomenal world) in
terms of absolute quantities than men do, and that therefore women
can turn the *asadhya* (the undoable) into the *sadhya* (the doable),
the *asambhav* (the impossible) into the *sambhav* (the possible).
Women are commonly described as *shaktidayinis* (givers of power/
strength), as being *sampoorna shakti* (full of strength/energy).
Women are said to control and direct the family and the flow of life
(they are *samsarore chalak*), they maintain the family and the world
(*samsaroku sambhaliba*), they ensure peace and order (*shanti
shrunkhala rakhiba*).

Oriya Hindu Women and the Family

Most Oriya Hindus of the old town believe that social reproduction is the primary task of any group. They believe that the family represents the most appropriate site for social reproduction. Both men and women will say, 'We are born into this world to play our roles in *samsara*, to participate in the ebb and flow of life, to build families, to raise children'. They emphasize the impermanence of all things in this world, the fact that continual change is the only stable feature of life. They believe that only through procreating and raising children to responsible adulthood does a group achieve immortality.

Not surprisingly, therefore, Oriya Hindu women, and their menfolk too, regard the home and the family—the domestic domain— as an important sphere of human action. And with women controlling and managing all household affairs, this responsibility for enculturating the next generation rests almost exclusively in their hands, making them important and influential social actors.

We should mention that Oriya Hindus dichotomize space into domestic space or inner space (*ghare*) and public or outer space (*bahare*). According to their ways of thinking, domestic or inner space is sacred, for it is a space that doesn't progressively pollute the person. Public or outside space on the other hand is polluting, in the sense that continued and prolonged involvement in the world outside the home leads to a coarsening of the human being. That is why people in the temple town will say that men are coarser than women, less civilized, less refined, more *abhadra*. Men, it is argued, display their emotions, for instance, of anger (*raga*) or mocking laughter (*hasa*) more readily. Men, it is argued, are not reticent or respectfully restrained and are less capable of experiencing refined and refining emotions such as *lajya* or 'shame'. All such coarsening things are associated in the Oriya mind with the occupation of public or outside space.

Both men and women believe that men have only a peripheral role to play in achieving prosperity for the family and the well-being of its members. Men earn, but this marks the limit of their contribution. Whether what men earn is utilized effectively and productively depends on the sagacity and capability of the women of the household, particularly mature adult women.

Men readily acknowledge that women shoulder many more responsibilities than they do (*striro daitva purusa opekhya jvateshtha adhika*) and that the work women have to do is six times as much as that which men have to do (*stri jatinkoro karma chho guna adhika*). As one quite articulate informant put it: 'Look at a twenty-two-year-old man. What is he? He is nothing but a child, a twenty-year-old child. He knows nothing. He just roams here and there. But a twenty-year-old girl, she has become the mother of two children. She runs her household and family. She cares for the cows and calves under her care, the children and the house. She cooks and serves her husband. She cleans the children, dresses them and sends them to school, makes sure that they are well. She manages the parents of her husband. She cleans the house... Compared to a man, a woman's responsibilities are far more. When you compare men and women of the same age, that is what you find.'

Hierarchy and Difference as Natural and Moral

We wish to emphasize that in our view such popular Oriya recognition of the worth of women's work and such widespread acknowledgment of greater female effectiveness in this world is not equivalent to espousing a feminist viewpoint. For in Orissa very few men and women believe that men and women are equal, in any sense of the term. In fact, the preferred view in the temple town of Bhubaneswar is that gender relations are built on the logic of difference and solidarity rather than on equality and competition. Most residents of the temple town would find the notion of 'gender equality' either incomprehensible or amusing or perhaps even childlike. For these people the most common and cogent metaphor for society is the human body, where no organ is exactly substitutable for any other and yet all work together so that the body functions efficiently, survives and lives. Temple town men and women believe that male and female are the only two *jatis* or 'castes' in the world whose differences can never truly be transcended.

For Oriya Hindus then, difference and inequality are natural and moral facts, although the particular prerogatives and privileges enjoyed, and the power exercised, are fluid, and as A.K. Ramanujan (1990) has suggested, vary with particular contexts. Men, in terms of the constitution of their substances, have disproportionately more of the *sattva guna*. They are thus regarded as 'purer', and because of their relative purity they enjoy greater privileges in some contexts. Women, on the other hand possess more *guna*s in

absolute terms. They thus exercise more power and control than
men in other contexts.

This fluidity in the privileges enjoyed and the power exercised by
men and women relative to each other complicates any description
of the relations that exist between husbands and wives. At one,
perhaps the most obvious level, Oriya Hindu husbands in the temple town do dominate their wives and they are the absolute unquestioned heads of their households. In terms of public presentation, the Oriya Hindu wife is extremely careful to display the
utmost respect and deference to her husband. Women explicitly
refer to their husbands as their gods (*ame tanku amor debata
manuchu*, we accept them as our gods) and publicly display rituals
of deference and worship. In fact, the Oriya word for 'husband' is
swami—meaning 'lord'—while the Oriya word for 'wife' is *stri* or
'woman'. Thus, wives in the old town will commonly say, 'For a
woman, her husband is her god...we [that is, people/everyone] call
to *parameshwar*, *bhagwan*, but for a wife her husband is every
kind of god' (*gote nariro pati hela tar devata, ame jo parameshwar, bhagwan dakuchu, nari paiin tar swami hela sabu kichi
bhagwan*). Thus, traditional wives will perform an *aarti*—the wor-
shipful gesture of honoring by holding out and circling a lit flame—
to their husbands every morning before eating anything, and even
for those who fancy themselves 'modern', the very first duty of the
morning is to bow their heads to God and then touch the feet of
their (often sleeping) husband.

This acceptance of inequality by Oriya Hindu women is rooted
in their belief that they are continually in a state of relative physical
impurity. The fact of menstruation, a natural process that is difficult
to regulate through fasting or any other cultural means, reinforces
the belief in the natural inferiority of women. Perhaps this point
may seem arguable to a 'Western mind' suspicious of the idea of
natural hierarchies, but we believe that Oriya women voluntarily
acknowledge the existence of natural gender hierarchies, and that
they would themselves describe this acknowledgment as a mature
recognition of a natural fact. Alternatively stated, Oriya men do not
need to exert brute force to ensure this recognition of a hierarchical relationship between men and women.

But men are often unworthy superiors. Confident in their 'natural' lordship, they see no need to control their desires or their pas-

sions. They are often untruthful and treacherous. Women, on the other hand, will tell you that women are different. They will tell you that when they voluntarily subordinate themselves to men, when they serve men, they have to exercise self-discipline, they have to control their emotions, they cannot let their passions sway them. They may suffer but such suffering, because it is voluntarily accepted, ennobles rather than degrades them.

Such self-discipline has its inevitable impact on women. According to the more articulate Oriya Hindu women informants, an exercise in self-control strengthens and develops the capacity for further self-control. In terms of emotional functioning and moral development, they believe they become superior to men. They grow in moral stature. They gain such moral authority that finally even their 'natural' masters are ready to acknowledge and respect it.

The logic appears to be that in terms of nature (or physiology), man is superior to woman, but in terms of culture he is not. Women may start off as 'naturally' inferior. But they work upon that inferiority. They rework themselves to transcend that inferiority. And ultimately, as cultural artifacts they make themselves superior to men.

Thus we partially agree with Reynolds (1980: 35-57) when she says, in her paper on 'The Auspicious Married Woman', that for Hindus power lies in subordination. But we would contend that this subordination is not the result of explicit male domination but rather a voluntary subordination. Within the Oriya Hindu worldview only such a subordination that comes from within is truly moral, completely ennobling, and carries with it real power.

The Meaning of the Icon

And it is here that the meanings that Oriya Hindus attach to the icon of Kali (Figure 1) become particularly relevant. Men and women in the temple town of Bhubaneswar say that the goddess was morally justified in her murderous rampage because the male gods had betrayed her, sending her in to do battle with the buffalo demon, Mahishasura, without telling her that the boon the demon had received from Brahma protected him from every living being but a naked female and that to kill him, she would have to strip. But they also say that she became calm, regained her composure, not because of anything Shiva did but because of a sense of her duty as a wife to Shiva, and as a mother to the world. Shiva, after all, they argue, could have done nothing to prevent her from continuing on her murderous rampage. If she had wished, she could have crushed him and gone on with her destruction. According to them, this story exemplifies voluntary subordination, a deliberate exercise in self-control. It is such self-control that is culturally valued and it is through such self-control that women gain power.

Therefore, when it comes to Oriya Hindus, Sherry Ortner's 1974 formulation 'nature is to culture as woman is to man' does not really seem to apply. For Oriya Hindus a woman derives her power from her natural substance but such power gathers its full significance only because it is subject to cultural, ultimately moral, control that originates from within herself. As Ramanujan points out, the Lévi-Straussian opposition between nature and culture is itself culture-bound: in the Hindu alternative, and here we quote him, 'culture is enclosed in nature, nature is reworked in culture, so that we cannot tell the difference' (1990: 50). This is another of the reversible 'container-contained relations' (1990: 50) that extend to other Hindu concepts and ideas.

And so, to end, the Oriya Hindu answer to the question 'Is the Great Goddess of Hinduism a feminist?' should probably be 'no'. Oriya women and men see the goddess as full of power. But it is a power that is reined in and held in check. It is a power that is controlled from within. It is a power that is capable of destroying men and all of creation. It is a power that is exercised most responsibly by enduring the sacrifices and hardships that are necessary to keep the social order from tumbling down. Thus, while it is conceivable that in Marin County, California, these days Kali may have become a symbol of feminism, among Oriya Hindus in the temple town of Bhubaneswar, the Great Mother of us all stands for neither gender equality nor for any transformation of society.

Bibliography

Menon, Usha, and Richard A. Shweder
    1994   'Kali's Tongue: Cultural Psychology and the Power of "Shame" in Orrisa, India', in S. Kitayama and H. Markus (eds.), *Emotion and Culture* (Washington, DC: APA Publications): 241-84.

1998   'The Return of the White Man's Burden: The Encounter Between the
            Moral Discourse of Anthropology and the Domestic Life of Oriya
            Women', in R.A. Shweder (ed.), *Welcome to Middle Age! (And Other
            Cultural Fictions)* (Chicago: University of Chicago Press): 139-88.

Ortner, Sherry B.
1974   'Is Female to Male as Nature is to Culture?', in M. Rosaldo and L. Lam-
            phere (eds.), *Women, Culture and Society* (Stanford: Stanford
            University Press): 67-81.

Ramanujan, A.K.
1990   'Is There an Indian Way of Thinking?', in McKim Marriott (ed.), *India
            through Hindu Categories* (New Delhi: Sage): 41-58.

Reynolds, Holly
1980   'The Auspicious Married Woman', in Susan Wadley (ed.), *The Powers
            of Tamil Women* (Syracuse, NY: Maxwell School of Citizenship and
            Public Affairs): 35-60.

Shweder, Richard A., and Usha Menon
forthcoming 'Dominating Kali: Hindu Family Values and Tantric Power', in Rachel
            McDermott and Jeffrey Kripal (eds.), *Encountering Kali: Cultural
            Understanding at the Extremes.*

Tuttle, Lisa
1986   *The Encyclopedia of Feminism* (Harlow, Essex: Longman).

Miranda Shaw

Is Vajrayogini a Feminist?
A Tantric Buddhist Case Study

Vajrayogini is the supreme goddess of the Tantric Buddhist pantheon. As a fully enlightened being, or female Buddha, she embodies the pinnacle of spiritual attainment. Vajrayogini offers a visually striking portrayal of enlightenment in female form. Her body is bright red in color, bespeaking the heat of her yogic fire and her plenitude of primal energy (*sakti*). She has an intense yet rapturous expression as she gazes into the depths of reality. Vajrayogini appears in dynamic lunging, leaping, and soaring poses with her long hair swirling around her, naked except for delicate bone ornaments. The goddess cups in her left hand a skull-bowl that contains the nectar of bliss that she distills from every experience. In her right hand she brandishes a curved knife that she uses to sever all illusion and duality at the root. The crook of her left arm supports a staff, signifying that she has integrated eroticism into her spiritual path.

Tantra is a religious paradigm, found within both Hinduism and Buddhism, that emerged to historical view within both traditions at about the same time, namely, the seventh and eighth centuries CE. The central premise of Tantra is that the world is intrinsically radiant, blissful, and pure. The goal of Tantric practice is to remove the veil of illusion that obscures the pristine perfection of the world and thus to experience the innate ecstasy of being at the heart of reality. Toward this end, one of the main Tantric methods is to visualize oneself as a deity in order to discover one's divine qualities and powers. Another method is to envision the world as a mandala, the residence or palace of a deity, and everyone within it as divine beings. Mantra recitation is used to focus and purify the mind. The body is affirmed as the abode of bliss and vehicle of spiritual insight. Inner yogic methods, known in Hindu Tantra as kundalini yoga and in Buddhism as perfection stage yoga, channel the subtle energies of the body in order to kindle an inner fire of psychic heat that burns away karmic residues and literally transforms the body into the adamantine body of a deity, or, in Buddhist terms, enables one to become a living Buddha. Because of its world-affirming ethos, Tantric practitioners do not turn away from the world but rather immerse themselves in the dynamic stream of life. Accordingly, erotic experience falls within the purview of Tantric practice, and the relationship between lovers is seen as a path to spiritual awakening. One of the hallmarks of Tantra is the honor that is accorded to women in its philosophy and practice. This gynocentrism is gaining recognition in scholarship on Hindu Tantra (Gupta 1991), and I contend that this holds true for Buddhist Tantra as well.

Vajrayogini is featured in some of the earliest Tantric Buddhist scriptures (c. seventh–eighth centuries CE), remained important in India through the twelfth century, and is still prominent in the living traditions of Tibet and Nepal. Before proceeding to the question of whether Vajrayogini and her cultural purview might be considered to be feminist, and in what sense, I will describe some methodologies that I have used and outline their role in shaping my conclusions.

My work has addressed both women and goddesses in Tantric Buddhism, because I find their interpretation to be closely intertwined. My research was initially motivated by the discrepancy I perceived between the vibrant vision of female dynamism presented in Tantric iconography and the undocumented theory of gender exploitation universally espoused in Western scholarship. The prevailing Western view has been that the women of Tantric Buddhism were dominated, marginalized, and exploited by their male cohorts. Earlier scholars pronounced female Tantrics to be prostitutes, sluts, and witches, while more recent scholarship has temporized that they were low-caste unfortunates who were used by male Tantrics in sexual rituals. The corollary of this view is that the Tantric Buddhist goddesses have been relevant only for male psychology and religiosity. A recent contribution on the topic reiterates:

> Any valorization of the feminine is primarily of benefit to the male practitioner... The feminine sky-dancers or dakinis are a powerful representation of the repressed feminine aspects of the male psyche (Sponberg 1992: 28).

The denial of any relationship between women and Tantric goddesses like Vajrayogini has long foreclosed upon any attempt to discover whether women might have been their creators or exemplars or even whether goddesses might have figured in women's religious lives as models of inspiration and objects of meditative and yogic transformation.

My discoveries on this topic were made possible by explicitly feminist historiography and hermeneutics. I applied modes of historical and textual analysis that have already been under refinement for decades in fields such as biblical and classical scholarship, although their application in the discipline of Buddhist studies is a relatively recent development.

In terms of historiography, my operative principle is to treat women as historical agents, that is, as active shapers of history and interpreters of their own experience, rather than as passive objects or victims of male historical agents.

Making women subjects rather than objects of history shaped the questions I asked. I focused on women's practices, beliefs, and writings, rather than on men's views of, projections upon, and real or imagined restrictions upon women. Because I place women at the center of my inquiry, my research occupies the cusp of an emerging phase of scholarship on women in Buddhism, namely, the transition from investigation into the portrayal of women in male texts and the roles ascribed to women by male authority figures and institutions to the exploration of women's contemplative and ritual practices, oral and literary traditions, doctrinal emphases, institutions, and self-understanding as gendered beings and religious seekers.

This feminist revisionist approach required a range of hermeneutical strategies that would enable me to break free from the strong grip of androcentric analysis upon my field. For example, when reading Tantric Buddhist literary sources, I did not presume that every statement reflects male viewpoints or interests. Since the scriptures and meditation manuals were generated within communities of both men and women, I searched them for, and found, evidence of women's views and experiences. I extrapolated from descriptions of men's attitudes and behavior toward women, reanalyzed accounts of interactions from the women's perspective, and highlighted passages written from a gynocentric perspective, that is, from the point of view of female embodiment, sexuality, and active concern for women's well-being—passages generally voiced by a female deity.

I also brought gender to the forefront in my approach to translation. In the case of translations that are already available, I discovered that generic (gender neutral), ambiguous, and plural grammatical constructions in the original texts are consistently rendered as male terms and pronouns in English translations. For example, the generic term 'Tantric practitioner' might be rendered as 'yogi' in an English translation, followed by gratuitous use of the pronoun 'he', creating a false impression of the male exclusivity of Tantric texts. I opted for neutral or inclusive translations that more closely approximate the grammar and meaning of the original, and this allowed for dramatic reinterpretation. Moreover, when a Tantric text is available in both Sanskrit and Tibetan versions, the Sanskrit original will typically be more highly inflected for gender and number, whereas plural and case endings were often dropped in the Tibetan translation. Consulting the Sanskrit original of a given text sometimes reveals that what started as a female reference in the Sanskrit ends up as a male reference in the English translation. In several cases, 'yogini' in the Sanskrit was rendered as 'yoga practitioner' in the Tibetan and then translated as the male 'yogi' in the English version. In a more frequent occurrence, 'yoga practitioners', a gender–inclusive plural in Sanskrit and Tibetan, is commonly translated as 'yogis' in English works, even when the practice under discussion requires the participation of both men and women, such as certain sacramental feasts (*cakrapuja*) and the yoga of sacred union.

Another key element of my methodology was to find and translate sources by women. Their meditation manuals, theoretical treatises, ritual texts, and poetic anthologies represent a rich legacy of profound learnedness, meditative and ritual expertise, and visionary experience. These works and the level of brilliance, creativity, and innovation reflected in them enabled me to delineate the religious milieu of Vajrayogini as a movement in which women were gurus, leaders, and pioneers (Shaw 1994: chs. 4–5).

In evaluating scholarship on goddesses and their relationships to women, I no longer consider it sufficient to consult only male sources, to presume male authorship of sources generated by communities of men and women, or to analyze such sources only with reference to male psychology, sexuality, or social roles. Such andro-centric interpretations should not be regarded as universally valid but only as partially valid for the limited topic of inquiry, namely, men. Further, the question of whether a given goddess might em-body a female perspective requires inquiry into women's oral, visual, and written interpretations of that goddess and the practices in which women worship, contemplate, or body her forth, as well as the role the goddess might play in women's self-understanding and path to liberation.

Feminist methodologies helped me to elicit a gynocentric design within which it is meaningful to ask whether the goddess Vajrayo-gini is a feminist who acts to empower, advocate on behalf of, or liberate women on any level—psychological, social, sexual, or spiritual. In the case of Vajrayogini, this question can be answered unambiguously in the affirmative. She closely identifies with and allies herself with women, evincing great concern that women should appreciate their spiritual capacities. Vajrayogini declares that women participate in her divinity and announces: 'Wherever in the world a female body is seen, that should be recognized as my holy body' (George 1974: 32). The goddess imparts that she adopts a female form so that women, upon seeing her, will recognize their own innate divinity and potential for enlightenment. She invites women to meditate upon their identity with her as a direct avenue of self-affirmation and enlightenment, without reference or recourse to male approval or legitimation of their religious progress or au-thority (George 1974: 96, 121).

Vajrayogini is an emphatic, impassioned advocate of women and prescribes how men are to view and treat them. She insists that since all women are her embodiments, they should all be respected, honored, and served without exception:

> I am identical to the bodies of all women.
> There is no way that I can be worshipped
> Except by the worship of women (*stripuja*) (George 1974: 123).

Vajrayogini instructs a male Tantric in how to approach and behave toward his female companion. Regarding her as an embodiment of Vajrayogini, he should prostrate himself to the woman, circumam-bulate her, and give her clothing, incense, flowers, lamps, perfume, and sacramental meat and wine. In their daily interactions he should cook for her, feed her, and wait until she has eaten to partake of her leftovers (George 1974: 78, 83). He should regard every substance discharged by her body as pure and should be willing to sip sexual fluid and blood from her vulva and to lick any part of her body if requested to do so. Vajrayogini also insists that the man must satisfy his female partner sexually, with a mind free from lust, meditating upon her identity with Vajrayogini, making the pleasure of sexual union his offering to the goddess within her (Shaw 1994: 152-59; 1997: 120-24). He must cultivate his erotic repertoire, taking special care to incorporate the female superior position.[1] He should never mentally or verbally criticize her and should always 'speak with pleasant words and give a woman what she wants'.[2]

Apparently this goddess feels very strongly that men on the Tantric path must not disrespect women, if we are to judge from the following pronouncement:

> Chattering fools...who disparage women out of hostility,
> Will by that evil action remain constantly tortured
> For three eons in the fathomless Raudra hell,
> Wailing as their bodies burn in many fires (George 1974: 70).

The same work and other Tantric writings contain many condemnations of men who fail to honor women (Shaw 1994: 47-53). Vajrayogini's consort in this text, Candamaharosana, joins her in her strong advocacy on behalf of women. He agrees to punish those who transgress against women. Always portrayed with a sword and noose, he assures her that he keeps his weaponry at the ready as he scouts for men who fail to pay homage to women, so he can slash the scoundrels to pieces (George 1974: 66).

Clearly Vajrayogini is a strong supporter and champion of women, but she does not promote this philosophy at the expense of men. A woman on this path does not seek to dominate or exploit the man or crush him into submissive service. In Vajrayogini's vision of ideal relationships, the women who manifest her presence in the world

---

1.   On the extensiveness and specificity of the sexual repertoire, see George (1974: ch. 6). On the importance of the female superior position, see *Cakrasamvara-tantra*, sDe-dge 368, fol. 237a. 2-3.

2.   *Candamaharosana-tantra*, sDe-dge 431, fol. 319a.1-2. For a more complete discussion of the forms of homage and honor that Tantric yogis are to render to their female companions and to women in general, see Shaw (1994: 39-47).

are to dispense kindness, happiness, bliss, insight, and *sakti*, or spiritual nourishment, helping men overcome their arrogance, intellectual pride, and alienation from life. By virtue of her own spiritual attainments, a woman may provide insights and energy that a man needs to attain enlightenment, but she does so freely—not out of duty, obligation, or coercion. Women on this path are never required to do anything to assist, appeal to, seek the approval of, or gain legitimacy in the eyes of men. Women are enjoined only to pursue their primary purpose, which is to attain enlightenment.

In the diverse literary genres and historical sources I consulted, I found no evidence of the male exploitation previously posited in works in my field. Rather, the women's writings, scriptures, and biographical literature consistently portray women as free spiritual agents, in the sense that they sought out teachers, pursued their religious practices, and taught others at their own initiative. There is no point on their journey where their energies were diverted into the service of men or they could progress no further because they were women, nor was there a structure of male authority to limit or legitimate women's progress. On the contrary, there is evidence that women zealously guarded their hegemony in Tantric practice. They imposed numerous requirements of esoteric etiquette, displays of respect, and specific forms of homage from men who would approach, practice with, or apprentice themselves to them. Only the most sincere male seekers would be admitted to the women's ritual gatherings and feasts, and the men's behavior in this context was surrounded by proscriptions and requirements (Shaw 1994: 45-46, 83). I interpret these elaborate requirements as women's strategy for safeguarding their religious sovereignty, individually and collectively, in the Tantric sphere.

In this gynocentric tradition, goddesses such as Vajrayogini served women as divine prototypes and archetypal images of their own potential. Women embodied goddesses in a range of ritual contexts and meditated upon them as personifications of their own enlightened essence. Women's ultimate spiritual identity as female Buddhas is the cornerstone of the ideological understanding of femaleness in this movement, giving rise to an ethos of honor that women accorded to themselves and demanded of men. During my field research, I observed the survival in the living tradition today of many of the gender dynamics depicted in the historical sources.

My feminist approach raises the question of whether I simply projected what I was looking for onto the sources that I investigated, translated, and analyzed. I feel confident that this is not the case, because what I discovered was nothing I could ever have imagined. What I had sought, based on expectations shaped by Western feminism, was perhaps a religion of equality, in which men conceded respect, dignity, and religious opportunity to women, or at most a subaltern or liminal female tradition of resistance or subversion against a prevailing patriarchal structure. I never doubted that the overarching religious framework would be designed and governed by men. Therefore, my own assumptions were continuously overturned as I delved into the primary literary sources and encountered a clarion stream of triumphal female voices, a treasury of female interpretation and creativity within Buddhism in which women themselves explored, defined, and celebrated their femaleness, sexuality, and spirituality without any concession whatsoever to male interests, approval, or legitimation—a 'women's Buddhism', to which large numbers of men flocked because of the promise that it held for their deliverance, as well as for the liberation of women. Similarly, nothing in my Indological training or cultural background prepared me for my observations, during my fieldwork among living practitioners, of how the understanding of women as female deities in human form continues to shape attitudes and interactions in myriad ways. Therefore, although my discoveries were made possible by feminist methodologies, they ran counter to my expectations and did not conform to any of the hypotheses I had formulated beforehand.

This Tantric feminism—or, more properly, gynocentrism—was not previously recognized in androcentric scholarship, I believe, because the evidence was rendered invisible by the absence of an interpretive framework in which to locate it. The historical hypotheses and conceptual categories that might make it possible to do so were not present, for several reasons. One reason might be termed an 'ethnocentric fallacy', a largely unconscious tendency to project the interpreter's cultural values upon other historical period and cultures. Western scholars on the whole have simply interpreted the gender dynamics of Tantric Buddhism in accordance with their own cultural norms, according to which female images and women themselves function as objects of male desire and consumption.

The presumed universality of this pattern has made it unnecessary for those who have posited it of the Tantric movement to provide any documentation of their claims.

Another reason might be termed the 'patriarchal fallacy', or presumption that male dominance is a universal cultural invariant. This essentialization of patriarchy arbitrarily privileges men in any given topic of inquiry. Assuming that women's lives are circumscribed by patriarchal social and ideological structures renders women's experiences as derivative at least and oppositional or transgressive at most vis-à-vis the enveloping patriarchy. However, enshrining patriarchy as universally normative is a tendentiously blunt and inadequate interpretive tool for illuminating the varieties of cultural constructions of gender and gender relations throughout the world and human history. It prevents the recognition of venues in which women have created for themselves a hegemonic domain of freedom of action, experience, and expression. A dramatic case in point is Tantric Buddhism, in which women charted the course of their religious lives with ultimate principles and divine beings as their reference points, enjoying complete freedom of movement, lifestyle, livelihood, relationship, and spiritual progress with no discernible external constraints.

Another reason that the claim that women were oppressed in Tantric Buddhism gained such easy acceptance and wide circulation is that it accords with a general image of Indian women as a collectively oppressed group. The theoretical construct of the 'oppressed Indian woman', which operates as a powerful, deeply entrenched stereotype of virtually unquestionable and 'self-evident' status in Western cultural discourse, has a specific history, like all ideas. Its colonial patrimony can be traced to the British period in India. It is now well recognized that colonialism is not simply a political or economic agenda but a self-promoting ideological one as well. The colonizing agent achieves its self-representation as civilized and culturally and racially superior through its very contrast to the imputed depravity, backwardness, and inferiority of the colonized. The superiority of the imperialist aggressor in turn justifies empire-building and economic exploitation under the guise of the bearing of the gift of civilization (Nandy 1983: 1-18, 29-42). When the British government sought to galvanize public support for the colonial mission in India and plan to usurp governance of that nation, the tactic at hand was to craft a convincing portrait of the depraved, barbaric, uncivilized condition of the people. In the case of the Raj, the winning stroke of this strategy was the claim that Indian women needed British assistance to be liberated from their horrible oppression. The reports of British missionaries, administrators, ethnographers, art historians, religious historians, and journalistic writers all promoted this agenda, sufficiently fictionalizing and sensationalizing the so-called plight of Indian women that the British citizenry were at last convinced of the moral imperative of British rule in India.

Thus, the oppression of Indian women became the predominant trope for the depravity of the Indian race, which was in turn invoked to justify the paternally benevolent intervention of the British. The colonial encounter did open new spaces for women's political agency in India. Contrary to what was promised, however, recent scholarship has also documented numerous ways in which the status and freedom of Indian women declined under British rule (see, for example, Banerjee 1990). Colonial policies deprived many women of their property, livelihood, legal rights, social status, religious roles, and artistic expressions. A case in point is the fate of the temple dancers, or 'women consecrated to deity' (*devadasis*). The use of dance in religious worship, the existence of economically independent, unmarried women, and the high respect and even veneration accorded to women whose sexuality was not controlled or owned by men were all anathema to the Victorian mentality. The British confiscated the land and property of the temple dancers and made the performance of their sacred dance illegal, rendering the women destitute and condemning their ancient art form to near extinction (Marglin 1985 and Srinivasan 1990). The complex history of this period has just begun to be told, but it demonstrates the need for reevaluation of the scholarly categories and truisms generated in that context.

Indology still bears the stamp of its colonial genesis. Many of the operative assumptions regarding the cultural construction of gender in India and lives of Indian women, past and present, carry the imprint of that legacy. The baleful image of the 'oppressed Indian woman', mute and powerless and eternally downtrodden in her cage of patriarchal suppressions, is so deeply entrenched in the Western psyche in large part because of the powerful motives that set and keep it in motion. Originally designed to justify colonial domination, it is continually manipulated in our popular media today to perpetuate the myth of Western superiority, as well as to commend Western patriarchy as moderate in comparison to other, more virulent 'oriental' forms. The resultant hermetically sealed paradigm is so firmly fixed in the Western psyche that it has become literally 'unthinkable' that Indian women should enjoy any form of agency or exercise any type of power, be it social, economic, political, religious, sexual, or psychological.

It is this reigning paradigm that makes any work such as mine, which documents a tradition significantly pioneered by Indian women who enjoyed forms of wholeness, affirmation, and empowerment of which modern Western women can barely dream, seem so radical and even, to the minds of some, impossible.

Western feminists (often under the rubric of 'global feminism') have also colluded in cultural imperialism by purveying a monolithic, denigrating portrayal of non-Western women (read: women of color, Third World women, women in 'undeveloped' societies) around the world. White feminist discourse and scholarship emanating from Europe and America often proceed with the assumption that, after millennia of unmitigated oppression, Western women have finally 'discovered' female dignity, worth, and equality and thus are unprecedentedly enlightened, powerful, and emancipated. The conviction that contemporary Western women have a unique and privileged perspective on femaleness is an ethnocentric claim that plays directly into the hands of the imperialist myth of progress to be bestowed upon a benighted world by the enlightened West.[3]

Argentinian feminist Marta Savigliano protests the new feminist frontier of cultural colonization:

> Third World women are addressed by Eurocentric or Westernized feminists full of good intentions, offering their sisterly hands to fight universal subordination, but in the same move we see ourselves depicted as victims of backwardness, barbarism, and underdevelopment who need to be enlightened about these very facts... We smell betrayal and violence behind misrepresentations and insensitivity. Global feminism starts looking like a new trick of Western imperialism (Savigliano 1995: 228).

3.   On the complicity between the nascent feminist movement in Britain and the imperialist agenda of the Raj, see Burton (1994).

Indian feminist Chandra Mohanty further claims that Western feminist discourses actually capitalize upon the devaluation of Third World women, achieving their self-representation as liberated, autonomous agents precisely through their contrast with the homogeneous portrayal of Third World women as powerless victims of male exploitation:

> This average third world woman leads an essentially truncated life based on her feminine gender (read: sexually constrained) and her being 'third world' (read: ignorant, poor, uneducated, tradition-bound, domestic, family-oriented, victimized, etc.). This, I suggest, is in contrast to the (implicit) self-representation of Western women as educated, as modern, as having control over their own bodies and sexualities, and the freedom to make their own decisions (Mohanty 1991: 56; see also 57, 74).

Insofar as Western feminism capitalizes and indeed depends for its very self-definition upon the hypothesized universal oppression of third world women, it is invested in research projects that further 'document' and 'prove' such oppression. In Mohanty's view, the antidote to this monolithic, homogenizing 'ethnocentric universalism' is more carefully nuanced, sophisticated feminist scholarship that acknowledges 'the material and historical heterogeneities of the lives of women in the third world' (Mohanty 1991: 53). She calls for geographically localized, culturally contextualized, historically grounded analyses of specific groups of women in which they may emerge as 'authorial subjects' who engage in self-definition, exercise the power of choice, actively pursue their interests and desires in their discrete social and political networks, attach specific meanings to their material and cultural environments and activities, and may in fact be powerful and central in their concrete milieu (Mohanty 1991: 55, 59, 64-68, 72). Such scholarship should not proceed with a preestablished, ethnocentric definition of power or an a priori premise of the powerlessness of the women under discussion but should be alert to the potential diversity of ways to define and exercise power. Similarly, the cross-cultural monolith of 'patriarchy' as 'that stable, ahistorical something that apparently oppresses most if not all the women in these countries' must be deconstructed (Mohanty 1991: 53-54). Analytic concepts such as 'dominance', 'exploitation', 'inferiority', and 'repression' must be problematized and specifically documented, contextualized, and defined in each case (Mohanty 1991: 68, 70-71, 73).

With Mohanty, I believe that feminist methodologies, freed from commitment to Western supremacism and the perpetuation of imperialist psychology, can be of great assistance in critiquing the politically motivated premises of colonialist discourse, revealing what had been concealed by androcentric scholarship. The evidence that I have found is, and has been, available for all to see, but it was rendered invisible by Western understandings of gender and ongoing disparagement of Indian women.

For me, the discovery of the Tantric Buddhist version of feminism, flourishing under the divine aegis of Vajrayogini, is a welcome corrective to the widespread misconception that feminism is a distinctively modern and Western achievement. In addition to doing a disservice to Indian (and other 'third world') women, this self-congratulatory stance ultimately disempowers Western feminists by robbing our efforts of a history and a tradition of women of all races who have blazed paths to freedom. It may be that feminism is, after all, a *philosophia perennis*. I am honored to bring the voice of this ardent Indian feminism into our contemporary and increasingly cross-cultural dialogue. If we learn to acknowledge, respect, and celebrate the power that women throughout history and around the world have wielded in diverse ways to change, direct, and shape their own consciousness, personal lives, and societies, we may one day attain a feminism that is truly global.

The achievement of intellectual integrity requires the willingness to relinquish the posture of sovereign ontological and epistemological subject in the process of inquiry, to renounce the power-dynamic of domination and sense of superiority that this entails, and to concede to 'cultural Others' the status of ontological and epistemological agents who may possess insights, values, and visions of femaleness and humanity against which we may be measured, judged, and found lacking.

Western culture in general and Western feminism in particular must cease to be the yardstick against which all others are measured. Therefore, I believe that asking whether Vajrayogini can be considered a feminist is not the most pertinent question. I believe that we rather should ask: by her standards, can we?

Bibliography

Banerjee, Sumanta
1990   'Marginalization of Women's Popular Culture in Nineteenth Century
               Bengal', in Kumkum Sangari and Sudesh Vaid (eds.), *Recasting
               Women: Essays in Indian Colonial History* (New Brunswick, NJ:
               Rutgers University Press): 127-79.
Burton, Antoinette
1994   *Burdens of History: British Feminists, Indian Women, and Imperial
               Culture, 1865-1915* (Chapel Hill: University of North Carolina Press).
George, Christopher
1974   *The Caṇḍamahāroṣaṇa Tantra, Chapters 1-8: A Critical Edition
               and English Translation* (trans.; American Oriental Series, 56; New
               Haven: American Oriental Society).
Gupta, Sanjukta
1991   'Women in the Śaiva/Śākta Ethos', in Julia Leslie (ed.), *Roles and
               Rituals for Hindu Women* (Rutherford: Fairleigh Dickinson Univer-
               sity Press): 193-209.
Marglin, Frédérique Apffel
1985   *Wives of the God-King: The Rituals of the Devadasis of Puri* (Delhi:
               Oxford University Press).
Mohanty, Chandra Talpade
1991   'Under Western Eyes: Feminist Scholarship and Colonial Discourses',
               in Chandra Talpade Mohanty *et al.* (eds.), *Third World Women and
               the Politics of Feminism* (Bloomington, IN: Indiana University Press):
               51-80.
Nandy, Ashis
1983   *The Intimate Enemy: Loss and Recovery of Self under Colonialism*
               (Delhi: Oxford University Press).
Savigliano, Marta E.
1995   *Tango and the Political Economy of Passion* (Boulder: Westview
               Press).
Sponberg, Alan
1992   'Attitudes toward Women and the Feminine in Early Buddhism', in
               José Ignacio Cabezon (ed.), *Buddhism, Sexuality, and Gender*
               (Albany: State University of New York Press): 3-36.
Srinivasan, Amrit
1990   'Reform or Conformity? Temple "Prostitution" and the Community in
               the Madras Presidency', in Bina Agarwal (ed.), *Structures of Patri-
               archy: The State Community and Household* (London: Zed Books):
               75-98.
Shaw, Miranda
1994   *Passionate Enlightenment: Women in Tantric Buddhism* (Prince-
               ton: Princeton University Press).
1997   'Worship of Women in Tantric Buddhism: Male is to Female as
               Devotee is to Goddess', in Karen L. King (ed.), *Women and Goddess
               Traditions: Studies on Asia, the Ancient Mediterranean, and Con-*

temporary Goddess Thealogy (Minneapolis: Augsburg Fortress Press): 111-36.

Walters, Jonathan S.

1994   'A Voice From the Silence: The Buddha's Mother's Story', *History of Religions* 33.4: 358-79.

Stanley N. Kurtz

In Our Image: The Feminist Vision of the Hindu Goddess

My first research in India led me to study the newly popular Hindu goddess Santoshi Ma (Kurtz 1990, 1992). The rapid rise of Santoshi Ma to popularity throughout much of the subcontinent had occasioned tentative theories of her origin from a variety of scholars; but certainly the bulk of scholarly interest in Santoshi Ma came from feminists (Kurtz 1990: 205-25). The relation between feminist scholarship and the study of South Asian goddesses stimulated that research, and continues to provoke reflection. It also requires contextualization.

All of us, over the last twenty-five years, have witnessed revolutionary changes in our society's system of gender difference. Gender roles that had once seemed fixed, ranked, and naturally differentiated increasingly appear to us as flexible, equal, and capable of being merged into complex forms of androgyny. It is not surprising that social change on this scale should have given rise to a new kind of scholarship. History, in revealing gender's contingency, has bid us look again, through the lens of gender, at every familiar thing. This is what feminist scholarship has done.

Yet the vastness of the change we are living through itself poses a problem for our scholarship. How are we now to understand cultures in which gender roles often are seen as fixed, ranked, or differentiated by nature? As we look at these varied societies from our new perspective, are we to see in them the image of the world we have just left behind, or do these many societies represent something different than the past that we are even now outliving? Or are these very alternatives not alternatives after all? Perhaps we have come so far that we no longer remember what it is that we have left behind.

I understand feminism as an advance in Western individualism. This seems surprising in light of feminist rejections of Western individualism on behalf of a more relational perspective. But even relational feminism is centered on the individual actor—she who must finally choose how and with whom to build her network of care and concern, and she who must finally choose when and if such relational bonds must be broken. To choose for oneself what bonds to make and what bonds to break is to throw off the yoke of ranked and predetermined social roles. Thus, the feminist quest for equality is linked to a form of individualism. Individuals are equal when they cannot be placed, against their wills, into a particular social role. Individuals are free when they can choose whether, and for how long, to adopt a particular role—a particular set of relationships. From my perspective, then, feminism is a consistent development of the underlying egalitarian individualism upon which liberal democracy rests. In effect, feminism extends egalitarian individualism into the family, the last stronghold of hierarchical collectivism in our society.

As with gender, the consistent extension of egalitarian individualism to all levels of contemporary society has led to profound changes in the conception and practice of religion. Just as we now reject the notion of involuntary imprisonment in some fixed gender role within a permanent family, so, too, do we reject the notion that we must retain our membership in a single, permanent, and inherited religious community. Increasingly we pick and choose our religious affiliations, breaking the boundaries of customary religious communities by combining images and archetypes from a range of traditions in a way that suits our individual tastes. And as our individual tastes shift and proliferate, so, too, do our preferred combinations of image and archetype.

In the midst of this cultural sea change, feminism has found something of worth in the image and archetype of the Hindu Goddess. Increasingly, the image of the Hindu Goddess has suggested to feminist scholarship the outlines of a future being born in our own society. After all, in India, God can be a woman, an extraordinary transgression of our customary gender roles. In India, moreover, this female embodiment of God can sometimes be superior to a male embodiment of God, perhaps the ultimate transgression of our customary gender roles. And, finally, in India, God can be, now a man, now a woman, now this woman, now another woman, now androgynous, and now neither man, woman, nor man-woman, but something beyond and yet encompassing all of these things. This is more than mere gender transgression. It is the overcoming of the very notion of fixed, ranked, and differentiated gender roles—perhaps the ultimate goal of many feminists. And so the archetype of the Hindu Goddess has been taken into American feminism at every level, from the most popular to the most scholarly.

Nonetheless, there is a difficulty—a difficulty clearly recognized by feminist scholarship. The archetype of the Hindu Goddess, while in many ways epitomizing the developing characteristics of Western feminism, is nonetheless the product of a male supremacist society. How can this contradiction be explained?

In recent years, an explanation of the apparent paradox has emerged—an explanation modeled on our understanding of our present situation. Might not the Hindu Goddess be the Hindu woman's intimation of a better future—a future that she longs for, both because of, and in spite of, her imprisonment in her own gender role? Might not the Hindu woman's dream of redemption provide a road map for our own lived experience of gender liberation? And might we not, by making good use of this Goddess archetype, return it, with interest, to the Hindu woman? Could we not infuse the Hindu woman's archetype with our own hard-earned experience of a new way of life and offer it back to her as a guide? Thus has feminist scholarship discovered the distinctive world of the Hindu woman's religion—a world hidden under her superficial obeisance to male religious authority.

And yet, a difficulty remains. How can we know that the Hindu Goddess is really the shared intimation of our own feminist future, and not something different from this? How can we know that the pattern of female cooperation with both ordinary and authoritative male devotees is in some important sense a veneer over a deeper yearning for an independent, female form of religious expression? This feminist interpretation of the Hindu Goddess would be more persuasive if we could detect the beginnings of a change in Hinduism. If we could discover modern Hindu goddesses who had more clearly extracted themselves from the unified tradition—if we could show that these goddesses were more obvious and evident examples of an incipient Hindu feminism, then we could validate the notion that even the more traditional Hindu Goddess is a kind of prototype of a hidden feminism waiting to be born.

This is where I came in, arriving in India to study Santoshi Ma (Kurtz 1990, 1992). As noted, among those who proposed various theories of this goddess's origins, feminist scholars were the most prominent (Kurtz 1990: 205-25). The common claim of these feminist scholars was that Santoshi Ma was less bound up in the male religious tradition than other godesses. It was said that her worshipers were exclusively, or almost exclusively, female. It was said that Santoshi Ma's bounty was directed to young women just married into oppressive joint families, or, alternatively, that Santoshi Ma was the goddess of the new, urbanized Indian woman. It was said that her worship was performed by women themselves, independently of the supervision of priests. It was said that Santoshi Ma possessed chiefly women, who thereby became the focal points of this goddess's worship.

There was some limited notice on the part of these feminist scholars of male participation in the worship of Santoshi Ma, but male involvement was invariably interpreted as a late development —and not only late. Male participation in the worship of Santoshi Ma, either by priests or by ordinary devotees, was seen by many scholars as an effort to appropriate Santoshi Ma's distinctive female power and draw her into the controlling sphere of the dominant male strand in Hinduism.

My own field research, however, led me to conclude that neither Santoshi Ma nor her worshipers answered to this description (1990: 205-95). Men were heavily involved in the worship of Santoshi Ma, even if not as a majority. Moreover, the percentage of men worshiping Santoshi Ma did not seem to differ significantly from the percentage of men worshiping other goddesses. And men had been involved from the start, although their approach to Santoshi Ma tended to be through image worship or attendance at possession sessions rather than through Santoshi Ma's *vrat*, or ritual fast. Male participation appeared secondary and appropriate for two reasons. First, scholars had focused on the text of Santoshi Ma's *vrat* ritual at the expense of other modes of worship. Second, because Santoshi Ma had been defined from the start as a woman's goddess, male participation could only appear to be minimal, accidental, or even antithetical to the central principles of this goddess's worship.

So the question of the sheer statistical proportion of men involved in Santoshi Ma's worship only begins to get at the deeper problem—the problem of separating a presumed religion of Hindu women from a religion of Hindu men. What are we to make, for example, of a man seeking business success who is told by a man possessed by Santoshi Ma herself to have his wife perform Santoshi Ma's *vrat*? What are we to make of a woman who performs Santoshi Ma's *vrat* so that her son will have success at his exams and thereby secure a subsidized apartment for the entire family? What are we to make of the male director and creator of Santoshi Ma's famous film, who discovered Santoshi Ma when he assisted his wife in her fast for Santoshi Ma after she herself learned about this fast from her male Brahman priest? And above all, what are we to make of a goddess who, like all goddesses, continually shifts her identity, merging into and splitting off from other goddesses, who, in turn, are linked with this or that male deity or male devotee?

In my own view, when a Hindu woman asks her husband for permission to perform Santoshi Ma's *vrat*, or to accompany her to a local temple, she sees herself neither as submitting to his oppressive dominance, nor as buying him off with token obeisance while she goes off to worship in a world of female religion. She asks for her husband's permission or accompaniment because she sees herself *in* him. And she sees in him not only herself, but a whole host of relations. By the same token when a man asks his wife to perform Santoshi Ma's *vrat* on his behalf it is because he sees himself in her and even sees a sphere in which he is but a part of her larger whole. There is hierarchy here, to be sure, but it is a hierarchy pervaded by a sense of the unity of the whole, and therefore of occasional reversal of rank (Dumont 1980: 239-45). Of course, there is tension within this whole. There is pain and complaint. Most often, however, I think the pain and complaint are about the abuse of roles within the system, rather than resistance to the system itself.

So, in my view, when we see that the God of the Hindus can be male or female, when we see that the female deity is sometimes higher than the male, and when we see that male and female deities are often found beside and even within each other, we are not seeing the apotheosis of an egalitarian subversion of gender roles. On the contrary, we are seeing the very antithesis of our advanced egalitarian individualism. We are seeing an enactment of the underlying unity that alone makes comprehensible what we too often perceive as simple and intolerable domination. This Hindu way of thinking, this Hindu way of life, may or may not be pervaded by false consciousness. That can be argued. But whether or not this Hindu life stance is oppressive in spite of its own self-understanding, it is not an intimation of egalitarian individualism's emerging transcendence of gender. The seeming contradiction between Hinduism's glorification of the Goddess and its system of gender hierarchy is no contradiction at all. The Hindu Goddess is the secret of hierarchy itself. She is the unity upon which Hindu hierarchy is based.

So in my view, the alliance between feminism and the Hindu Goddess is a misplaced alliance. Feminism, whether in India or the United States, grows out of an egalitarian individualism rooted in the West. When we see in the Hindu Goddess the image of our own struggles over gender, then, we are in fact appropriating the Goddess for purposes quite alien to her own. That is why the feminist appropriation of the Goddess is so persistently troubled by the continual emergence of hierarchy within the world of the Goddess and her devotees. The Hindu Goddess cannot be separated from hierarchy. And this is why we see that at times the feminist idealization of the Goddess shifts, and becomes instead a disappointed rejection.

Ultimately, though, I think we need to see the Hindu Goddess as neither our dream nor our nightmare. She belongs to another cultural world—a world quite apart from the egalitarian individualism of advanced liberal democracies. In the world of the Goddess, separation is ultimately an illusion, and the relation of low and high is based on this deeper unity of opposites. We may wish to adopt insights from this world, or we may wish to reject this world. But we shall first have to learn how to understand it.

Bibliography

Dumont, Louis
    1980   *Homo Hierarchicus: The Caste System and its Implications* (Chicago: University of Chicago Press [1966]).
Kurtz, Stanley N.
    1990   'A Goddess Dissolved: Toward a New Psychology of Hinduism' (PhD dissertation; Cambridge, MA: Harvard University).
    1992   *All The Mothers Are One: Hindu India and the Cultural Reshaping of Psychoanalysis* (New York: Columbia University Press).

Tracy Pintchman

Is the Hindu Goddess Tradition a Good Resource for Western Feminism?

As feminist critiques of religion have gained strength in recent decades, several scholars have turned the critique on traditional images of God, arguing that male hegemony in Western cultures can be correlated directly with the centrality of a single, all-powerful male God in the dominant strands of the predominantly Jewish and Christian religious heritage of Europe and the United States. In a seminal article on this topic Carol Christ asserts that religions centered on the worship of a male God generate conditions that keep women in a state of dependence on males and legitimate the political and social authority of men. She argues further that '[r]eligious symbol systems focused around exclusively male images of divinity create the impression that female power can never be fully legitimate or wholly beneficent' (Christ 1979: 275). Underlying her points is a broader, twofold argument: first, that religious symbols influence social behavior, and in turn are influenced by it; second, this means that male-dominated theologies encourage male-dominated social systems, and the two become mutually reinforcing. So, Christ argues, the symbol of God as exclusively male leads people to believe that men should hold all significant and legitimate power in society; and reciprocally, the fact that men hold most of this power reinforces the notion that God is most appropriately symbolized as male (Christ 1983: 234). Mary Daly offers a similar criticism in *Beyond God the Father*:

> The symbol of the Father God, spawned in the human imagination and sustained as plausible by patriarchy, has in turn rendered service to this type of society by making its mechanisms for the oppression of women appear right and fitting. If God in 'his' heaven is a father ruling 'his' people, then it is in the 'nature' of things and according to divine plan and the order of the universe that society be male-dominated (Daly 1973: 13).

Many would argue further that given this situation, it is important for women with feminist goals to recover or create empowering female symbols to help combat the ones that support patriarchy. As part of this program, some feminist scholars celebrate goddesses and goddess symbolism in particular as highly affirmative of women's power. The accompanying argument in this case follows from the first: that is, since religious symbols and social behavior influence one another, and since male-dominated theologies and male-dominated social systems therefore reinforce one another, then images of powerful goddesses may help counter this effect. Hence Christ, for example, argues that 'the affirmation of female power contained in the Goddess symbol' supports the power of women in family and society, and 'the work that feminists are doing to transform the image of God has profound…consequences for social life' (Christ 1979: 278; 1983: 231).

In seeking spiritual resources upon which to draw, some Jewish and Christian feminists have turned to religious traditions other than their own, both present and past, and have extolled and even appropriated the goddesses revered in these traditions. Some have sought solace in the strong goddesses of Hinduism. Christ, for example, argues that the Hindu tradition (among others) is a rich source of goddess symbolism (1979: 276). In another key article Rita Gross also turns East, arguing that for women in traditions that lack goddesses, the powerful goddesses of the Hindu tradition can, within limits, serve as 'a resource for the contemporary rediscovery of the goddess'. Cautioning that she is not advocating a 'wholesale transplant' of Hindu goddesses to the West, she does, however, suggest that 'if approached critically and carefully, and if intelligent selection and borrowing are utilized, the Hindu goddesses can be the greatest stimulant to our imagination and to our speculation about the meaning of the goddess' (Gross 1983: 217-18).

One point of challenge to the celebration of selected Hindu traditions is that the female-empowering perspective that Christ, Gross, and others offer with respect to powerful Hindu goddesses appears to be generally lacking in the dominant currents of Indian religious and social history. Brahmanical Hinduism, the 'orthodox' core of the Hindu tradition, for example, recognizes many powerful female divinities who play various important roles and are highly revered, yet predominant male attitudes toward women in Brahmanical Hinduism are generally at least as repressive as those found in cultures that do not have strong goddess traditions, and Hindu women tend to play fairly traditional social roles comparable to those played by women all over the world.

If there is a potent connection between reverence for powerful goddesses and the social and political empowerment of women, then why is it that given the strong goddesses of the Hindu tradition, women in Hindu society are not on the whole a good deal more socially and politically empowered than they are in societies that lack a strong goddess tradition, such as ours? And given this situation, what evidence is there that Hindu goddess traditions would be a better resource for Western feminist agendas than, for example, Christian Marian traditions? In other words, is the Hindu goddess tradition really a good resource for Western feminism?

In order to address these questions, it is helpful to consider them in the context of the larger issues involved, namely, (1) whether or not powerful, independent goddesses are naturally conducive to female empowerment in the social realm, and (2) whether or not religious symbols—in this case, goddesses—can be powerful motivators regardless of cultural and historical context because their meaning and power are not finally context-dependent.

Are Powerful, Independent Goddesses Naturally Conducive to Female Empowerment in the Social Realm?

In building an argument for why women need the Goddess, Christ outlines the more general theoretical and methodological framework on which her argument is based. In explaining the role of religion in human life she draws on the description that Clifford Geertz gives of religion as 'a system of symbols that act to produce powerful, pervasive, and long-lasting moods and motivations' in the people of a given culture. As Christ describes the terms 'mood' and 'motivation', 'mood' refers to psychological feelings and attitudes—respect, trust, fear, awe, and so forth—while 'motivation' refers to the social and political trajectory that these psychological attitudes—moods—establish and that 'transforms mythos into ethos, symbol system into social and political reality'. Christ argues that 'symbols have both psychological and political effects' because they generate attitudes and feelings that lead people to feel comfortable with and accepting of social and political arrangements that correspond to symbols. She also makes the point that such

effects do not depend on rational assent since symbols often function in non-rational, even unconscious ways (Christ 1979: 274;
Geertz 1972: 206).

If I am correct in identifying the guiding methodological principles in Christ's argument, then I agree with Christ that religious
symbols can be powerful vehicles for both expressing and reinforcing psychological, socio-political, and cultural realities. Religious cosmologies and portrayals of divinity can communicate and
reinforce truths concerning human imagination and experience
and are often invoked to justify all manner of socio-political arrangements. I don't agree, however, with Christ's apparent understanding of the extent to which religious symbols in and of themselves,
as opposed to human acts of interpretation and appropriation, have
the power to motivate behavior.

In interpreting Geertz's description of religion as a cultural system, Christ seems to imply that there is a direct line from symbol to
mood to motivation to effect. Geertz, in fact, does not place these
elements in such a direct cause/effect relationship; this seems to be
Christ's interpretation of Geertz. In her discussion of gender symbols, Caroline Walker Bynum suggests that Christ's understanding
of Geertz's formulation is a partial misinterpretation of his theory.
But she notes, too, that Geertz's formulation is itself problematic in
suggesting too close a relationship between symbol and social condition (Bynum 1986: 18 n. 15). Instead, Bynum finds Paul Ricoeur's
discussion of symbol to be more adequate in conveying the complex and polysemic nature of symbolic modes of meaning when it
comes to gender (Bynum 1986: 8-10). Ricoeur argues that symbols
are rooted in non-linguistic dimensions of experience that cannot
be reduced to language; hence symbols cannot be merely explained,
but must be interpreted. Furthermore, symbols are multivalent;
they are tied into a rich and complex web of meanings and associations, some of which might even contradict one another (water,
for example, has symbolic associations with both life and death), so
symbols can be interpreted in many different ways. As Ricoeur puts
it, symbols contain a surplus of meaning, and they give rise to endless exegesis. No given categorization, says Ricoeur, 'can embrace
all the semantic possibilities of a symbol' (Ricoeur 1976: 55-57).[1]

---

1.   Bynum also emphasizes Victor Turner's understanding of symbols as
'polysemic', noting that both Turner and Ricoeur 'agree in emphasizing two

Ricoeur's observations have implications with respect to the understanding of religion as a symbol system. In and of themselves symbols can 'mean' almost everything and nothing at the same time. Because symbols are tied into complex webs of association, what a particular symbol means is not predetermined in the symbol but unfolds dialectically in relation to experience and interpretation, whether personal or cultural. Thus any religious symbol can engender a variety of different and even contradictory moods or motivations, depending on the context and how the symbol is interpreted. It is the set of interpretations and the ways in which these are appropriated by an individual or culture—not the symbol itself—that finally shape a symbol's social and ethical implications or 'meaning'. As Christ herself notes, 'symbols have a richer significance than any explications of their meaning can express' (1979: 279).

Hence there is no inherent, invariable relationship between powerful goddesses and the advocacy of women's empowerment. Rather, there are potentially empowering interpretations of goddesses that may or may not be articulated or effectively appropriated, just as there are potentially disempowering interpretations of the same goddesses. I would suggest that the reverse is also true: male god symbolism has tended to be sexist and anti-feminist not because it is inherently so but because it has been interpreted and appropriated in ways that make it so. In his insightful discussion of feminist uses of goddess symbolism, Larry D. Shinn notes that literalistic interpretations of religious symbols, especially when such symbols are understood 'primarily (or only) as explicit models of sacred realities to be emulated...usually reflect social or political realities and interests' and have been used to justify repressive social or political agendas, including those pertaining to gender. But he also charges that scholars who acknowledge only sexist interpretations of god symbolism and champion the Goddess as a uniquely feminist symbol are equally guilty of using a literalistic interpretation of religious symbols to justify a socio-political agenda. 'Ironically,' he remarks, 'it would seem that those who would save women from such politically or socially motivated literal inter-

---

aspects of symbols: their capacity to refer simultaneously to many levels of human experience and their capacity to bring users to appropriate that to which the symbol points' (Bynum 1986: 10). See also Turner (1967).

pretations of religious symbols, commit the very same mistake in offering the Goddess as the explicit embodiment of feminine roles and/or attributes' (Shinn 1984: 192).

In the Hindu tradition, goddess symbolism has sometimes been appropriated in ways that are quite sexist. As many scholars have noted, for example, Hindu traditions tend to portray female gender on both divine and human levels as inherently very powerful. Yet because the female is powerful, she is also portrayed in some contexts as dangerous and needing to be controlled. It has been argued by many scholars that in some strands of Hindu religious symbolism, the female's destructive potential manifests itself as sexual voraciousness, and submission of females to male dominance, especially through marriage, tends to domesticate and neutralize their potentially dangerous power. In Brahmanical environments, the most beneficent Hindu goddesses—Lakshmi, for example—tend to be portrayed as married, sexually controlled, and subservient to their husbands; more ambivalent and potentially destructive goddesses—Kali, for example—tend to be sexually freer, and when associated with a male they are less likely to submit easily to masculine authority.[2] Sudhir Kakar notes a disjunction in Hindu mythology between images of the nourishing, beneficent, good mother, and the threatening, destructive, and sexually demanding bad mother (1981: 79-103). On the human level, women too, like goddesses, are often portrayed in Brahmanical texts with some ambivalence, and here, too, scholars have argued that this ambivalence can be linked to issues concerning female sexuality. Some Hindu social treatises, such as the *Manu-Smriti*, describe female sexuality as being uncontrollable and irresponsible, so that women are apt to place sexual gratification above family well-being. The *Manu-Smriti* claims that because of their passion for men and their natural heartlessness, women are prone to be disloyal to their husbands (*MS* 9.15; also Leslie 1989: 320).

Such Brahmanical interpretations of female nature represent just one perspective on these issues, and some scholars have noted the existence of alternative portrayals of female nature, especially

2.   See, for example, O'Flaherty (1980: 90-91); Babb (1975: 219-26); Shulman (1980: 223-26); Wadley (1977: 112-16); Brown (1990: 124-27); Pintchman (1994: 194-214). Brown quotes both Babb and Shulman in his own discussion of this problem.

among Indian women. Ann Gold, for example, articulates a perspective on female sexuality and maternality in Indian folklore that
she argues 'persuasively offers images of female nature that include
a sexuality not rampantly destructive but seeking mutuality with
males'. In the women's folk songs she explores, Gold argues, 'the
sexual and maternal aspects of female nature seem fused rather
than split, and generative rather than destructive images of female
power emerge' (Raheja and Gold 1994: 66-67). Similarly, it is tempting to think that Hindu women would offer empowering, feminist
interpretations of their goddesses, but this is not always the case. In
interviews with priestesses (*pujarins*) of goddess temples in the
city of Benares in December 1995, for example, I found that women
acting as officiants in these temples made little connection between the powerful goddesses they serve and the empowerment of
women. These priestesses view themselves as the vehicles of the
Goddess, who possesses their bodies to communicate with devotees. Because of their connection to the Goddess these women
enjoy heightened prestige among temple devotees. As temple
priestesses, they also hold positions of religious authority that are
usually reserved for men. Despite all of this, however, these
women do not make any explicit connection between their relationship to the goddess and social, political, or even religious empowerment of women in general.

Durgadevi, the priestess of the Shailputri Devi temple at the out-
skirts of Benares, for example, believes that the goddess she serves
shares the same type of devotional bond with all devotees regardless of gender. Durgadevi does hold that it is more appropriate for
women to serve at goddess temples than for men to do so, but the
explanation that she gives for this has nothing to do with feminist
impulses. It pertains instead to the Goddess's modesty. The temple
priestess must bathe and dress the icon of the Goddess daily, and
the goddess might be offended if a man were to place his hands all
over her body. Nonetheless, Durgadevi was reluctant to carry her
claims too far:

> When a woman touches another woman, she [the one who has been
> touched] is happy. For example, if I am your mother—like Devi is
> my mother—and you are my daughter, and you touch me, then I like
> it. But if you [a woman] can't do it, then a man can do it...She
> [Devi] is pleased if anyone does it [the worship or *puja*], but she is

more pleased if it is a woman. But men can also do it. Men are like sons, so they can also do it.

Madhavi, the priestess at the Skanda Mata temple in the city, holds similar views, proclaiming that women should serve as ritual officiants at goddess temples because, as she puts it, 'Men should not look at the Goddess's body... Her body is like my body. Men should not see it. A man should not put a sari on her.' With respect to the relationship between the goddess and women's empowerment, however, Madhavi is vehement in her defense of traditional values:

> Women should do *pativrata dharma* [duties and behaviors incumbent upon a good, obedient wife]. They should serve their husbands, and they should serve their in-laws. They should serve the Mother [Devi] the way I do... They should not have bad thoughts. And even if the husband is a leper, they should serve him. Even if he is very bad, whoever he is, you must be with him... No matter how the husband is, one must serve one's husband.

It may seem ironic that a woman who has dedicated much of her life to serving a powerful goddess should insist that women must hold service to the husband as the highest goal. But for both Durgadevi and Madhavi, serving the Goddess is in fact in keeping with the traditional *pativrata* or 'good wife' ideal. Both women became priestesses because they married into families that owned and presided over goddess temples traditionally served by female religious officiants. In both cases, their husbands' families expected the new daughters-in-law to assume the role of temple officiant when the presiding matriarch became incapable of continuing the job. Similarly, Durgadevi and Madhavi now expect their incoming daughters-in-law to succeed them. For both women, service in the temple is not a chosen profession but essentially an extension of their service to their husbands and their in-laws, who own the temples and benefit from the women's labor. In this regard, Madhavi denies the suggestion that women who are dissatisfied with their traditional gender roles might view her as a role model. When she dies, she told me, 'My daughter-in-law will be doing the worship (*puja*), no one else. When there is a birth, death, and so on, she will be doing the worship, no one else.' Because Madhavi's position as temple priestess is a matter of family duty, not personal choice, she does not perceive her role as one that other women might emulate.

Perspectives like those detailed above do not uphold a feminist interpretation of Hindu goddesses. Such views are not, however, definitive, and it is possible to interpret Hindu goddesses in completely different ways. Lina Gupta, for example, argues that 'patriarchal understanding has appropriated the Goddesses and the feminine aspects of the Ultimate Reality at the heart of Hinduism in ways that sanction the unequal treatment of women'. She invokes Kali as a role model and suggests an 'alternative vision' of the goddess as 'a dramatic embodiment of conflicts found in the struggle of women to assert their social rights through spiritual freedom from within the limiting structure of a patriarchal society'.[3] As Kathleen Erndl notes, there is now a feminist Indian press called 'Kali for Women', a name that clearly links the goddess Kali with feminist values and goals. There are also examples of women who have drawn on apparently traditional, subservient images of goddesses and heroines to sanction non-traditional, non-subservient roles and activities for Hindu women. Lou Ratté describes Sarojini Naidu as one such example. Naidu was an activist in the Indian nationalist movement at the turn of the century when India was still under British rule. To support her work in the nationalist movement, she invoked the models of Sita and Savitri, who are both usually interpreted as representing the ideal of the perfect, devoted wife and are seen as anything but feminist role models. Naidu, however, reinterpreted what these goddesses represent, arguing that, like traditional 'good' Hindu women, Western-educated and politically active women were also acting out the traditional ideals of service and sacrifice that Sita and Savitri embody (Ratté 1985: 367-69):

> By invoking the heroines to represent all Indian women, including the group of western-educated women whose behavior did not conform to traditional patterns, Sarojini Naidu provided nationalist society with a new view of gender which sanctioned non-traditional behavior through traditional references, but took account of the real ways in which women's lives had been changed (Ratté 1985: 368).

In a similar vein, in interpreting Christian symbols Mary Daly sees in the Virgin Mary—who like Sita and Savitri is often seen as any-

---

3. Gupta (1991: 16-17). I disagree, however, with Gupta's apparent willingness to universalize her own alternative vision of Kali and uphold it as 'a model and image that could be used to fit the needs of today's women' regardless of cultural context (16, 36-38).

thing but feminist—more feminist implications than might at first appear. Daly recognizes the long history of sexist interpretations imposed upon the Virgin Mary by the Christian church but also argues that the symbol of Mary has been a 'two-edged sword' that for some women has represented female strength and independence:

> The image of Mary as Virgin has an (unintended) aspect of pointing toward independence for women. The woman who is defined as virgin is not defined exclusively by her relationships with men... The message of *independence* in the Virgin symbol can itself be understood apart from the matter of sexual relationships with men. When this aspect of the symbol is sifted out from the patriarchal setting, then 'Virgin Mother' can be heard to say something about female autonomy within the context of sexual and parental relationships. This is a message which, I believe, many women throughout the centuries of Christian culture have managed to take from the overtly sexist Marian doctrines (Daly 1973: 84-85; see also Kinsley 1989: 256).

These examples suggest that there is no inherent correlation between any particular representation of divinity and any particular social or political attitude toward women, although some representations might lend themselves more easily than others to sexist interpretations. In the quest to expose and root out sexist and repressive religious ideologies in religious traditions, it might be helpful instead to focus on questions of interpretation and look carefully at who is doing the interpreting for whom and for what purpose. The core scriptures of the world's major religious teachings, sanctioned non-canonical writings, and other sources that have been used to transmit religious traditions have been largely controlled by males who were writing for other males. It is understandable that sexist perspectives have flourished in such conditions. Many women may accept and perpetuate sexist ideologies themselves, ignoring alternative interpretations that may be more empowering. But in the hands of feminists, the same content can acquire completely different significance. As Rita Gross notes in her article in this volume, if the devotees of the Goddess are feminists, then the Goddess will be feminist. It seems to me, however, that the same should hold true for God. Bynum notes that 'even traditional symbols can have revolutionary consequences...old symbols can acquire new meanings, and these new meanings might suggest a new society' (1986: 15-16).

Are Religious Symbols—in This Case, Hindu Goddesses—Powerful Motivators Regardless of Cultural and Historical Context?

There are many kinds of 'power', of course, and many ways of interpreting the terms 'power' and 'powerful'. In terms of the ability of religious symbols to motivate or influence behavior, however, it seems to me that there are two levels on which the power of religious symbolism is most frequently interpreted by those who invoke the symbol of the Goddess: the personal and the socio-cultural.

On the level of personal empowerment, some women do find the goddess symbol to be quite potent. Many testify that the goddess symbol has great therapeutic or spiritual power for them regardless of whether or not the particular goddess or goddesses in question are part of the cultural context in which these individual women function. The rise in the United States in recent years of feminist religious movements that focus on female images of the divine suggest that many women find goddess symbolism to be affirming. Many feminist artists, too, claim to have found inspiration in goddesses and goddess symbolism (see, for example, Gadon 1989: 257-307).

With respect to the motivational power of religious symbolism on the communal, socio-cultural level, the effectiveness of goddess symbolism when it is taken out of its cultural context is less clear. The sort of inspirational and motivational power that the goddess symbol tends to provide Western devotees is essentially private and individual, not public or social. Hence it has little communal potency outside of a small circle of already committed individuals, and therefore probably can do very little to advance directly the cause of feminism in the public domain. In fact, too much emphasis on the private and therapeutic dimensions of religion with little attention to its shared, public character runs the risk of making religion so personal a matter that it is no longer relevant to discourse about the public realm and therefore has little power to change it (Bellah 1985: esp. 219-49). I would argue, in fact, that much of the social and political power of any religious symbol depends on a cultural context that imbues it with meaningful interpretations tied into a network of shared beliefs, values, and stories. In other words, symbols can be invoked persuasively because they are not only private, but also public—they are part of the common fabric of a culture. It is the shared dimensions of symbols that imbue them with motivational power beyond the individual level. Hence, for example, Martin Luther King's invocation of the Hebrews' exodus from Egypt as symbolic of the struggle of African-Americans worked because the story was part of the shared cultural and religious heritage of those whom King wished to reach.

With respect to goddess symbolism, it would seem that reverence for a powerful goddess or goddesses could effectively support and advance public dimensions of feminism if such goddess symbolism were to be meaningful to the community at large and were to be accompanied by pervasive, empowering cultural interpretations and appropriations of these goddesses in relationship to women. By extracting another culture's goddess or goddesses for one's own individual purpose, one loses the context that makes that deity or deities meaningful to a community, and the religious symbol loses its social and cultural power. Hence it loses the power to motivate beyond an individual level. In this regard, of course, Hindu goddesses are imbedded in a larger cultural system that is rooted in India's Hindu heritage, not in the West. Although it is quite possible that empowering interpretations of these goddesses may help advance feminist causes in the public domain among Hindus, such interpretations would probably not be very effective in supporting or advancing the same causes in mainstream American or European culture. As Rachel McDermott notes, 'It is hard to import the worship of a goddess from another culture: religious associations and connotations have to be learned, imagined, or intuited when the deep symbolic meanings embedded in the native culture are not available... The lack of public reinforcement of one's chosen religious symbolism makes the path difficult' (1996: 305).

Finally, one must ponder the ethical and intellectual implications of the kind of cultural borrowing that occurs when Western feminists appropriate Hindu goddesses for their own purposes. In her study of the feminist spirituality movement in America, Cynthia

Eller notes that '[t]he joy of feminist religious syncretism is marred somewhat by the fact that when one borrows religiously, one is borrowing *from* someone (or some culture), and often without their permission' (Eller 1993: 74-75). While women who engage in such borrowing might see it as a compliment to the culture, it is not always received as a compliment. Eller cites specifically the anger expressed by one Native American woman over perceived exploitation of Native American spirituality among white spiritual feminists (pp. 75-76). A history of oppression makes such borrowings especially sensitive, and as Eller notes, '[t]he people spiritual feminists worry about offending are the people that white culture has already offended very deeply: Native Americans and African-Americans' (p. 77). But perhaps the same concerns should be applied to the borrowing of Hindu goddesses, especially in light of South Asia's colonial history. In his essay, '"Conceptual Resources" in South Asia for "Environmental Ethics"', Gerald J. Larson notes the problematic nature of 'resource' language when applied to Asia, whether those resources be natural or conceptual. While Larson's comments refer specifically to issues concerning environmental ideas and concepts, his remarks are nonetheless germane here as well:

> Since the eighteenth century, European nation-states have been utilizing Asia to supply a variety of resources: spices, tea, cotton, minerals, oil, natural gas, cheap labor, and hosts of other commodities. Now it seems that we are setting out again, only this time we are on the lookout for 'conceptual resources'... What is methodologically loaded and seriously misleading about such an economic metaphor of raw materials is the corollary component of such a metaphor, namely, that we are not really interested in the raw materials in their natural state. We want, rather, to appropriate the raw materials so that we can use them for making what *we* want... when we proceed by using an economic metaphor in this fashion, we are committing ourselves to a comparative enterprise of external appropriation. Ideas and concepts come to be construed as 'things' or 'entities' that can be disembedded from their appropriate frameworks and then processed and made to fit into our own frameworks (Larson 1989: 269-70).

The adoption of goddess traditions from Hindu and other religious systems to support Western feminist ideals helps fill a void for some women. But feminist interpretations of these goddesses tend neither to represent the dominant perspectives of the religions from which these goddess traditions spring nor to be concerned with the lives and experiences of adherents of those religions. Such appropriations generally tell us more about the persons who use goddess images for their own purposes than they tell us about the socio-cultural, religious, and historical contexts in which the borrowed goddesses arise and function, or the ways in which goddesses and their relationships to women are understood in the cultures and institutions that shape these goddesses and give them life. Whether or not one finds strong Hindu goddesses to be empowering feminist symbols, it is important not to overlook the women for whom these goddesses are a living reality. And in seeking to empower oneself, one should not fail to recognize and acknowledge interpretations of goddesses that serve to perpetuate patriarchal hegemony in their original cultural settings.

Bibliography

Babb, Lawrence A.
1975   *The Divine Hierarchy: Popular Hinduism in Central India* (New York: Columbia University Press).
Bellah, Robert.
1985   *Habits of the Heart* (New York: Harper & Row).
Brown, C. Mackenzie.
1990   *The Triumph of the Goddess: The Canonical Models and Theological Visions of the Devi-Bhagavata Purana* (Albany: State University of New York Press).
Bynum, Caroline Walker
1986   'Introduction: On the Complexity of Symbols', in *idem*, Steven Harrell and Paul Richman (eds.), *Gender and Religion: On the Complexity of Symbols* (Boston: Beacon Press): 1-20.
Christ, Carol P.
1979   'Why Women Need the Goddess', in *idem* and Judith Plaskow (eds.), *Womanspirit Rising: A Feminist Reader in Religion* (San Francisco: Harper & Row): 273-87.
1983   'Symbols of Goddess and God in Feminist Theology', in Carl Olson (ed.), *The Book of the Goddess: Past and Present* (New York: Crossroad): 231-51.
Daly, Mary
1973   *Beyond God the Father* (Boston: Beacon Press).
Eller, Cynthia
1993   *Living in the Lap of the Goddess* (Boston: Beacon Press).
Gadon, Elinor W.
1989   *The Once and Future Goddess* (San Francisco: Harper & Row).

Geertz, Clifford
1972   'Religion as a Cultural System', in William L. Lessa and Evan V. Vogt.
            (eds.), *Reader in Comparative Religion: An Anthropological Approach* (New York: Harper & Row, 2nd edn): 167-78.
Gross, Rita M.
1983   'Hindu Female Deities as a Resource for the Contemporary Rediscovery of the Goddess', in Carl Olson (ed.), *The Book of the Goddess: Past and Present* (New York: Crossroad): 217-30.
Gupta, Lina
1991   'Kali the Savior', in Paula M. Cooey, William R. Eakin, and Jay B. McDaniel (eds.), *After Patriarchy: Feminist Transformations of the World Religions* (Maryknoll, NY: Orbis Books): 15-38.
Kakar, Sudhir
1981   *The Inner World: A Psycho-Analytic Study of Childhood and Society in India* (Delhi: Oxford University Press).
Kinsley, David
1989   *The Goddesses' Mirror* (Albany: State University of New York Press).
Larson, Gerald J.
1989   ' "Conceptual Resources" in South Asia for "Environmental Ethics" ', in J. Baird Callicott and Roger T. Ames (eds.), *Nature in Asian Traditions of Thought: Essays in Environmental Philosophy* (Albany: State University of New York Press): 267-77.
Leslie, I. Julia
1989   *The Perfect Wife: The Orthodox Hindu Woman According to the Stridharmapaddhati of Tryambakayajvan* (Delhi: Oxford University Press).
McDermott, Rachel Fell
1996   'The Western Kali', in John S. Hawley and Donna M. Wulff (eds.), *Devi: Goddesses of India* (Berkeley: University of California Press): 281-313.
O'Flaherty, Wendy Doniger
1980   *Women, Androgynes, and Other Mythical Beasts* (Chicago: The University of Chicago Press).
Pintchman, Tracy
1994   *The Rise of the Goddess in the Hindu Tradition* (Albany: State University of New York Press).
Raheja, Gloria Goodwin, and Ann Grodzins Gold
1994   *Listen to the Heron's Words* (Berkeley: University of California Press).
Ratté, Lou
1985   'Goddesses, Mothers, and Heroines: Hindu Women and the Feminine in the Early Nationalist Movement', in Yvonne Y. Haddad and Ellison Banks Findly (eds.), *Women, Religion, and Social Change* (Albany: State University of New York Press): 351-76.
Ricoeur, Paul
1976   *Interpretation Theory* (Fort Worth: Texas Christian University Press).
Shinn, Larry D.
1984   'The Goddess: Theological Sign or Religious Symbol?', *Numen* 31.2: 175-98.

Shulman, David
  1980   *Tamil Temple Myths: Sacrifice and Divine Marriage in the South Indian Saiva Tradition* (Princeton, NJ: Princeton University Press).
Turner, Victor
  1967   *The Forest of Symbols: Aspects of Ndembu Ritual* (Ithaca, NY: Cornell University Press).
Wadley, Susan S
  1977   'Women and the Hindu Tradition', in Doranne Jacobson and Susan S. Wadley (eds.), *Women in India: Two Perspectives* (Colombia, MO: South Asia Books): 111-35.

Brenda Dobia

Seeking Ma, Seeking Me

In the cremation ground of my heart
You are Queen.
A field once verdant with innocent promise
Now smoulders, and I,
Inflamed still with your beauty,
Fall swooning into ashen obscurity.

Ah, Mother!
What strange blessings you bring:
Relief in the sweet fruit of nihilism,
Joy in your gift of melancholy,
Naked truth beaten in and out of me
By the blows of your trampling feet.

Mother.
Mother.
Cruel and wonderful Mother—
Who can understand this sublime torment?
This aching purity of Love,
The depth of You in me,
The tender restless heart that reels at the tide
Of human havoc and destruction,
And yet would drink it all in
Just to hasten the divine alchemy—

If only it could.

If only I could (August, 1994).

Mount Road, Madras.[1] To a Western tourist it's a little hard to imagine Mount Road as heaven, the abode of the gods. The footpath, such as it is around the Commander-in-Chief Road intersection, is broken and crumbling. It requires careful attention to pick your way gingerly among rocks, street vendors and beggars. The children tug at you, hands outstretched for money. 'Ma!' they say plaintively. Their eyes plead, too.

---

1. Madras is now known by the Tamil name, Chennai.

Walking on the roadway is a little easier, and faster—as long as you don't mind mingling with streams of pedestrians, cyclists, and auto-rickshaws as you vie for space to proceed while trying to breathe as little as possible of the toxic fumes that are spewed from traffic exhausts. Though Madras is neither as polluted nor as crowd-ed as other large Indian cities (notably Calcutta), avoiding polluting fumes is still a losing battle. After a trip to Mount Road the usual requirements are a bath and rest.

I had braved the expedition, by cycle, a few days before I was scheduled to return to Australia. This was my first visit to India (that is, if you exclude an unscheduled and unwelcome stopover in Bombay on a flight home from London thirteen years before) and I wanted to buy gifts to take to family and friends at home. Jewellery, silk scarves, kurtas, woolen shawls from Kashmir, brassware—there were so many beautiful handicrafts to choose from, I was sure I would have no trouble finding the range I needed for a variety of family and friends.

I had come to Madras to meet and study yoga with T.K.V. De-sikachar, and had been very privileged to receive thoughtful instruc-tion as well as warmth and hospitality. But my interest in India was strictly secular. While I saw yoga as a legitimate spiritual path, I was not about to betray the foundations of my Jewish upbringing by investigating Hinduism's emphasis on idol worship. Yet in the very unlikely 'temple' of Mount Road I was ultimately forced to recon-sider.

In spite of my insistent conscious resistance I suddenly and in-escapably found myself mesmerized by an image of Devi—the Hindu Goddess. At the time I had no idea who She was. With no knowledge whatsoever of any Hindu mythology, and an express intention not to seek it, I found myself repeatedly attracted to a particular statue of Her. Every time I walked into a handicrafts shop in search of gifts a statue of this Goddess would irresistibly catch my eye. Finally I determined to avoid going anywhere near the icons, and I put on a mask of vigilance before entering the next shop. I headed directly for the silks, without so much as turning an eye—until I was stopped in my tracks by an insistent magnetic force that tugged at my shoulder and made me turn around. There She was again, staring me in the face.

Eventually I asked a shopkeeper:

Who *is* this?
That's Goddess Parvati.
Who? Who is she?
Parvati, you know.
Please, write it for me. I must find out.

So it was the Goddess as Parvati who first enticed me into the realm of Hindu mythology. With the help of an introductory text I discovered that She was the daughter of the mountain who had taken up yogic austerities in order to win the hot-tempered ascetic god, Shiva. I also discovered that, once married, 'they frequently quarreled. Often these disputes were caused by Shiva wishing to curse someone whom Parvati wished to bless' (Ions 1986: 88).

This was the big revelation for me, the cosmic joke: So, I thought, I'm not the only one who has to deal with a wild hothead of the male gender. I had come to India to find a way to move beyond being too closely involved with a certain Shiva character. And there She was pointing to my role in this particular pas-de-deux and revealing it as Act I of the Divine Dance. I burst out laughing. So, the relationship struggle I had felt stuck in was actually enacting an archetypal dynamic. If the Goddess Herself had trouble dealing with machismo in Her male counterpart, who was I to imagine I should have single-handedly overcome it all by now? According to Mircea Eliade,

> myth relates a sacred history, that is, a primordial event that took place at the beginning of time, *ab initio*. But to relate a sacred history is equivalent to revealing a mystery... [Myth] speaks only of *realities*, of what *really* happened, of what was fully manifested. Obviously these realities are sacred realities, for it is the *sacred* that is pre-eminently the *real* (Eliade 1959: 95).

How then do we recognize the sacred? How do we know when something is 'pre-eminently real'?

My initial experience of the Goddess in Madras was one of mystery, of something inherently unfathomable and yet intimately present, a direct link with eternity that left no doubt as to its reality. Without prior experience or knowledge I was immediately convinced of the truth I was being offered. In the *Yogasutra* the term for this kind of direct knowing is *pratyaksha*, a knowing that needs no outside reference or process of inference in order to claim inherent validity.

The timeless quality of my experience of Her and the mythic characterization of gender issues in relationship persuaded me both that I had tapped into an archetypal dimension, and that there was something valuable to be learned here. Mircea Eliade again: 'the supreme function of the myth is to "fix" the paradigmatic models for all rites and all significant human activities' (1959: 98)— 'it is in the myth that the principles and paradigms for all conduct must be sought and recovered' (1959: 102).

But this analysis comes long after my initial experience…

When I returned to Adelaide, Australia, together with my new bronze image of Parvati, never having read Mircea Eliade and not being a Hindu, I had no idea how to further my relationship with her. I wasn't even sure I wanted to. There no longer seemed to be any particular meaning or purpose hidden within this dark metallic figure, however exotic and graceful she appeared as she gazed across my room from above the fireplace. Surrounded by the strange familiarity of the Australian landscape and culture, Adelaide soon dimmed my conscious awareness of whatever it was that had touched me in Madras.

Or so it seemed. And yet something inside me had changed, if imperceptibly. Was it India alone, or was there anyway some residue of Her? Speaking of religion, Santayana considered that 'the vistas it opens and the mysteries it propounds are another world to live in (quoted in Geertz 1973: 87). Though it was some time before I began any kind of formal inquiry into the religious and philosophical system from which this Goddess had emerged, it seems likely now that there was something in me from that first moment that opened to a subtler, more immediate truth, allowing the mythic dimension to unfold, to live through me even while I remained unaware of its influence.

> [I]n one way or another one 'lives' the myth, in the sense that one is seized by the sacred, exalting power of the events recollected or re-enacted. 'Living' a myth, then, implies a genuinely 'religious' experience, since it differs from the ordinary experience of everyday life… What is involved is not a commemoration of mythical events but a reiteration of them. The protagonists of the myth are made present, one becomes their contemporary. This also implies that one is no longer living in chronological time, but in the primordial Time, the Time when the event *first took place* (Eliade 1963: 19).

Whether or not as a result of my tapping into primordial time, my first meeting with Parvati occasioned a year's reflection and a living out of the depth of her essential feminine benignity. Although my religious sensibilities and the strength of my personal *tapas* (mental and physical purification) were undoubtedly enhanced by this particular inquiry, it eventually became very clear that the world of men, or at least of those I had met, was very far from actively valuing the sacred dimension of feminine virtue—except perhaps in poetry. Eventually, the painful consequences of my extreme efforts to remain virtuously giving in the face of others' failed appreciation brought me back to my feminist roots, and to India.

In Sri Aurobindo's prose it is Mahalakshmi who personifies the tender, loving beauty that is so often extolled by male poets as the epitome of the divine feminine:

> For she throws the spell of the intoxicating sweetness of the Divine: to be close to her is a profound happiness and to feel her within the heart is to make existence a rapture and a marvel; grace and charm and tenderness flow out from her like light from the sun and wherever she fixes her wonderful gaze or lets fall the loveliness of her smile, the soul is seized and made captive and plunged into the depths of an unfathomable bliss (Aurobindo 1989: 45).

What to me is most important in Sri Aurobindo's intuited account of this one aspect of the multi-faceted Divine Mother is that there are very specific conditions under which Mahalakshmi consents to manifest:

> If she finds herself in men's hearts surrounded with selfishness and hatred and jealousy and malignance and envy and strife, if treachery and greed and ingratitude are mixed in the sacred chalice, if grossness of passion and unrefined desire degrade devotion, in such hearts the gracious and beautiful Goddess will not linger. A divine disgust seizes upon her and she withdraws, for she is not one who insists or strives; or, veiling her face, she waits for this bitter and poisonous devil's stuff to be rejected and disappear before she will found anew her happy influence (Aurobindo 1989: 46-47).

Contemporary feminists may find cause for aggravation in the lofty and idealizing words of Sri Aurobindo. Yet if, in our dissatisfaction with patriarchal definitions of femininity, we approach these words as religious teachings that require women to conform to over-idealized notions of what 'the feminine' ought to be, then we will have succeeded in turning into a tool of oppression the work of an inspired mystic devotee of the Goddess and foremost advocate of women's embodiment of Her for the transformation of society. His words are more constructively taken as invitations, pointers to a subtler reality that we are beckoned towards in order to be fully present to our own experience of the divine.

Taken in this light, Sri Aurobindo's Mahalakshmi can be appreciated as a symbolic representation of a gentle, loving beauty who also shows very clearly that Her demand for honour and respect must be met if She is to provide the grace of Her presence and nurture. The Mother archetype here is understood as potentially available to all, while being embodied and expressed in a particular way in women's grace and devotion.

Mahalakshmi as a divine feminine embodiment makes it clear that she will not tolerate abuse, and, since all women are sparks of Her, then neither must they. Her intent toward gracious tenderness does not require that women should allow themselves to be exploited as all-giving martyrs. She demands, rather, a true honouring of love received and given. Love, in its divine purity, is a sacred gift to be bestowed and received with great reverence and care.

Sri Aurobindo's essay *The Mother,* in which both fierce and gentle personalities are combined as aspects of Her, was also my first introduction to the conception of the Goddess as Shakti, Power. Shakti in her universal, cosmic aspect is the force behind all creation. This perspective forms the basis of Hindu Shaktism, in which the Goddess is worshipped as the ultimate deity: 'By you this universe is borne, by you this world is created. By you it is protected, O Devi, and you always consume it at the end' (Jagadiswarananda 1953: 17).

What more fundamental challenge to the politics of patriarchy than the understanding that power itself is feminine?

> Sakti means power, force, the feminine energy, for she represents the primal creative principle underlying the cosmos. She is the energizing force of all divinity, of every being and every thing. The whole universe is the manifestation of Sakti (Mookerjee 1988: 11).

Or, as Sir John Woodroffe put it—

> There is no word of wider content in any language than this Sanskrit term meaning 'Power'. For Sakti in the highest causal sense is God as Mother, and in another sense it is the universe which issues from

Her Womb. And what is there which is neither the one nor the other? (Woodroffe: 1987: 17).

Embedded in this conceptualization I discovered a very profound and far-reaching spiritual challenge to the gendered social constructs which our culture has used to civilize and deny the primal feminine forces (and for that matter the primal masculine), subverting them into neurotic, constraining distortions of a subtler, deeper truth.

In Hindu cosmogony, especially in Shaktism and Tantra, when Shakti constructs the world she informs all manifestation by means of subtle cosmic sound vibrations, *nada*. It is Shakti in her transcendent aspect who provides the impetus and divine will to bring forth creation from the ultimate formless source. In her immanent aspect (universal Shakti in Sri Aurobindo's terms) she continues to sustain it, manifesting herself as a subtle field of resonance through which 'she enters into the worlds that she has made [so that] her presence fills and supports them with the divine spirit and the divine all-sustaining force and delight without which they could not exist' (Aurobindo 1989: 29-30).

Elsewhere the special power of Shakti to manifest form has been described as that of a finitizing principle because her 'job' is to 'give form and limits' (Svoboda 1993: 79). Since there is no manifestation without her it is said that 'Without Shakti Shiva is *shava*'. The god Shiva, who, as pure consciousness, represents the polarity to Shakti as cosmic energy, is no more than a corpse without the power of Shakti to provide life and form. This doctrine is often seen depicted in art and iconography where Shiva lies in trance underneath Kali's trampling feet.

Such representations in myth and in visual art may help our conceptual understanding, but it is especially through sacred sound, through mantra, that one is offered the means to attune to the vibrations of Her divine energy. When first introduced to Vedic chanting, I was a long way from any theoretical formulation or intellectual understanding of Shaktism or the significance of mantra. It was my second visit to India, and I was somewhat interested but not yet convinced of the power of subtle sound vibrations as a healing force. Committed to trying it, I learned several hymns that Desikachar taped for me before my departure so as to help guide my practice. Then, as an afterthought, he added an additional chant, one I hadn't learned. 'You get depressed sometimes, don't you?' he said. 'If you listen to this it will help.'

Whether feeling depressed or not, I found later that there was something especially powerful in this particular hymn and I tried to learn it by simply mimicking the sounds from the tape. Soon I wrote for corrections. By return I received a transliteration of the *Durga Suktam*, together with a rather obscure sounding translation:

> I take refuge in Her, the Goddess Durga, who is fiery in lustre and radiant with ardency, who is the Power belonging to the Supreme who manifests manifoldly, who is the Power residing in actions and their fruits rendering them efficacious [or the Power that is supplicated to by the devotees for the fruition of their work]. O Thou Goddess skilled in saving, Thou takest us across difficulties excellently well. Our salutations to Thee (Vimalananda 1979: 95).

Sraddha, faith, is the term used in the *Yogasutra* to describe the primary requirement for sustained advancement towards the state of yoga in which the quality of mental clarity allows for a direct, undistorted link with a greater consciousness (*Yogasutra* I-20). To secular Western minds the notion of faith seems most often equated with belief. At the time I first learned chanting I was very far from having any sense of a specific object, or even a creed, in which to believe. I had no background in Hindu cosmology and no context within which to understand the power of sound as a cosmic conduit, the means whereby all manifestation spills over from the Source into being. Yet there I was sensing some profound reality, whether with or without the conceptual tools for understanding all of my experience.

No doubt my particular faith then, and since, was influenced by the conception of divinity articulated in the *Yogasutra*:

I-24   God is the Supreme Being whose actions are never based on misapprehension.

I-25   How can God be so extraordinary?
        He knows everything there is to be known.
        His comprehension is beyond any human comparisons.

I-26   Is God, according to Patanjali, timebound or timeless?
        God is eternal. In fact he is the ultimate teacher. He is the source
        of Guidance for all teachers: past, present and future (Desikachar
        1987: 14).

Notwithstanding the wrongly-gendered language, the perspective here expressed in the *Yogasutra* became the basis for my deepening inquiry into the Goddess and Her various forms. Developing a relationship with Her as the ultimate teacher was the avenue to growing beyond the cultural limitations imposed by a society that institutionally seeks to limit women's power and influence. This was also the context in which She became my chief inspiration for finding a way through the personal gender politics that, for me anyway, constitute the field where the most intense battles are played out. Through the media of my yoga practices, reflections on mythical accounts of Her, and those aspects of Her that I encountered on my subsequent travels in India, She has provided many rich insights and lessons.

Mythologically, She is said to manifest periodically as a particular incarnation or embodiment in order to achieve a specific purpose in aid of Her creation. In personalized form, then, 'Individual, she embodies the power of these two vaster ways of her existence [the transcendent and the universal], makes them living and near to us and mediates between the human personality and the divine Nature' (Aurobindo 1989: 27-28). Yet, for those who would seek to further feminist values regarding women's status, how are we to interpret stories of Her when they derive from (apparently) patriarchal sources?

Thomas Coburn pointed to the more vexing practical paradox represented by the discontinuity between the empowerment of Indian women and the power of the Hindu Goddess:

> Broadly speaking, it now appears that the oppression of women is independent of the dominant theology or thealogy of a given culture. India provides vivid evidence in support of this conclusion, for nowhere else on earth has there been as long and broad a tradition of Goddess worship and yet the struggles that Indian women face are legion (1994: 6).

As Sandra Robinson (1985: 186) noted, 'in the brahmanic paradigm femininity is designated to be intrinsically powerful but positionally subordinate'.

These issues speak both to the pervasiveness of the patriarchal value system and to the complexity entailed in relating spiritual symbolism to human activity. Mythical material, by its nature, is intrinsically open to a range of interpretation. It is this broad multivalence that provides the basis for the richness and appeal of myths. However, when the exoteric meaning ascribed to a particular reading is appropriated to justify patriarchal dominance and thus serves to codify the subordination of women to the (apparent) self-interest of the male elite, its deeper significance, and therefore also its liberative potential, is eroded.

The feminist critique of religion is thus well founded, but this need not necessarily require us to discard Hindu Goddess mythology as male-derived and therefore inherently unusable. Though not identified as a feminist scholar, Wendy O'Flaherty (1980: 8) noted that 'It is possible to extract an "operational code" from a myth, a code whose pattern may be suggested by similar patterns elucidated in the fields of psychology, philosophy, and even the natural sciences... We *can* see patterns that are obscured by the mythmakers' views of themselves'. Thus, notwithstanding their Sanskritic origins, I have found mythic depictions of Devi in Her various forms profoundly illuminating tools for inquiry into archetypal manifestations of female power and its relation to the male.

I do not intend here to refer to Jungian archetypes. Jung's concepts of *anima* and *animus* have been critiqued for their heavily culture-bound and patriarchal values (see Wehr 1985). This is especially apparent when Jungian notions of gender are cross-referenced with the gender constructions denoted in Shaktism. What I am referring to is something akin to Bina Gupta's elaboration:

> Sexual archetypes are not merely categories of human experience indicative of the psychological structuring of the human mind. They should be understood more on the model of Platonic ideas; not in the sense that they exist in some transcendent sphere, but in the sense that they are rooted in the objective order of reality...
>
> Like Platonic ideas in which reality participates, archetypes also refer to something supra-temporal, eternal, or perennial. That is, if we find discernible structures in the male-female interaction, we treat them rather as instantiations of a more primal relation. The reality provides the grounds for such an instantiation. Instantiation means that the biological, cultural, and psychological dimensions of the male/female polarization are equally to be viewed as dimensions of a more primordial reality (Gupta 1987: 2-3).

If the Goddess is to be related to as the teacher *par excellence* and also as primordial reality, then whatever human conceptions we might have of Her must be subject to continual reshaping and refinement. Myth therefore need not be taken as a once-and-for-all prescription for shaping the world of outer forms. It is for us to enter into the archetypal dimensions through which She manifests as a means of developing our relationship with Her and of deriving Her illumination. This requires that we cultivate an attitude of surrender to Her greater wisdom and power, while yet embracing the struggles and strivings intrinsic to our being human. We are not the originators of the archetypal patterns but we may participate in giving them form—and in bringing them to life for ourselves.

It was through chanting the *Durga Suktam* that I first came into contact with a primordial sense of the Goddess. There was something about the visceral resonance of the hymn itself that evoked strength and resilience, even without my cognitive understanding.

The *Durga Suktam* praises Her as the Fire Goddess; She is also like a boat that carries us safely across stormy waters. Her name, Durga, means the unassailable one. She is unequivocally the personification of courage and justice, as my Indian friend, Kshama, explained once after she had taken me on a visit to Her temple just out of Pune, and I had asked what it meant for her as a woman to worship Durga.

Reading the *Durga Saptasati*, known also as the *Candi* and the *Devi Mahatmya*, what is most striking to me, as a Western woman, is the fierceness of Devi. She is no mere divinely gentle and benevolent female. She *is* Shakti, and those who would mistake Her for a demure beauty, beware!

6.6   Seeing the Goddess standing on the snowy mount,
       He bellowed in a loud voice: 'Come into the presence of Shumbha
       and Nishumbha!
6.7   If you do not come with delight to my master right now,
       Then I will immediately take you by force, upsetting you by drag-
       ging you by the hair.'
       The Goddess said:
6.8   'Sent by the lord of demons, mighty, and surrounded by your
       army, You take me by force. What can I do about it?'

       The seer said:
6.9   'Thus addressed, old Smokey-Eyes rushed at her.
       Ambika reduced him to ashes with the menacing sound of
       'Hmmmmmm!' (Coburn 1991: 59).

Her defeat of the demons who lust after Her is a clear message that Her power is not to be subverted for ego-driven or *adharmic* ends, yet She remains in the service of Her devotees. By outward standards She is a violent warrior Goddess, but Her standard is such that She never initiates combat. She simply responds to the situation and the need for which She has been supplicated. On the battlefield She is relentless, a consummate warrior—and She is invincible.

Classic interpretations of the *Devi Mahatmya* deriving from Indian sources, such as that by Vasudeva Agrawala (1963), have emphasized the cosmogonic implications of Devi's role in the great battles, which are described in the text in full gory detail. This stance was affirmed in Thomas Coburn's study, in which he concluded that

> ...ultimate reality is understood by our text as feminine, as the Goddess. Although this seems to be the first occasion on which such an understanding is articulated in Sanskrit, the DM does not argue that ultimate reality is feminine, nor does it propose it as a deliberate alternative to understanding ultimate reality as masculine. Feminine motifs are, of course, pervasive of the DM. But insofar as the DM is concerned to 'demonstrate' anything, it is that ultimate reality is really ultimate, not that it is feminine (Coburn 1984: 303-304).

Yet, at least for women, another interpretation is possible. It seems to me that a good heroine story such as is presented in the *Devi Mahatmya* cannot help but influence our perspective on power relations between the genders, and this at the very least. Taking a woman-oriented slant in her scholarship, Wendy O'Flaherty (1980: 97), commented: 'When Saktism finally effloresces, the pattern of male dominance is turned inside out. Now all the helpless gods prostrate themselves before the Goddess and beg her to help them.'

In the Mahishasura myth told in the *Devi Mahatmya*, the Gods have been defeated and therefore require an expression of concentrated, pure Shakti to overcome the demon at whose hands the world is in grave peril. She appears, resplendent, out of the collective fire of their anger, and, armed with weapons they lay before Her, goes off singlehandedly to accomplish what all the Gods and their armies have been unable to do. Against the advancing army of Mahishasura She hurls torrents of weapons, and laughs derisively as She fends off counter-attacks. In the final battle:

3.33   Then the angry Candika, mother of the world, quaffed a superior
        beverage,
        And again and again she laughed, with reddened eyes.

3.34 The Asura, puffed up and drunk with might and power, bellowed
And with his horns hurled mountains at Candika.

3.35 Pulverizing what he threw with a volley of arrows,
With passion in her face that was flushed with intoxication, she
uttered fevered words.
The Goddess said:

3.36 'Roar, roar for a moment, O fool, while I drink (this) nectar!
When you are slain here by me, it is the gods who soon will roar!'
The seer said:

3.37 Having spoken thus and springing up, she mounted the great Asura.
Having struck him with her foot, she beat him with her spear.

3.38 Then he, struck with her foot, came forth out of his own mouth,
Completely hemmed in by the valor of the Goddess.

3.39 That great Asura, who had come forth halfway fighting, was felled
by the Goddess,
Who had cut off his head with a great sword (Coburn 1991: 47).

So much for our traditional notions of gender attributes! Clearly, here, assertive is not the word. What comes through loud and clear in such stories of the Goddess's battle prowess is that power and force are not male preserves.

If aggressive force can take form as a manifestation of the female principle, directly and independently of male attribution, then what *is* its nature? Is it just force, ungendered and hence expressed in the same way in Goddess or God, woman or man?

If we read the text with a view to reflecting on these questions, then we may find in Her a model of embodied female power that takes decisive and deliberate action in support of the cosmic female principle. As Mother of the Universe She is also its defender. Unlike the ascetic pursuits of the Gods, Her deeds express a complete and consistent commitment to the world of form She has created. She is gracious and forgiving, always first allowing the *asuras* the opportunity to surrender or desist, and only responding with force when the situation calls for it. Her army of *shakti*s all work in concert under her skilful direction. There is no argument over who is the greater warrior here; rather, Her many differentiated manifestations demonstrate a harmony of purpose and action. Though She is profusely lauded by the Gods She does not seek personal aggrandizement—once Her task is complete, She disappears from the scene. Her moves are swift and unequivocal, executed always with the ultimate poise and command.

Though not willing to lay claim to such a bold interpretation on the place of *female* cosmic power for the *Devi Mahatmya*, Cheever Mackenzie Brown concluded his comparison with the *Devi Bhagavata*, a more recent Shakta text that recounts and embellishes the myths presented in the *Devi Mahatmya*, with the observation that: 'The *Devi Bhagavata* clearly insists that of the two genders, the feminine represents the dominant power and authoritative will in the universe' (Brown 1990: 217). This is so because only She can remain as Her transcendent Self while at the same time manifesting in all Her immanence.

From his Shakta tantric perspective on the Goddess Durga-Kali, Wendell Beane eloquently expressed a complex argument related to this same issue:

> The dimension of preservation-and-destruction in Creation is present in the paradoxical sense in which one might say that the Primordial Totality (*Samvit*) of the goddess is seemingly 'destroyed' by the cosmogonic emanation, concatenation, and fractionalization of the Undifferentiated Essence of the goddess. Yet the paradox tends to be complete, because our understanding is that the ontological depreciation that would seem inevitably to be intrinsic to the *anuttarayogic* cosmogony of the goddess does not occur. Here lies the mystery of the staticity and dynamicity of Ultimate Reality and its translogical realization by the devotee of the goddess; for in soteriological terms it means both the acceptance *and* transformation of perennial sensuous-spatial existence into spiritual existence *as religious experience*. Moreover, the goddess continues to have her own Ultimate Being, Identity, and Power behind, within, and beyond the actions of all divinities of all universes, even such Lords and Sovereigns that make the Trimurti (i.e., Brahma, Visnu, and Siva (Beane 1977: 261).

This perspective is unambiguously expressed in the powerful *Devi Suktam*, which concludes the recitation of the *Candi*:

> I move in the form of the Rudras, the Vasus, the Adityas and all the other gods.
> I support both Mitra and Varuna, Indra and Agni, and the two Ashwins.
> I support the foe-destroying Soma, and I Tvastr, Pushan and Bhaga.
> I bestow wealth on the institutor of sacrifice who is ready with oblations and offers homage.
>
> I am the sovereign power, wise queen over all the worlds, foremost among those worthy of sacrificial homage.

The gods in all places worship but me. I am diverse in form and permeate everything.

Whoever eats food, or sees, or breathes, or hears what is spoken, does so through me.
Unknowing they depend on me. Hear, O famous one—I speak of a most profound faith.

I myself proclaim this that is favoured by gods and men.
Whomsoever I wish I make mighty, a Brahman, a seer, a sage.

I draw the bow for Rudra, so his arrow may slay the foe of sacred speech.
I incite people; I pervade heaven and earth.

On the summit of this world I give birth to the father; my origin is in the waters, in the ocean.
Thence I spread through all the worlds, creating the sky's infinite expanse.

I blow forth like the wind, grasping all worlds.
Beyond heaven, beyond this earth, in my greatness such have I become (translation after Coburn 1991 and Kartik Patel, personal communication).

Interestingly, this hymn, given in the first person, comes from the *Rig Veda* and was composed by a female *rsi*. In the chanting it is the *aham*, the I, that gives the hymn such a powerful immanent resonance. Here She is all-pervasive; I, as woman, am but a spark of Her. 'All the various knowledges, O Goddess are portions of you, as is each and every woman in the various worlds' (Coburn 1991: 74). When Her syllables resound in my body it is She as transcendent communicating with Her immanence in me, necessarily embodied, necessarily gendered.

She has a similar relationship with her various incarnations: Sati, for example. To a secular, occidental way of thinking it seems difficult to understand how Sati, a female figure portrayed as the perfect docile wife of Shiva, could be conceived as a great Goddess when, caught in the argument between her father and husband and seeking to redeem her husband's honour, she is ultimately driven to self-immolation. This hardly seems to be the powerful act of the one who is revered as World Mother, *Jagadamba*.

But, if we take a step back to reflect on the cosmological context in which the saga unfolds, we discover that Sati is in fact a particular incarnation of Devi, who has consented to be born in the world for the purpose of enticing the ascetic God Shiva into worldly pursuits. Her acceptance of Brahma's request, according to the *Shiva Purana,* is granted with one stipulation: 'O Prajapati, you have to take a vow. It is a precondition... If in future you were to be less respectful to me I will cast off my body. I shall withdraw myself to my soul or take to another form. It is true' (J.L. Shastri 1970: 327).

As World Mother, both immanent and transcendent, She plays an integrative role in ensuring that all dimensions of the cosmic order remain in harmony. Shiva, the ascetic God, is unconcerned with the social realm. But the withdrawal of his primal energy from worldly creation represents a threat to its very vitality. Devi therefore incarnates as Sati, daughter of Daksha, a lord of the godly realm, and succeeds in Her mission of marrying Shiva, thus engaging the auspicious God of the *lingam* (phallus) in worldly life. Daksha, however, is more concerned with appearances at his court than with maintaining respect for the anti-social character of Shiva. Only Sati, it seems, is aware of the threat posed by this disjunction of primal male energy from the civilized world governed by outer form.

When She arrives at Daksha's court, incensed that he would have debarred Shiva from attending an important ceremonial sacrifice, She is snubbed as an unworthy daughter. This provides the occasion for Sati to implement Her vow. She creates from Her yogic *tapas*[2] a great fire and burns off her mortal body.

On hearing of this, Shiva is enraged. He descends from Kailash and destroys the sacrifice. The *Devi Bhagavata* at this point tells of Shiva dancing uncontrollably while clasping the charred corpse of Sati, and of the land becoming sacralized when her dismembered body falls to earth as, bit by bit, Vishnu cuts her corpse out of his arms. Ultimately, since Shiva is finally brought into relationship with Daksha and afforded proper respect, Sati succeeds in achieving Her purpose.

Taken in their larger context, it is apparent that the gender issues implicit in Hindu myths are framed within a perennial spiritual quest to understand the relationship between forces of transcendence and immanence. What is also evident, and a lot of what makes these tales so engaging, is that the Gods and Goddesses in their

---

2.   Austerity, or purification practices associated with yogic *sadhana,* through which great heat is generated.

numerous incarnations don't always have the answers. In these, their relative forms, they must learn as they go.

Through her various births as consort of the god Shiva, including that of Sati, Parvati struggles to retain the perspective of the transcendent Goddess while dealing with social constraints associated with the worldly female role. Her mother, Mena, is repeatedly distressed at her unconventional conduct, first when Parvati announces that She plans to take up penance (*tapas*) to win Shiva's devotion, then again when She is to marry the ashen-smeared, mendicant god, and later when She takes up residence with him in the wilds at the top of the world (*Shiva Purana, Rudrasamhita*). It is thus not only Shiva himself, but also the prevailing force of cultural expectations with which She has to contend in order to break free of social stereotyping.

But She persists, with the aid of her yogic *tapas*. At one stage, clearly post-honeymoon, She decides that it will not do to have Shiva barge into her apartment, so She fashions a young boy, Ganesha, from the scrapings of her skin, informing him that he is to stand as a sentinel at her door. But Shiva remains intent on gaining access to Parvati's chamber rather than being disgraced at not being allowed into his own house. He is infuriated with Ganesha, argues with him, and finally beheads him. At this, Parvati becomes enraged and lets loose an army of terrible *shakti*s to devour all and sundry. The gods finally get the message: 'When the hips of all the gods are broken and Parvati is fiery in rage, none of them dare stand before her' (*Shiva Purana* II, *Rudrasamhita* IV-17.22, J.L. Shastri 1970: 785). An elephant head is then found and placed on the boy and, in accord with Parvati's demand, he thereafter becomes the chief of all the gods' hosts.

In surveying 'the shifting balance of power in Indian hierogamies' Wendy O'Flaherty noted the tension inherent in Parvati's status and gave the following explanation:

> Parvati's ambiguous status as mortal/immortal is the pivot of the myth, the focal point of transition between male-dominated and female-dominated hierogamies. Below Parvati is the figure of the merely mortal worshiper of the God; but above her, and infusing her with power, is the figure of Devi, the Goddess herself, regarded not only as *a* divinity but as *the* divinity. Thus, depending upon the point of view of the particular text telling the story, Parvati may act more like her mortal counterparts (totally subservient to Siva) or more like

her immortal alter ego (totally dominant over Siva). In fact, on all
three levels she is a single goddess, but, as the context shifts, different aspects of her are brought into play (O'Flaherty 1980: 92).

Her relationship with Shiva certainly provides Parvati with plenty
of opportunities to test her mortal mettle, through which She
shows herself to be much more than a compliant devotee or dutiful
wife—and her resolve and independence (at least from my perspective) grow along with her spiritual development. It is as a result of
worldly incarnation that She remains susceptible to and has to
struggle with the limitations of cultural norms. In this regard the
mythic story lines of these accounts are without doubt influenced
by the cultural assumptions of their (male) authors. Yet there is no
question that She commands the respect and reverence of gods and
men alike.

Issues of gender and appropriate corresponding behaviour are
addressed explicitly in the myth of Minakshi. My introduction to
Her came on a tour of South India in 1991 with an all-woman group
of yoga students from Australia and New Zealand. For one reason
or another, all beyond our control or conscious intention, we found
ourselves repeatedly drawn back to the town of Madurai.

The area surrounding Madurai is principally rural and there, in
the midst of Tamil Nadu state, the effects of the Westernization that
is intruding on Madras appear much less. Madurai is also the oldest
city in Tamil Nadu, being over 2500 years old,[3] and is known as a
seat of highest Tamil culture. People there, I'm told, speak a far
superior Tamil to that spoken in Madras. The town itself encircles
the Minakshi Sundareshwarar temple, built on the site of a pre-exist-
ing shrine to Shiva in the 12th century CE (Meena n.d.)

The atmosphere of the huge temple permeates the whole city. It
is a majestic presence to be seen for miles, with its multiple ornate-
ly carved towers, including the four nine-storey *gopura* built over
each of the temple gates. Whether it is the ancient beauty and
mystique of the temple or of Minakshi herself, I found myself capti-
vated, spellbound by its allure.

According to Tamil legends Minakshi, the fish-eyed Goddess, was
born as a three-breasted girl, Tatatakai, to a Pandyan king and

---

3.   This information comes from information supplied by the Department
of Tourism, Government of Tamil Nadu.

queen of Madurai. Their concern at her third breast was responded
to by Shiva himself, when he announced from the heavens:

> O King! Treat your daughter as though she were a son:
> Perform for her all the rites as specified in the Vedas.
> Give her the name, 'Tatatakai'. Crown her queen.
> And when this woman, whose form is golden, meets her Lord,
>   one of her breasts will disappear (*Tiruvilaiyatarpuranam* I.4.25,
>   quoted in Harman 1989: 45).

Tatatakai is educated accordingly, learning all the martial arts,
and is eventually crowned ruler of the kingdom. Soon after the king
dies and Tatatakai, now Minakshi, assumes full responsibility as
queen. When the king's widow, Kancanamalai, goes to temple to
worship the Goddess, it is revealed to her 'that it is due primarily to
her virtue (*karpu*) as the king's wife that Siva's consort Parvati was
born miraculously in the form of Tatatakai/Minakshi'. The myth continues, as summarized by William Harman:

> The fifth chapter opens with Minakshi as Pandya monarch: her rule
> is just and beneficent, but she rules as an unmarried queen, a situa-
> tion which, the commentator notes (I.5.1, 2), is not proper for an
> Indian monarch. Her mother laments her unmarried state (4), but
> Minakshi assures her that there are better things to do now, such as
> conquer the world (5).
>
> The female monarch then prepares her impressive array of sol-
> diers for their assault on the guardian deities of the eight directions
> (6ff.). She herself leads the cavalry, followed by horse-drawn char-
> iots, rutting elephants, and decidedly vicious hand-to-hand combat-
> ants. Significantly, the three southern kingdoms (Pandya, Cera and
> Cola) are portrayed as united under the Pandya queen's command
> as, together, they set out to conquer the rest of the universe (verse
> 18).
>
> The attacking army is so impressive that its first scheduled combat
> with Indra, king of the gods, never occurs: he flees at the sight of the
> troops (23), and his white elephant and wish-granting tree are taken
> as booty. In fact, the same occurs with the other seven guardians
> of the directions: the troops march directly to the abode of Shiva,
> Mount Kailasa, where they encounter their first real resistance.
>
> Mount Kailasa is first beseiged. Then a genuine battle between
> Minakshi's forces and the demigod (*bhutagana*) armies commanded
> by Nandin, Shiva's bull vehicle, ensues (27-31). Blood and gore
> abound on the battlefield (32-38), and the Pandya queen appears par-
> ticularly savage in the fray. Nandin's forces are completely routed;
> he has no choice but to appeal to Shiva for help. With appropriate

fanfare, Shiva graciously appears to survey the carnage (42). Then the miracle occurs:

The moment She saw him Her [third] breast disappeared.
She became bashful, passive, and fearful.
She leaned unsteadily, like the flowering branch of a tree under the weight of its blossoms.
Her heavy dark hair fell on Her neck.
She looked downward, toward Her feet, with collyriumed eyes that were like kentai fish.
And there She stood, shining like lightning, scratching in the earth with Her toes. [43] (Harman 1989: 46-47; quotations from *Siva's Sacred Games*).

Notwithstanding the patriarchal bias in the tone of the text, Harman points out that the story of the marriage of Minakshi and Sundareshwarar is anyway about the triumph of the Goddess. It is certainly evident that their marriage site, originally a Shiva temple, was many centuries ago wholly reconsecrated to Her. At the time of the festival that celebrates their marriage She is the daughter, the Goddess and the home-coming queen of Madurai. She is the chief deity; Shiva is worshipped as Her consort.

What is especially intriguing to me, in spite of the overlay of traditional gender roles in written accounts of the myths, is that Her post-nuptial relationship with Shiva is egalitarian. This is of no small consequence to the local culture. Harman commented 'that among Tamilians Minakshi, despite her representation in *Shiva's Sacred Games*, is the dominant figure in the pair. Indeed, the marriage of the Madurai divine couple is regarded as the classic instance in the south of the female-dominated marriage, an arrangement referred to as "a Madurai marriage" ' (Harman 1989: 65). As Sundareshwarar, Shiva is the Lord of Beauty, and he devotes himself fully to Her and Her kingdom. In contrast with other incarnations in which Parvati has to contend with the more ferocious and hot-headed aspects of Shiva, here he is portrayed as the perfect husband.

What is it about Minakshi that makes this particular enactment of the divine marriage such a match? The classic interpretations strike me (again) as very androcentrically oriented. It is assumed, in line with Lawrence Babb's (1970) distinction between malevolent and benevolent goddesses, that Minakshi is a dangerous warrior goddess who needs to be subdued by marriage to Shiva. A.K. Ramanujan (1986), drawing from Jungian theory, referred to the distinction between goddesses of the breast and goddesses of the tooth. Commenting on this distinction, O'Flaherty wrote, 'Goddesses of the breast provide role models for the wife: they are subservient to the husband. Goddesses of the tooth do not provide such models; though they have consorts, they dominate them and play nonfeminine, martial roles as well' (O'Flaherty 1980: 91).

Curiously, the symbolism gets reversed in interpretation of the myth of Minakshi, where the third breast is typically assumed to be an indication of her excessive masculinity:

> The commentator of our text, Venkatacami Nattar (1:357), says that the disappearance of the third breast is indicative of a change from male to female. Up to the moment she met Shiva, Minakshi's father had treated her as his male heir: training her as a man would be trained in the sciences and martial arts. She ruled powerfully over Madurai and conquered all the regions of the world. In short, she acted like a man (Harman 1989: 49).

David Shulman (1980) allowed her a measure of femaleness but concluded that the third breast symbolized Minakshi's 'bisexual nature' (p. 211). While it seems clear that the mythology of Minakshi has to do with the issue of gender attributes, this argument seems to require that she is somehow reduced from her androgynous state in order to be subdued in marriage. Yet throughout the tale Minakshi is hailed as a triumphant queen. Her story does not seem to suggest that something has gone wrong in her expression of 'masculine' behaviour, but rather that something has gone right.

It may be that the interpretation hinges on whether one takes a predominantly Shaiva or Shakta perspective, and also on the personal emphasis one places on gender issues. Kathleen Erndl, for instance, in her study of local northwestern Indian Goddesses, found that the dichotomous categories proposed by Lawrence Babb and A.K. Ramanujan were of limited applicability. She commented: 'What Babb perceives as malevolence could simply be called realism. Devi is closely connected with the realities and ambiguities of life' (Erndl 1993: 158).

An alternative explanation of the myth of Minakshi is that, in fact, this particular incarnation is intended for Her to overcome the constrictions of socially sanctioned feminine behaviour, and that it is because She is successful in doing so that Shiva appears in his Sundareshwarar form. Since Her *shakti* is not bound by the restrictions of excessive femininity—since, by Her sovereignty and war-riorship, She incorporates and transcends the masculine sex role—Shiva, as her divine consort, can equally balance the feminine in Him. In their common transcendence of the limitations of gender roles the auspicious beauty of the divine is revealed.

Recall that it is Shiva himself who instructs the Pandya king to educate his daughter as a male. Recall, also, that it is revealed to Kancanamalai that, due to her virtue, her daughter is actually an incarnation of Goddess Parvati. Can the third breast be a symbol for an excess of femininity which in this incarnation She is challenged to overcome? When Minakshi arrives at Mount Kailasha and gazes on Shiva, he tells her:

> 'From the moment You started out
>   intending to triumph over the eight directions,
>   from that moment We and Our forces also left Madurai,
>   accompanying You all the way here.
> On the coming Monday I will marry You at the auspicious hour,
> and as prescribed in the Four Vedas...' (*Siva's Sacred Games*, V-45,
> from Harman 1989: 175).

All along, it seems, there has been a divine purpose in Her bat-tles. Reaching Kailasha, the heavenly abode of the Gods, Minakshi is in conquest of the transcendent abode of the phallic God Shiva. In the process She has won knowledge (*vidya*) of the masculine realm. Then, not only does She win and marry Shiva, thus engaging him in worldly pursuits, She also succeeds in enthroning him with-in the human world where his auspicious beauty (Shiva Sun-dareshwarar) becomes widely accessible. Here again, both the tran-scendent and the immanent are incorporated in the triumph of the Goddess.

> She appeared as the holy Daughter of a Pandya king,
>   learned all the sciences,
>   and assumed the royal crown,
>   with responsibility for ruling the kingdom.
> She conquered the entire world,
>   defeating Nandin and his servant forces in battle.
> She placed on that Lord Whom all worship
>   a beautiful, fragrant wedding garland
>   and Her crown.
> She graciously gave Him Her crown,

and prospered from the wealth so gained.
All this She did, this Woman-king
  whose lotuslike feet are worthy to be placed
on the heads of us all (*Tiruvilaiyatarpuranam I. Katavul Valttu*
  11, quoted in Harman 1989: 62-63).

Though folk culture in South India, as elsewhere, may at times
express an ambivalent stance towards the Goddess who asserts
with force Her feminine power—revealing what Beane (1977: 268)
referred to as the 'matrifocal-patrifocal schizophrenia' of Hindu religion and society—tantric worship is single-minded in its embrace
of the wild and dark Mother Kali.

> O Mother, even a dullard becomes a poet who meditates upon Thee
> raimented with space, three-eyed, Creatrix of the three worlds,
> whose waist is beautiful with a girdle made of numbers of dead
> men's arms, and who on the breast of a corpse, as Thy couch in the
> cremation-ground, enjoyest Mahakala (*Karpuradi Stotra—Hymn to
> Kali*, v. 7, in Woodroffe 1981: 301).

As one of Sri Aurobindo's four manifestations of *The Mother*,
Mahakali inspires with the majesty and brilliance of her power of
action:

> There is in her an overwhelming intensity, a mighty passion of force
> to achieve, a divine violence rushing to shatter every limit and
> obstacle.
> The impulses that are swift and straight and frank, the movements
> that are unreserved and absolute, the aspiration that mounts in flame
> are the motion of Mahakali. Her spirit is tameless, her vision and will
> are high and far-reaching like the flight of an eagle, her feet are rapid
> on the upward way and her hands are outstretched to strike and to
> succour (Aurobindo 1989: 40-42).

I find Sri Aurobindo's words breathtaking. And yet my own relationship with Her Kali form was not so easy to enter into as was my
reading of Sri Aurobindo's sweeping prose.

In the mythology of the *Devi Mahatmya*, Kali's finest hour is in
the defeat of the demon hordes after She springs from the fur-
rowed anger of Ambika's brow and forges into battle:

> 7.6   She carried a strange skull-topped staff, and wore a garland of
>   human heads;
>   She was shrouded in a tiger skin, and looked utterly gruesome
>   with her emaciated skin,

7.7   Her widely gaping mouth, terrifying with her lolling tongue, With sunken reddened eyes and a mouth that filled the directions with roars,

7.8   She fell upon the great asuras in that army, slaying them immediately.
         She then devoured the forces of the enemies of the gods (Coburn 1991: 61).

Having demolished the whole demon army, Kali brings the severed heads of its commanders triumphantly back to lay before Devi. She is indispensible when it comes to vanquishing Raktabija, whose every drop of blood spilt generates further demon hordes. Kali defeats him by drinking up all his blood. In some accounts, and in Bengali iconography, her taste for blood and intoxication with battle set her off on a frenzied victory dance (Kinsley 1975).

It was one thing to be inspired by the poise and courage of Durga, or by the determination of Minakshi. It was quite another to invite ferocious, bloodied Kali into my life.

She, of course, was quite insistent.

In 1992, on a lone pilgrimage to various Shakta temples, I had imagined that I would slip through Calcutta on my way to visit Kamakhya, the temple of the *yoni*. I discovered, however, that one does not just 'slip through' Her city, Kalighat, without paying due respects. I got a red light on my attempted visit to Kamakhya.

Stop. Do not pass go.

What *I* had intended was of no consequence. *Her* plan was evidently that I should be with Her in Kalighat. So, eventually, I found my way to Her temple, where a priest insisted on walking me through a formal ritual to Her.

I began to warm to Kali-Ma. After all, when she gives you a direct message there is little choice. As yet I was not sure what to make of Her, or of the special worship I had offered. She, however, would not let me get away with my doubts. On my return to Madras, after some deliberation I finally decided to get an icon of Her. She, as if to say, 'Who do you think you are to doubt Me?', brought on in me a sudden and extreme menstrual flood that continued until I got safely back home. Three times I very narrowly escaped public embarrassment, saved only by the absorbency of my blood-drenched cotton petticoat and the rich purple of my sari. In public I managed to hide it, but in private there was no denying Her blood initiation.

The modern Bengali saint Ramakrishna is reported to have said:

> The Divine Mother is always playful and sportive. This universe is
> Her play. She is self-willed and must always have Her own way. She
> is full of bliss. She gives freedom to one out of a hundred thousand
> (Nikhilananda 1942: 195).

Ramakrishna being perhaps one of those one in a hundred thousand, his surrender was complete, expressed in the devotion of a child. 'There is only one Guru, and that is Satchidananda. He alone is the Teacher. My attitude towards God is that of a child toward its mother' (Nikhilananda 1942: 199). This attitude of deep and total devotion is imbued with tantric symbolism in the iconography of Dakshinakali, which portrays Shiva inert under Her feet.

> As the Purush, or Soul, [Shiva] is Consort and Spouse of Maya,
> Nature, the fleeting diversity of sense. It is in this relation that we
> find Him beneath the feet of Kali. His recumbent posture signifies
> inertness, the Soul untouched and indifferent to the external. Kali
> has been executing a wild dance of carnage. On all sides She has left
> evidences of Her reign of terror. The garland of skulls is round her
> neck; still in Her hands She holds the bloody weapon and a freshly-
> severed head. Suddenly She has stepped unwittingly on the body of
> Her Husband. Her foot is on His breast. He has looked up, awakened
> by that touch, and They are gazing into each other's eyes. Her right
> hands are raised in involuntary blessing, and Her tongue makes an
> exaggerated gesture of shyness and surprise, once common to
> Indian women of the villages.[4]

> And He, what does He see? To Him, She is all beauty—this woman
> nude and terrible and black who tells the name of God on the skulls
> of the dead, who creates the bloodshed on which demons fatten,
> who slays rejoicing and repents not, and blesses Him only that lies
> crushed beneath Her feet.

> Her mass of black hair flows behind Her like the wind, or like time,
> 'the drift and passage of things'. But to the great third eye even time
> is one, and that one, God. She is blue almost to blackness, like a
> mighty shadow, and bare like the dread realities of life and death.
> But for Him there is no shadow. Deep into the heart of that Most
> Terrible, He looks unshrinking, and in the ecstasy of recognition He
> calls Her *Mother*. So shall ever be the union of the soul with God
> (Nivedita 1989: 34-36).

4. Rachel McDermott (1993) provides evidence that this interpretation of Kali's lolling tongue demonstrates the extent to which She has been domesticated in popular Bengali culture.

There lies Shiva, inert, a corpse on the ground at Her feet, yet filled with ecstasy in recognition of Her. She, wild and bloody, bears the ornaments of her play with death and destruction with an air of triumph. There is no doubt of her superordinate power, yet She is revered as Mother, one who nurtures and protects as well as destroys. In Her resides the power of the *yoni*, the dark womb from which She manifests the world and to which She again withdraws it at the end of time. She is the fertile and fallow ground of creation and destruction. Into the world of forms, Her playing field, She pours the immanent force of all-sustaining *shakti*.

Of what use is a purely transcendent, disembodied power? In death there is nothing to transcend. One can only place oneself, as does Shiva, at the lotus feet of the Mother in the hope of becoming one of the vessels for Her creation. In the words of Ramprasad Sen,

> O Mother, who really
> Knows Your magic?
> You're a crazy girl
> Driving us all crazy with these tricks.
>
> No one knows anyone else
> In a world of Your illusions.
>
> Kali's tricks are so deft,
> We act on what we see.
>
> And what suffering—
> All because of a crazy girl!
>
> Who knows
> What She truly is?
>
> Ramprasad says: If She decides
> To be kind, this misery will pass (Nathan and Seely 1982: 40).[5]

She may be a crazy girl. As for me, I am just crazy enough to be smitten by Her wildness, the primal, fiery force that surges through me, dares me to trust the flashes of illumination that arise under pressure of Her lightning Kundalini energy, dares me to believe that Hers may be the way to remedy the insanity of chaos let loose in this dark age of Hers.

5.   From 'Grace and Mercy In Her Wild Hair', by Ramprasad Sen, translated by Leonard Nathan and Clinton Seely, ©1982 by Leonard Nathan and Clinton Seely. Reprinted by arrangement with Shambhala Publications, Inc., Boston, www.shambhala.com.

To me She is the ultimate defender of Love's Truth, the *Mahavidya*[6] whose knowledge is complete because She remains fully engaged with all Her creation, whether it takes the form of beauty or of horror. She is the one, too, who reminds me 'with sharp pain, if need be' (Aurobindo 1989: 41) that it is only when I give over my personal desire to Her will that I can receive the grace of Her greater Truth.

In my struggles to stay open as Her vessel, I have often found myself in the burning grounds, hopelessly enamoured, and frequently scorched:

> So, now I see that
> I have been avoiding Her.
> Yet I know I cannot.
> The intensity builds.
> Something is demanded of me
> But I do not want to pay the price.
>
> When I am not in Her space
> Outer space closes in around me.
>
> And She—
> She waits.
> She awaits my call.
> (I only need to call.)
>
> Kalika. What is it you would have me do?
> I am burning, Ma (April, 1994).

Are we to define Truth (*Sat*) in terms of the social constructions in which we keep entrapping ourselves? Is life to be lived in conformity to the outer dictates of a painfully shallow culture that knows not how to retain the sacred raw majesty of existing naked and close to the source with Love our only shelter? How did we get to this place? How to make the return?

In 1992 I arrived in San Francisco from India reverberating with a question that had been haunting me for weeks: How does She go from being Sati to Kali? The question was not one to be solved by historical analysis of puranic accounts. Unknowingly I had slipped into primordial time, the place where the myth takes over and I am lost to Her veiling *maya*, oblivious to the drama being recreated in me.

---

6.   Literally 'the great knowledge', as She is known and worshipped in Tantra.

Almost two years later I found that indeed She had not forgotten my question, that She was using her favourite means to teach me: the fire of direct experience. I had somehow created a situation that had me choking on my attempts to shape love to meet social pressures, when Shiva appeared to challenge me. 'Where is the passion?' he asked. Suddenly I was burning up. I had become the myth.

> You have pared me to the core,
> Insisted on Truth.
> I am cut.
> I am bleeding.
> And still I would offer myself up
> To Your blows.
> Am I to be a sacrifice to the Father?
>
> Ma, I would return to You,
> Crawl to You.
> O Ma, let me set myself ablaze with Your Glory.
> I will be Your Truth.
> I will heed Your Call.
>
> Sat.
> Satî.
> Throw me on the pyre, Ma, if You will.
> I am Yours (April, 1994).

And then—

> O Mother. Here I have been grovelling at Your feet,
> A crawling infant, crying fitfully for Mother's comfort,
> And You so cruelly deserting.
>
> Kali, in Your wild, dishevelled abandon
> You have let loose the goblins of havoc,
> Left me cowering
> Alone,
> In panic—
> Easy prey for their spiteful tricks.
>
> You may be at home, Ma,
> In the thick of this dark squalor,
> But I want more than to drown
> In Your cess-pool,
> Smothered by the waste of unanswered desires.
>
> That's it, Ma.
> I'm not waiting for You.

I've spent long enough prostrate
On my knees,
Being lashed at freely
With Your scorn.
No more, Ma.
I'm out of here.
On my feet.
No more waiting.
I'm stepping out.
I'm gone.
I'm—

What?
No, it couldn't be.

Mother.

Radiant in Her wickedest ways,
Mother grinning.

Mother applauding.

Mother holding out her hand
In drunk and riotous delight.

Could this really be
The Dance? (September, 1994).

Two years after She led me to Her, the force of Kali as Mother had come to represent for me the fullest, most passionately embodied expression of the unconditioned, primordial Feminine.

As the *Devi Suktam* proclaims, She arises from the depths and presides at the summit; She exists both before and beyond Her apprehension by the male psyche.

Tameless Mother of Time,
I return again, and again,

To You.

The temple of the Goddess Kamakhya is in the state of Assam in northeast India. It is sacred to the *yoni*, and it was this association with the 'sex organ of the Goddess'—as the Sanskrit term *yoni*, meaning vulva, is often rendered in English—that drew me there. I had heard that the Kamakhya temple marked an ancient site in which the inner sanctum, deep within a natural cave, housed a *yoni* stone which was kept moist by a natural spring that flowed up through the cave. For hundreds and probably thousands of years this rock has been worshipped as a symbol of the Goddess, and held to be especially sacred during the *ambuvachi* festival when the spring is reddened with mineral deposits flushed out by the monsoon rains, symbolizing Her menstrual blood.

Kamakhya's name means Goddess of Desire, an epithet which reflects her association with love and sexuality. The Sanskrit term *kama* may also mean any kind of desire, a quality often regarded in the mainstream Hindu orthodoxy as a human weakness to be overcome.[7] It is accordingly not surprising to find that worship of the Goddess of Desire is tantric. A poster which I discovered in the Assam tourism bureau in Delhi during my unintended lengthy preparation for the pilgrimage to Kamakhya attests to the tantric preeminence of the Kamakhya temple with the caption: 'the famous Kamakhya temple where tantricism still practices' (sic).

However, my own original desire to visit Kamakhya was prompted not by the mystique of tantric sex[8] but by the *yoni* as a symbol of female fertility. I was thirty-something and struggling with doubts and fears about my potential for motherhood. As an outsider to the Hindu world I had not quite put together that my seeking in this regard could just as well be directed to any of Her aspects. This is because Motherhood is so very fundamental to the Goddess's identity; She is, after all, addressed as Ma. In the end it was my much adored Kali who blessed me, and after a visitation by Jagadamba, the World Mother Herself, my little Uma was conceived in Pondicherry.

So when I finally made the approach to Kamakhya in 1996 I brought my almost one-year-old daughter along to receive the Great Mother's blessing for our journey and our life together. We were joined by five co-pilgrims, women scholars from both India and the US whom I had invited to collaborate on this *shakti yatra*.

---

7.   Krishna's teaching in the *Bhagavad Gita* is explicit in its advocacy of *niskama karma*, action which is not motivated by desire. Later the *Mahabharata* suggests that Arjuna's sexual weakness for women is the only blemish on his otherwise noble character.

8.   Tantra is of course a much more complex and sophisticated practice than its much publicized association in the popular understanding with sex. See, for example, Gupta, Hoens and Goudriaan (1979).

The climb to Nilachala, the blue hill on which the Kamakhya temple stands, takes you through lush vegetation to a magnificent outlook over the surrounding farmlands and across to the town of Gauhati and the great Brahmaputra river. These days there is a road that leads to the top, though once it was accessible only by foot. Kamakhya is at the pinnacle, a large, low stone canopy built over the steep cave in which the *yoni* stone rests.

Nilachala is also home to the *Dasa Mahavidya,* the ten tantric manifestations of the Goddess who are the keepers of the Great Wisdom. Each one has a shrine established on the surrounding hillside; several of these house womb-like caves similar to that of Kamakhya herself. We were interested also to hear that there were in addition many more caves dotted around the hill and that some had become home to tantric mystics engaged in ascetic practices.

As part of our collaborative research we met with priests, held discussions, participated in rituals and immersed ourselves in the significance of the place. But the most striking experience was that accumulated through the act of crossing each threshold and entering into the Mother's sacred cave. Here was a meeting with Mother as source that made vital sense of the link between Mother, Earth, ecology, and the body and soul of Woman.

When I later read the *Kalika Purana* account of the naming and significance of Kamakhya, it was this experience of female Source that came back to me.

> *Siva said:* As the goddess has come to the great mountain Nilakuta to have sexual enjoyment with me, she is called Kamakhya, who resides there in secret. Since she gives love, is a loving female, is the embodiment of love, the beloved, she restores the limbs of Kama and also destroys the limbs of Kama, she is called Kamakhya. Now listen especially to the great glory of Kamakhya who as the Primordial Force puts the entire world into motion (*Kalika Purana,* ch. 62).

Kamakhya's special powers are those of love, attraction and sexual fulfilment. In this capacity she reserves the power to either restore or destroy the limbs of Kama. She thus not only embodies the quality of love, but establishes its cosmic law, differentiating between that desire which arises from love and that which arises simply from lust. Whereas in the hands of the male god, Kama, a lesser deity burnt to ashes by Shiva's anger, the power of love is circumscribed, Kamakhya wields her power in a way that defines love as the supreme principle of the cosmos. She presides over love and sexual relationships not because She is disposed to doing favours to gods or men but because this is central to Her nature as the primordial creative force.

As the cosmos has its cycles, so too does the Goddess engage in cycles of sexual desire:

> Mahamaya is called Kamakhya by gods and men because of her coming to the mountain (Nilakuta) for enjoying sexual pleasure... When the goddess Mahamaya comes for having sexual enjoyment her body turns into yellow by the red saffrons applied for arousing the sexual excitement. When it is time for love-making she abandons her sword and willingly adorns herself with a garland, when she is no more in amorous mood (*kama*) she holds a sword. When it is time for love-making she stands on a red lotus placed on (the bosom of) Siva, who is in the form of a corpse and when free from the sex desire she stands on a white ghost (*Kalika Purana*, ch. 58: 54-58).

Kamakhya is both world lover and protector. She invokes no authority but her own in determining the appropriate time for intimacy or detachment, and the gods are beholden to Her. This contrasts with the story of Sati whose death comes about as a result of a lack of authority in relation to her husband, Shiva, and father, Daksha. But when She reemerges as Kamakhya, as out of the womb of the earth itself, the Goddess has undergone a transformation that makes her story of relational integrity a triumph for the innate wisdom of the female principle. And she does not forget the lessons learned.

The *Kalika Purana* recounts how Keshava (an epithet of the god Vishnu) once failed to pay his respects as he travelled by her mountain mounted on his vehicle, Garuda. 'Kamakhya, who is Mahamaya herself, the mother of the world, made Keshava immobile with Garuda in the sky.' Keshava then became angry and tried to move Mount Nilachala out of the way. When She observed this Kamakhya became angry and bound both Keshava and Garuda with a special thread before throwing them to the bottom of the sea. Without the Goddess's help Keshava was unable to surface and he subsequently began to rot. When Brahma then came looking for Vishnu he in turn suffered the same fate.

Notwithstanding Her being the embodiment of love it is clear from this that Kamakhya does not brook any disrespect—from anybody. The gods are ultimately freed from their predicament only when they learn the sacred *kavaca* of the Goddess from Shiva. With this they propitiate Her, whereupon she responds:

> O Kesava! today you along with Brahma and the host of gods take the bath in my vaginal-water and sip from that water without delay. Your pride will be purged after you have done this (*Kalika Purana* ch. 72).

Significantly, the humbling of the gods is not finally achieved through aggressive action on the part of the Goddess (though She is clearly well able to wield this kind of force), but through the experience of unparallelled bliss that descends on them as a result of drinking from Her vaginal waters.

> Your blue throne,
> O Goddess of Desire,
> Is studded with the vaults of your Eternity
> From which you spill the waters
> Of your carnal bliss,
> Pouring nectar to your devotees:
> Save me.
>
> How strange that the One
> Who would fulfil Desire
> Has divested me of mine.
> In its place a seed of wisdom grows.
>
> To be with You
> Is as well to be free of you.
> The longing abates, leaving
> Only this sense of vast spaciousness
> And this taste—
> Liberation? (November, 1997).

Gods and men are enjoined to drink from the sacred waters that bestow the bliss of sacred sexual union on those who pay homage to Kamakhya Devi. But the secret of the *yoni* and of the mysteries of life and birth that manifest from the Great Womb, remain the preserve of the Goddess and of the female principle She embodies.

> Holy Mother—
> May your earth ground and support me,
> May your waters sustain and purify me,
> May your fire warm and ignite me,
> May your air breathe and inspire me,

May your sacred space surround and resound in me,
May your enlightened mind illuminate mine.
Holy Mother, may your divine spirit dwell always within me (May, 1997).

Bibliography

Primary Sources

Agrawala, V.S.
   1963   *The Glorification of the Great Goddess [Devi Mahatmya]* (Varanasi: All-India Kashiraj Trust).
Coburn, Thomas B.
   1991   *Encountering the Goddess: A Translation of the Devi Mahatmya and a Study of its Interpretation* (Albany: State University of New York Press).
Desikachar, T.K.V.
   1987   *Patanjali's Yogasutras: An Introduction* (Madras: Affiliated East-West Press).
Jagadiswarananda, Swami
   1953   *Devi Mahatmyam* (Madras: Sri Ramakrishna Math).
Shastri, Biswanarayan
   1991   *The Kalika Purana (Vols. I-III)* (Delhi: Nag Publishers).
Shastri, J.L.
   1970   *Siva Purana (Vols I-IV)* (Delhi: Motilal Banarsidass).
Vimalananda, Swami
   1979   *Mahanarayana Upanisad* (Madras: Sri Ramakrishna Math).
Vijnanananda, Swami
   1986   *The Srimad Devi Bhagawatam* (Delhi: Munshiram Manoharlal).
Woodroffe, Sir John
   1981   *Hymns to the Goddess and Hymn to Kali* (Madras: Ganesh & Co.).

Secondary Sources

Aurobindo, Sri
   1989   *The Mother* (Pondicherry: Sri Aurobindo Ashram).
Babb, Lawrence A.
   1970   'Marriage and Malevolence: The Uses of Sexual Opposition in a Hindu Pantheon', *Ethnology* 9.2: 137-48.
Beane, Wendell C.
   1977   *Myth, Cult and Symbols in Sakta Hinduism: A Study of the Indian Mother Goddess* (Leiden: E.J. Brill).
Brown, Cheever Mackenzie
   1990   *The Triumph of the Goddess: The Canonical Models and Theological Vison of the Devi Bhagavata Purana* (Albany: State University of New York Press).

Coburn, Thomas B.
1984   *Devi Mahatmya: The Crystallization of the Goddess Tradition* (Delhi: Motilal Banarsidass).
1994   'Experiencing the Goddess: Notes on a Text, Gender and Society', *Manushi* 80: 2-10.
Eliade, Mircea
1959   *The Sacred and the Profane* (New York: Harper & Row).
1963   *Myth and Reality* (New York: Harper & Row).
Erndl, Kathleen M.
1993   *Victory to the Mother: The Hindu Goddess of Northwest India in Myth, Ritual, and Symbol* (New York: Oxford University Press).
Geertz, Clifford
1973   *The Interpretation of Cultures* (New York: Basic Books).
Gupta, Bina
1987   *Sexual Archetypes, East and West* (New York: Paragon House).
Gupta, Sanjukta, Dirk J. Hoens and Tuen Goudriann
1979   *Hindu Tantrism* (Leiden: E.J. Brill).
Harman, William P.
1989   *The Sacred Marriage of a Hindu Goddess* (Bloomington: Indiana University Press).
Ions, Veronica
1986   *Indian Mythology* (London: Hamlyn).
Kinsley, David
1975   *The Sword and the Flute* (Berkeley: University of California Press).
McDermott, Rachel Fell
1993   'Evidence for the Transformation of the Goddess Kali: Kamalakanta Bhattacarya and the Bengali Sakta Padavali Tradition' (PhD dissertation, Harvard University).
Meena, V.
n.d.   *Madurai* (Cape Cormorin: Harikumari Arts).
Mookerjee, Ajit
1988   *Kali: The Feminine Force* (New York: Destiny Books).
Nathan, Leonard, and Clinton Seely
1982   *Grace and Mercy in Her Wild Hair: Selected Poems to the Mother Goddess—Ramprasad Sen* (Boulder: Great Eastern).
Nikhilananda, Swami
1942   *The Gospel of Sri Ramakrishna* (abridged edition; New York: Ramakrishna-Vivekananda Center).
Nivedita, Sister
1989   *Kali the Mother* (Calcutta: Advaita Ashrama).
O'Flaherty, Wendy Doniger
1980   *Women, Androgynes, and Other Mythical Beasts* (Chicago: University of Chicago Press).
Ramanujan, A.K.
1986   'Two Realms of Kannada Folklore', in S.H. Blackman and A.K. Ramanujan (eds.), *Another Harmony: New Essays on the Folklore of India* (Delhi: Oxford University Press).

Robinson, Sandra
    1985   'Hindu Paradigms of Women: Images and Values', in Yvonne Yazbeck
                  Haddad and Ellison Banks Findly (eds.), *Women, Religion, and Social
                  Change* (Albany: State University of New York Press).
Shulman, David D.
    1980   *Tamil Temple Myths: Sacrifice and Divine Marriage in the South
                  Indian Saiva Tradition* (Princeton: University Press).
Svoboda, Robert E.
    1993   *Aghora II: Kundalini* (Albuquerque: Brotherhood of Life).
Thompson, Edward J., and Arthur M. Spencer
    1986   *Bengali Religious Lyrics Sakta* (Delhi: Sri Satguru Publications).
Wehr, Demaris S.
    1985   'Religious and Social Dimensions of Jung's Concept of the Archetype:
                  A Feminist Perspective', in Estella Lauter and Carol Schreier
                  Rupprecht (eds.), *Feminist Archetypal Theory* (Knoxville: University
                  of Tennessee Press).
Woodroffe, Sir John
    1987   *Shakti and Shakta* (Madras: Ganesh & Co.).

Jeffrey J. Kripal

A Garland of Talking Heads for the Goddess: Some Autobiographical and Psychoanalytic Reflections on the Western Kali

> [W]e may wonder whether perhaps we are seeing today the emergence of a natural and healthy symbiosis of Hindu goddesses, on the one hand, and Western or Western-influenced women, on the other. This symbiosis may serve to increase the *sakti* of both—and at the same time, one hopes, to imbue men with a kind of energy they have often lacked in the past (Hawley 1996: 24).

Much of modern scholarship on Hindu goddesses, at least that inspired by historical-critical or anthropological methods, has been informed implicitly or explicitly by the political and social agendas of feminist thought. Indeed, it is probably no accident that the beginnings of Indological scholarship on the goddesses correspond roughly with, even if they run a bit behind, the rise of feminist thought in the academy of the 1960s and early 1970s. Usually this feminist subtext is just that, a subtext, but occasionally this general ideological spirit becomes more explicit and Hindu goddesses are studied, in Rita Gross's apt phrase, as a 'resource for the contemporary rediscovery of the goddess' (Gross 1994). There are numerous dimensions to this wide-ranging cultural project, most prominent among them a clearly and passionately articulated desire to reestablish a feminine aspect of the divine that can in turn function as a foundation for the social empowerment of historical women, whether in India or the West. One of the most sophisticated examples of such a project is the Hawley and Wulff edited collection, *Devi: Goddesses of India*, a state of the art series of essays that begins with an introduction by Hawley, who insightfully places the ensuing case studies within a discursive space defined by contemporary Western religious developments, particularly the desire of Western religion 'to make clearer contact with the feminine dimension in religious experience' (Hawley and Wulff 1996: 1), and appropriately ends with Rachel Fell McDermott's essay on 'The Western

Kali', which provocatively documents some of the more dramatic devotional attempts to transform Kali, history or no, into a modern feminist goddess (McDermott 1996).

And indeed, Kali in particular seems to be a particularly apt symbol for this general feminist project. She is usually portrayed as standing victoriously atop a supine passive male god, her husband Shiva. She wears a garland of (always male) decapitated heads and a mini-skirt of arms chopped off just below or above the elbows. Her four arms embrace the full terrifying sweep of the human life cycle: whereas her right arms promise boons and freedom from fear, her left arms promise death with an upraised sword and deliver it with the sign of yet another (male) decapitated head, usually held by the hair. The goddess's dominant position 'on top', her uncontrolled rage directed at (always male) demons, and her association with South Asian notions of 'power' (*shakti*) all come together to produce what seems to be an especially, indeed eerily, appropriate 'chosen deity' (*ishtadevata*) for the feminist position, at least in its more radical versions. I recall here a god-poster I have in my collection that shows Kali astride her prostrate husband on a gory (but quite colorful) battlefield; in the background an army of bare-breasted women are ferociously hacking the legs, arms and heads off a hapless group of mustachioed[1] men, all of whom look exactly alike, as if there was only one way to be a man. Something is clearly going on here 'in the background' of this visual text, and it has something to do with male fears of female sexuality or female rage at male oppression, or, more likely, with more than a little of both.

But does the South Asian textual, iconographic and ethnographic evidence lend itself so easily to such an obviously 'Western' reading of Kali? Although I have few quarrels with the intentions of the feminist theological project (indeed I share much of the vision), I would suggest that the answer to this question is an unequivocal and definitive 'maybe', and that the specifics of the feminist appropriation of Kali need to be doubly balanced by two separate but related psychoanalytic critiques.

The first involves the growing scholarly consensus that India's goddess traditions are in many cases *male* traditions in which the goddess's symbolism is often employed to express the interests,

---

1.   For eloquent discussions of the gender significations of the Indian mustache, see Cohen (1995: 292-93); Hiltebeitel (1998).

anxieties and religious experiences of South Asian men. Here Kali's
rage, uncontrolled sexuality, and dominant position are all expres-
sive, not so much of female emotional responses to oppressive
social structures, but rather of male fears of women writ large with
mythological lines. Kali, after all, is hardly what a South Asian
woman is supposed to be or even wants to be; rather, *she is everything that a woman should not be* or, put differently, *she is what
a man most fears a woman secretly to be*. Kali's symbolism, then,
far from being 'liberating' for South Asian women, is in fact often
supportive of the very social and gender constructions that the feminist critique so justly attempts to overcome. Kali, to put it bluntly,
is more a goddess *of* male fears and anxieties than she is a goddess
for oppressed women. In Caldwell's disarmingly honest phrase, she
is 'a male projective fantasy about feminine sexuality' (Caldwell
1995: 422). No doubt, many of the shortcomings and failings of this
Hindu goddess in terms of the feminist agenda arise directly out of
this often unrecognized discrepancy: Indian and Western females
are attempting to appropriate what are often South Asian male religious experiences, which in turn are driven, at least partly, by
misogynistic processes. Here, then, the psychoanalytic literature on
the goddesses can function negatively, as a warning, as a reminder
and as a correction to anyone who would uncritically read the texts,
witness the rituals or, more seriously, appropriate the goddesses
'on the surface'. In other places, psychoanalysis can function positively, offering striking insights into the possible childhood, pre-
oedipal origins of many features of Kali's *cultus*: its emphasis on
the emotional-devotional states of the infant or child, its stated goal
of mystically merging with the Mother, and its bewildering symbolic complex of beheading, motherliness, sexuality and violence
(more on this below).

The second critique is distinct from the first in that it moves out
of Kali's original South Asian context and into the modern West to
ask questions about the *Western male* appropriation of Kali. If the
feminist reading of the goddess has been driven by a desire to
'express and bring to articulation the feminist intuition that the
struggle for equal rights is supported by the nature of reality' (Christ
1994: 250), what sorts of psychological, social, theological and cultural processes are at work when Western males appropriate her in
their religious lives or, in the case of the academy, in their scholar-

ship? Are these different processes than are at work in the feminist project? Are these different processes than are at work in the South Asian male understanding? Why *are* Western male scholars interested in engaging in a form of scholarship that seems, at least on the surface, to have everything to do with the religious and social positions of women (or South Asian men) and little if anything to do with the existential conditions of Western men? Are we just astonishingly altruistic, enlightened and liberal-minded? Or are there deeper, more psychologically complex motives at work?

Part of the answer, of course, is that males, in South Asia or America, are not always the monotonously portrayed demons some of the more radical forms of feminism—not to mention the Kali posters—paint them as; they genuinely love and are therefore concerned about the well-being and happiness of the many women of their lives, be they mothers, wives, lovers, sisters, friends, daughters or simply fellow human beings. But there is probably more here as well, and it seems quite likely that the psychological lines along which Western male interests in Hindu goddesses, and Kali in particular, have developed are in general significantly different than both those that drive the feminist hermeneutics and those that originally created the symbolisms, rituals and mythologies of the goddess in South Asia. More specifically, I would suggest that the Hindu goddesses in general and the Tantric goddesses in particular offer the hope of something that is rare if not structurally impossible within the Western monotheistic traditions—a *heterosexually coded male mysticism*. At least in my own case, this Western heteroerotic search for the divine feminine Presence of the Hindu Tantra is not as straightforward and as simple as it might first appear, as much that in the beginning what seems obvious to the sincere but psychologically naive Western male turns out, on closer inspection, to be extraordinarily complex, rooted deeply as it is in sociological realities that are virtually inaccessible to him, that is, in the psychological dynamics of Indian child-rearing, the unique nuances of Indian socialization practices, and the specifically Indian sexualities and genders that all of this helps create. Such are my general conclusions, as they stand now quite unsubstantiated and speculative but nevertheless stated up front. The remainder of the essay will attempt to flesh out these tentative thoughts—or write out this goddess—through two separate but related paths: (1) autobiographical reflections on my own failed but frutiful search for a heterosexual Tantric mysticism; and (2) a brief discussion of psychoanalytic discourse on Indian male psychosocial development as it pertains to the question at hand. I imaginatively write, not as the goddess herself, but as one of the many male heads that constitute her gory garland. This male head, however, quite unlike the traditional heads, talks back. It speaks with a distinctively American accent and in the strange language of its own academic training. It reflects. It speculates. It warns. It remembers. It has something to say in the dark.

The Unimaginable Bride

I remember coming home for the summer after my first year of training in a Roman Catholic seminary. More than a few friends and family members seemed surprised to see me, as if the seminary was a kind of jail or penitentiary whose high steel doors shut and locked tight behind one until the famous white collar was firmly wrapped around the neck as a sign of one's permanent celibacy—a kind of prison sentence for life, I suppose, in some of their eyes. 'They let you out?' they seemed to say with their looks. I could only laugh to myself, since in fact the very opposite was true: the seminary, or at least this seminary, let one in but then immediately did everything in its power to question one's place there. The attrition rate was very high—only about 15–20 per cent of the entering class would ever become priests. This was no secret, and it was a mark of the process's wisdom. These, after all, were young men, many of them very young, who were entering the seminary with the assumption, hope or guess that they were being called to a life of celibate service—an unusual conclusion to say the least for eighteen-year-old American males who grew up in the age of disco and early MTV. Consequently, the training was intense and wise, much of it focusing on the big question: Could one, why would one want to, remain celibate for the rest of one's life? We were forced to ask hard questions about ourselves, taught to explore our pasts for hidden emotional and sexual conflicts, and encouraged to be honest with ourselves and our spiritual directors about what we found. It was a supportive, even loving, atmosphere charged with spiritual, psychological and sexual insight. Many left, but very few, I would guess, departed unmoved. It was a sacred place.

I was more confused than most, I think. There was something I just could not seem to understand. Forced to explore the interfaces between sexuality and spirituality and more than tortured by my own psychosexual pathologies (I was suffering from anorexia at the time), I naturally felt some attraction for ascetic and mystical strands within the tradition that symbolically dealt with the same themes. Christian bridal mysticism seemed especially interesting to me. Here, after all, was a mode of mystical discourse that collapsed the spiritual and the sexual within a single symbolic language. And yet somehow the texts resisted my imaginative appropriation of them. Something was not right. 'Let him kiss me with the kisses of his mouth!' sing the opening lines of the *Song of Songs*, that favorite biblical text of medieval mystical writers, many of whom used it to describe and theologize out of their own encounters with Christ, here understood to be the Bridegroom of the female soul. Male or female, they were brides.

But I was not. And I never could be. Such language simply did not 'fit' my sexual nature. Although I did not have the vocabulary and theoretical training to say it then, I would say now that I could not appropriate the bridal mystical tradition because its homoerotic structure was in conflict with my own heterosexuality. And this basic conflict, I later realized, was a function, not just of medieval bridal mysticism, but of Western monotheism itself. Doctrinally defined by the existence of a single male God with whom the human being communes or unites, such a tradition has—quite predictably —tended to produce orthodox male erotic[2] mysticisms that are homoerotic in structure. What else *could* they be? After all, any heteroerotic male system would have to define, or at least imagine, the divine Presence in feminine terms that were also sexualized, and this was simply out of the question for all but the marginal, heretical or wildly imaginative few (I am thinking of a Boehme or a Blake, two married men who imagined into being their own uniquely heterosexual mysticisms and suffered, either active persecution and censorship in the case of Boehme or contemporary anonymity in the case of Blake, for their boldness).[3] I thus came to a rather

2.   My model, although applicable to monotheism in general, applies strictly only to mystical traditions or texts that employ sexual symbolism in order to express the male mystic's relationship to the (male) divine.

3.   See especially Blake's *The Marriage of Heaven and Hell* (Blake 1975),

surprising conclusion in regard to my own mystico-erotic tradition: *heterosexuality is heretical*.[4] Or put differently and more carefully, Christian erotic male mysticism, by the gender logic of its own doctrine (with a male human being uniting with a male Christ or God), tends inevitably towards a homoerotic structure. Certainly such a (heterosexual) problem is not restricted to Christianity. Howard Eilberg-Schwartz has expressed the biblical logic of a very similar dynamic within ancient Judaism in this way:

> The primary relationships in Israelite imagination were between a male God and individual male Israelites, such as Moses, the patriarchs, and the prophets... Men were encouraged to imagine themselves as married to and hence in a loving relationship with God. A homoerotic dilemma was thus generated, inadvertently and to some degree unconsciously, by the superimposition of heterosexual images on the relationship between human and divine males (Eilberg-Schwartz 1994: 99).

And this can only create problems, of the deepest ontological sort, for heterosexual men, since 'being a husband to a wife is in tension with being a wife of God' (Eilberg-Schwartz 1994: 195), or, in the terms of my life in the seminary, being a heterosexual male was in significant tension with being a Christian mystic, at least one who did not wish to check his sexuality in at the door.

which in effect reverses Christian mysticism in its positing of a heterosexually active human male mystic. Interestingly, there is historical evidence for an Indian Tantric influence on this text (Schuchard 1998).

4. I am not, of course, suggesting that *every* Christian mystic was or is homosexually oriented: an individual's use or appropriation of a homoerotic symbolic structure does not necessarily imply a psycho-physiological homosexuality. I am arguing that the historical process of the Christian mystical tradition (and more particularly, the bridal tradition), with its constant tacking back and forth between individual psyches and public social structures, eventually created a symbolic, doctrinal and institutional structure that clearly privileged males who were so inclined. The issue, then, is not this or that case study (numerous exceptions can always be found) but the general orientation and sexual saliency of the symbolism as it was developed through countless individual psyches over large stretches of time. Put differently, I am after here what Obeyesekere, following Weber, would call 'ideal typical situations', that is, those psychosocial contexts that occur with sufficient frequency and psychic intensity to find their way into a publically shared projective system (Obeyesekere 1984: 428-40).

This was not a pleasant realization for me, as I was quite happy, if almost fatally neurotic, within the symbols and rituals of my indigenous religious tradition. At some point, however, I had to admit to myself that my religious life was quite literally killing me (my body weight was down to 125 pounds, a good 50 pounds below my normal body weight; I struggled to walk up a flight of stairs), and that any kind of healing would have to take place within a religious worldview that did not deny the most basic physiological and sexual facts of my precarious existence. It was at this point that I began exploring other religious worldviews as alternative ways of making sense of my life-experience. The engendered and doctrinal structures of the Hindu goddess traditions in particular seemed to offer heterosexual possibilities that did not seem to exist within my own Catholic tradition. Here, after all, the divine was imagined as feminine, the male aspirant was allowed his masculinity (even if keeping it was deemed 'heroic'), and the union of the two was, again, analogized (or literally described?) in sexual terms. I was culturally naive, gloriously uninformed, fascinated and hopeful.

And remained so, until I got to India and immersed myself in the textual and cultural details of an actual Tantric tradition, the Shakta Tantra of Ramakrishna Paramahamsa (1836–1886), a Bengali mystic, Kali devotee and famous Hindu saint whose life and teachings are richly recorded and explored in a large corpus of Bengali texts. It was not that the textual tradition or the saint disappointed or disillusioned me. Far from it—I remain, to this day, in a state of awe. It was just that I began to realize, as I shall soon explain, that things were far more complicated than I had assumed, and that one cannot easily appropriate a mystical tradition of another culture for a whole host of linguistic, political, historical and psychological reasons, many of which have been amply treated in the present volume. More specifically, I realized that sexuality and gender, and *especially* mystical forms of sexuality and gender (which tend to be unusually fluid, free or conflicted, depending on one's perspective), could not be mapped within a simple binarism, as if heterosexuality/homosexuality or male/female were the only possibilities. Quite the contrary, there are innumerable sexualities and genders, I learned, and all of them are deeply informed by culture, history and society, none of which human beings have radically shared in any truly global sense, until perhaps now.

I began my studies of Kali and the Bengali Shakta Tantra in which she was embedded, then, after being frustrated with the consistently homoerotic structures that I found working in my own mystical traditions. I could not imagine myself 'marrying' Christ, much less kissing him. The symbolism simply made no sexual sense to me. Consequently, I turned to Shakta Tantra because I imagined it to be a tradition structured around heterosexual rituals, divinities and experiences. Ironically, what I actually found was yet another male mystic engaging male divinities in homoerotic encounters as a symbolic female; in Christian mystical terms, I had found another bride-soul. More specifically, my work focused on a large corpus of nineteenth- and early twentieth-century Bengali texts and concluded that Ramakrishna's visions, mystical states and ecstastic flights were driven by mystico-erotic energies that he neither fully accepted nor understood. The saint's visions and ecstasies, I suggested, could only be properly understood by positing a homosexual orientation in the saint; only in this way could we make sense of the saint's fear of and rejection of (hetero)sexuality,[5] his literally ecstatic responses to his young male disciples (he would often go into mystical states of absorption or devotion while touching them, playing with them, or simply seeing them), and his tendency to go into trances before sexualized women (trance here functioning as a negative defensive mechanism) and young male disciples (trance here functioning as a positive sublimating mechanism). To encompass all of this, I developed a dialectical category I called 'the erotic', which I defined as 'a dimension of human experience that is simultaneously related both to the physical and emotional experience of sexuality and to the deepest ontological levels of religious experience' (Kripal 1998b: 23). Building on the work of Ricoeur (1970) and Obeyeskere (1990), I argued that the erotic functions in these texts as an essentially dialectical process that manifests both 'regressive' returns back to childhood and early traumatic experiences and 'progressive' leaps forward into vision, religious ecstasy, personal healing and deification (hence his ecstasies became the psychotheological ground for those who would

5.   I adopt this partially parenthetical expression from Parama Roy, who uses it in her remarkable essay on Ramakrishna, Vivekananda and Sister Nivedita, 'As the Master Saw Her: Western Women and Hindu Nationalism', to properly qualify Ramakrishna's rejection of (hetero)sexuality (Roy 1998).

later deify him as an *avatara* or 'descent' of God). The erotic here was rooted in a painful pathological past and yet branched out into a theological, even mythological, future. It was an entire life-process that was simultaneously sexual *and* spiritual, regressive *and* progressive, pathological *and* theological.

In short, I was back to a culturally distinct form of the mystical homoeroticism that I thought I had left behind in Christianity. As I looked into the hermeneutical mirror of the texts, I saw an image of the Hindu saint that both was and was not like me, a kind of reverse mirror-image, if you will. I was struck to learn that the very heterosexual symbols and rituals that first attracted my attention to Shakta Tantra Ramakrishna himself rejected. But this made good sense to me, as, not unlike my own experience of Catholic bridal mysticism, Ramakrishna found such symbols to be structured around a sexual orientation that he did not share, in his case a heterosexual one. Ramakrishna and I, in other words, were in a very similar structural dilemma, if for opposite reasons—I understood him precisely because we both were and were not alike. My search for a heterosexual Tantric mysticism thus ended in an ironic disappointment that paradoxically functioned as a source of hermeneutical and comparative insight. It was a fruitful failure.

Pondering the Heads: The Psychoanalytic Gaze

But was Ramakrishna's mysticism, which cannot be fitted into any heterosexual code, simply a sexual rarity within the tradition, a single unusual occurence into which we cannot read any normative or general conclusions about the Shakta Tantra? At first I assumed as much, but I now have my doubts, and this for two reasons. First of all, I do not believe it is a historical accident that Ramakrishna's maternal mysticism, with its attending anxiety over an active adult heterosexuality, became canonical within the Bengali Shakta tradition. Why, for example, did Ramakrishna's emphasis on the seemingly sexless state of the Child and his alliterative rejection of *kamini-kanchana* or 'lover-and-gold' become so central? The truth is that there were dozens, if not hundreds, of Shakta saints over the last two hundred years in the Bengal region, and only a very small handful became representative, and none, with the possible exception of Ramprasad, are half as famous and loved as Ramakrishna. Apparently, his teachings, his personality and his resolutions of psychosexual conflicts basic to the culture spoke to something very deep in Bengali life. When he taught that sex with a woman is to be avoided as an act of symbolic incest since, in his own honest words (which were, by the way, completely omitted from the canonical English translation) 'Every woman's vagina is Mother's vagina' (Kripal 1998b: 133-36), then, Ramakrishna was not simply expressing his own oedipal fears; he was explicitly revealing something that was already implicit, if never so clearly stated, in the culture's innumerable mother goddess traditions. He acted, in effect, as the culture's unconscious made conscious; he revealed that which was concealed, made manifest what was latent. In psychoanalytic terms, he was abreacting on behalf of his society, acting out in his person and *in extremis* the general psychological problem of wanting to identify with the mother (Obeyesekere 1984: 601). Ramakrishna, in other words, may have been extreme and excessive in his psychosexual reactions (most truly great saints are), but he certainly did not stand outside his own culture. Quite the contrary, he expressed that culture in a dramatic and culturally syntonic way with the bright colors and emotionally appealing strokes of mythology and mysticism. We can thus assume, with the usual cautions, that the patterns of his life both flow out of and in turn legitimate or sacralize at least some of the psychosocial patterns of the larger culture.[6] That is to say, we can assume that Ramakrishna is not alone in his mystical rejection of (hetero)sexuality. Still, I would not want to make too much of this claim until other psychohistorical case studies are carried out. We know so very little about the psychosexual lives of Shakta saints, and until we know far more nothing of general or normative import can be concluded. At this point, I am only guessing about what lies after and beyond the single case of Ramakrishna Paramahamsa.

6.   It would be a serious mistake to pretend that Ramakrishna somehow represents all of Bengali culture. The truth is that Ramakrishna has always been quite controversial within Bengali society, where Western-style social reform, Marxism, secularism, a profound poetic-literary tradition and different forms of religiosity have flourished in a complicated and conflicted mix of discourses and worldviews. It is best, then, to see Ramakrishna's specific religious resolutions of culturally constituted psychological problems as only one of many cultural options available.

But at least they are educated guesses, and guesses with more than a little support in one important Indological-hermeneutical tradition, the psychoanalytic study of Indian culture. Since this same hermeneutical tradition has much to offer our present discussion about the goddess's feminist potential, it would serve us well to spend a few pages outlining what psychoanalysis has to say about the Hindu goddesses and their psychosocial anchoring in the Indian male psyche.[7] Certainly psychoanalysis is an iconoclastic interpretive tradition that many would like to avoid—open talk about the defining powers of sexuality tends to make people very uncomfortable (rather like Kali's garland of heads or flagrant sexuality)—but such avoidance behavior, I would suggest, is a serious mistake, at least if we are genuinely interested in understanding the feminist promises and problems of the Hindu goddesses. How, may I ask, can psychoanalysis *not* be relevant for understanding a tradition that understands its central goddess to be both Mother and Lover? The truth of the matter is that Kali is an excessive goddess who flaunts wildly transgressive acts and images (dead fetuses for earrings, cremation grounds, decapitation, explicit sexuality, and so on) that many, if not most, South Asians themselves recognize as extreme. Any method that hopes to understand such a goddess must honor that same excess by taking it seriously, by reflecting on it theoretically, and, most importantly, *by not looking away*. Psychoanalysis is often unpopular, I would suggest, precisely to the extent that, like the Hindu Tantra itself, it focuses its hermeneutical gaze on those very truths that others most fear. It is, if you will, our Western Tantra. It transgresses in order to transcend.

Psychoanalytically informed thinkers have been writing about Hinduism for about eighty years now (Vaidyanathan and Kripal 1998). Freud himself knew more about Hinduism than is usually assumed, primarily through his friend and correspondent Romain Rolland, the French writer, perennialist mystic and social activist who praised Freud's attack on the common man's religion in *The Future of an Illusion* (Rolland believed in neither a personal God nor the immortality of the individual soul) and later sent him his

---

7.   My comments here are cursory at best. For a much fuller treatment, see my 'The Goddess in the Psychoanalytic Tradition: Or Why the Tantrika is a Hero', in Rachel Fell McDermott and Jeffrey J. Kripal (eds.), *Encountering Kali: In the Margins at the Center, in the West* (ms. in process).

biographies of Ramakrishna and Vivekananda (Ramakrishna, it seems, goes back to the very beginning of the psychoanalytic tradition). Freud, again *pace* the traditional assumptions, could express both his usual skepticism and a certain poetic admiration for mystical modes of subjectivity, and he was not above admitting that mysticism bears a striking resemblance to psychoanalysis in its attempt to upset the normal functionings of the human psyche in order to access the unconscious or hidden dimensions of the mind (Freud 1933: 79-80; Parsons 1999). A beautiful ivory statue of Vishnu, a gift from the Bengali analyst Girindrasekhar Bose and the Indian Psychoanalytic Society on the occasion of Freud's seventy-fifth birthday, sat on Freud's desk among his better-known Egyptian and Roman pieces. When it later developed cracks in its ivory form, Freud playfully analyzed them as symbolic signs of the cultural dissonance he felt between the two great civilizations (Vaidyanathan and Kripal 1998: 3).[8] This same rich ambiguity in regard to things mystical and Hindu—this same cracked but present Vishnu—has carried through the later psychoanalytic tradition down to the present.

Although this hermeneutical tradition is hardly monolithic in its conclusions—important dissenting voices can always be found on any particular subject—there is something, I think, that we can call the 'consensual model' of Indian male psychological development. One of the most remarkable features of this model is its radically cross-cultural genesis, that is, the fact that it was developed, from the very beginning, by both South Asian and Western thinkers. Far from being the imperialistic cultural imposition that it is often assumed to be, psychoanalytic Indology has generated and regenerated itself over the years through healthy dialogue and open debate across the seas. Beginning with the pioneering work of Girindrasekhar Bose, who, like Rolland, also corresponded at some length with Sigmund Freud (Bose and Freud 1997), the tradition developed in mid-century through the later studies of G.M. Carstairs (Carstairs 1957, 1983; Carstairs and Kapur 1976) and Philip Spratt (1966) and reached something of a contemporary consensual sum-

---

8. For a photograph of the actual statue, see the frontispiece to Vaidyanathan and Kripal (1998). For the minutes of the Society's meeting (6 May 1931) and a translation of the Sanskrit verses that were sent to Freud with the statue, see the Appendix of the same: 453-55.

mary in the analyst Sudhir Kakar, who trained with Erik Erikson at Harvard University and now lives and writes in New Delhi. For the sake of conciseness, we can ignore for a moment the many important debates of the field[9] and take Kakar's work as a jumping-off point for our present purposes of reflecting on the feminist possibilities and pitfalls of the Western Kali.

In Kakar's model, the Indian male child experiences infancy as a prolonged and intimate bonding with a loving mother. Two factors complicate this otherwise blissful existence: the tendency of the Indian family structure to deprive the mother of sufficient sexual access to her husband, and the social fact that the birth of a son raises her immeasurably in the eyes of the extended family. The mother thus experiences the newborn son as something of a savior and pours her sexually toned affections onto him, along with her aggressive, destructive impulses born of the culture's implicit misogyny. Kakar suggests that the infant son, far from developmentally ready for such a complicated and powerful complex of emotions, is overwhelmed with intense emotional states of love, merger and the fear of emotional-sexual engulfment (Kakar 1981: 29, 88-89). Following Melanie Klein and Carstairs before him, Kakar argues that the son eventually learns to 'split' this emotional ambiguity into two separate mother-figures, which corrrespond closely to the two types of goddess-figures found in Hindu mythology: the 'good mother', who is idealized as 'totally good' (Kakar 1981: 83), and the 'bad mother', who is imagined in myth and dream as an orally and sexually voracious figure determined to deny individuation to the son. Both are now said to exist, simultaneously, in the child's primary-process thinking (Kakar 1981: 108). According to Kakar, it is this 'maternal-feminine' complex, these years of blissful but conflicted merger with the mother, that functions as the hegemonic narrative of Hindu culture (Kakar 1989). The same complex also defines the Hindu male psyche as more or less androgynous and in touch with the maternal, primary-process wellsprings of imagination, fantasy and creativity. The result, for Kakar, is a certain psychic wholeness and internal gender balance, a 'more human' psyche (Kakar 1981: 109).

At the age of four or five, however, the male child is rather suddenly removed from this maternal-feminine Presence and is intro-

9. See, for example, Goldman (1978) and Kurtz (1992).

duced into the male, patriarchal world of the father and society, an event Kakar calls the 'second birth'. Kakar argues that such a traumatic shift in the boy's existential moorings sets the Hindu male up for 'regression to an earlier "happier" era and a tendency to consolidate one's identification with the mother in order to compensate for her loss' (Kakar 1981: 130). Here too Kakar places the relatively strong narcissistic tendencies of the Indian male psyche, that is, its tendency to isolate itself in a kind of maternal-mystical independence, which harks back to the early merger of infant and mother shortly after birth, or alternatively, in the invincible isolation of the *lingam*, an iconic symbol which for Kakar speaks to the boy's post-separation attempt to reconstitute his shattered sense of narcissistic security and pleasure (Kakar 1981: 155-60). With regard to the former maternal model, Kakar writes:

> The child's differentiation of himself from his mother (and consequently of the ego from the id) is structurally weaker and comes chronologically later than in the West with this outcome: the mental processes characteristic of the symbiosis of infancy play a relatively greater role in the personality of the adult Indian (Kakar 1981: 104).

Put religiously, the adult Indian male is more likely to be attracted to mystical systems that emphasize union or merger, especially with some kind of mother-goddess.

Also related to this second birth is Kakar's notion of the Indian oedipal complex and its 'passive' resolution in the male child's renunciation of his sexuality *vis-à-vis* his mother and his absolute submission to the elder males of the family (Kakar 1981: 134). Such a resolution is a product of the broader culture, which it in turn serves and supports through a psychological structure that can adapt well to hierarchical submission to male authority, such as the institutions of caste and patriarchy demand (Kakar 1981: 134).

Now all of this has some rather profound implications for our reading of the Hindu goddesses, and Kali in particular. For example, the numinous presence of the loving but emotionally ambivalent and sexually powerful mother in the experience of the infant male child helps explain the equally ambivalent and sexualized mother-goddess figures of the male-constructed and male-controlled mythologies. Kakar's narcissistic model of the Indian male psyche also helps explain why Hinduism continuously returns to the mother goddess, emphasizing all the while the blissful joys of maternal communion or absorption, childlike surrender and an adzring devotion (*bhakti*). Unlike the Western monotheisms, which tend to focus on the later stages of oedipal struggle and patriarchal identification (the sacrifice of the beloved son in the stories of Abraham and Isaac or the crucifixion of Jesus [Delaney 1998; Levenson 1993], the themes of guilt, forgiveness and salvation, and the 'virgin mother' [Carroll 1986, 1992]), the narratives and soteriologies of Hinduism often focus on maternal merger as mystical union—they thus go 'further back' along the life cycle to the maternal, the primordial and the ontological. Astonishingly, this pattern was seen as early as 1932 with the Schjelderup brothers' early study *Über drei Haupttypen* (1932). The Schjelderups drew on eighteen case studies of glossolalia to categorize the religious personality into three basic religious types—the oedipal, the pre-oedipal, and the narcissistic. They then demonstrated each type with a historical case-study: Martin Luther typified the oedipal stage of guilt, sin and redemption (the 'father-religion'), Ramakrishna exemplified the pre-oedipal stage of mother merger (the 'mother-religion'), and the Zen monk Bodhidharma modeled the narcissistic identification of the self with the universe (the 'self-religion'). Once again, it was Ramakrishna and Kali who entered psychoanalytic discourse to embody that 'mother-religion' defined by the bliss of physical intimacy and security and a 'tendency towards mystical unity with the Divinity' (Schjelderup and Schjelderup 1932: 58).

This same developmental model, with its emphasis on the hegemonic mother/goddess narrative (Kakar 1989), also throws considerable light on the 'dark side' of the Hindu goddesses and the male psyches of which they often speak so eloquently. Here we might mention, with Kakar, the fear of female sexuality, the prominence of menstruation taboos, the *vagina dentata* legends, and problems with sexual impotence that one finds repeatedly in Indian culture (Kakar 1981: 92-95: 98). Kakar explains such processes in the terms of this same hegemonic goddess narrative:

> Of course, in its defensive aspect, the maternal-feminine identification of men may serve to keep the sexes apart and may even contribute to discrimination against women. A precarious sense of masculine identity can lead to a rigid, all-or-nothing demarcation of sex roles; this kind of rigid differentiation is a means of building outer bulwarks against feared inner proclivities (Kakar 1981: 109-10).

The culturally constructed religious ideal of becoming one with the (divine) Mother, in other words, has its own social price—a fear of and potential rejection of the feminine for the sake of the 'precarious' masculine ego. I need not point out that we are hardly left here with an unproblematic feminism. Quite the contrary. Like the goddess herself, we are left with a deeply ambivalent, even split image—the feminine simultaneously deified and feared, gracious and furious, blessed and cursed, and all this from a decidedly male perspective.[10]

One also cannot help noticing that there are an awful lot of male heads lying around in the images and texts and rituals of the goddess. Goats and buffaloes, always male, get their heads cut off in her temples and sacrifices, and men commonly lose theirs in her myths and images. Carmel Berkson has written a powerful and moving study of this process by looking at, and genuinely siding with, Durga's arch-nemesis, the buffalo-demon Mahisha, as an archetype of the embattled male identity, which must always be sacrificed for the mother-goddess (Berkson 1995). From a Western perspective at least, it is a mythologically powerful but ultimately poignant story, for the Mahisha-male can never really win, that is, can never truly establish himself as a subjectivity independent from the (divine) mother; his symbolically horned head, that is, his masculine identity, must always be cut off for the sake of the larger cultural narratives of maternal absorption, mother-religion and communal identity.

We must also keep in mind that in Tantric symbolism the head is the storehouse of the semen, that the ascetic is literally 'he whose semen is turned up' (*urdhvaretas*), and that the rising of the *kundalini* energy is imagined as a quite literal 'upward displacement' from the genital region to the top of the skull, where it bursts out into a kind of mystical orgasm. To read decapitation as symbolic castration, then, is no wild Freudian speculation imposed from without for some hegemonic agenda; quite the contrary, such a hermeneutic, although quite distinct in its psychoanalytic self-reflexivity and style, is remarkably consistent with the culture's own

10. For a cogent discussion of this 'splitting' as it develops in South Asian cultures out of Brahmanic values, see Obeyesekere (1984), ch. 11, 'Virgin, Wife, and Mother'.

symbolism and *honors* that symbolism by taking it seriously (cf.
Kakar 1981: 102). Indeed, as Serena Nanda has pointed out in her
study of Hijra emasculation, the mother goddess as castrator of her
human lover or devotee is a common and well-studied theme in
Hindu mythology and ritual (Nanda 1990: 33; cf. O'Flaherty 1980:
81-86; Cohen 1995; Hiltebeitel 1995, 1998, 1999). We know, for
example, that Hijras often become possessed by a goddess and
enter an analgesic trance before they undergo the surgery that will
take away their male genitals (Cohen 1995: 276; Nanda 1990), certainly one of the more dramatic confirmations of the general psychoanalytic perspective now disciplined, corrected and enriched by
a multiplicity of other frames of reference—religious, psychological, sexual, economic, socio-political and physiological (Cohen
1995: 295).

Such a hermeneutic can certainly help us understand—if never
fully explain—why the male sense of Kali is often filled with a certain anxiety and dread: the goddess cuts off, takes away and absorbs
one's masculine identity back into herself; indeed, she boldly wears
a whole host of such male heads (all of which, usually, and quite
significantly, look exactly alike, as if they had no true identities of
their own) as her decorative garland. Kakar is quite clear about the
sacrifice of masculine identity that the goddess demands: 'In psychosexual terms, to identify with one's mother means to sacrifice one's
masculinity to her in order to escape sexual excitation and the
threat it poses to the boy's fragile ego' (Kakar 1981: 102). Or with
respect to Kali herself: 'the rapture of recognizing (and being
recognized by) the mother's affirming presence together with the
ambivalent anguish in response to her individuality-destroying embrace are the complementary affects evoked and condensed in the
worship of Kali' (Kakar 1981: 173).[11]

11. There is one important caveat in all of this, however, and it goes back
to Girindrasekhar Bose, who long ago argued that his Hindu male patients
displayed no fear of a castration threat but, on the contrary, manifested clear
signs of a castration *wish*, that is to say, they displayed a 'desire to be female'
(Bose 1956). Bose traced this back to the Indian familial structure and its
childrearing patterns, which encourage the male child to identify with both
parents at different stages of its development, an insight which Kakar later
confirmed in his own writings about the balanced and gender-fluid nature of
the Indian male psyche (Kakar 1981: 1989). This is an important point, and
one supported by the remarkable series of Tantric ritual paintings that Indra

Lawrence Cohen has eloquently and critically discussed the colonial, psychoanalytic and postcolonial readings of such emasculation imagery, its inversion in the hypermasculine discourse of the Hindu Right, which is essentially responding to the colonizers' demeaning use of the effeminate male trope, and its renegotiation in the work of Ashis Nandy (Nandy 1983), who accepts the psychological relevance of such discourse but seeks to embed its truths within a more positive, nonviolent and empowering androgynous identity inspired by Gandhian principles in which both the hypomasculine identification of colonial discourse and the hypermasculine defense are transcended in a precolonial, bisexual sense of self, or in Cohen's terms, in 'a liberatory poetics of encompassment and balance' (Cohen 1995: 292). I have nothing to add to this already sophisticated and developed discussion, except to ask the further question: What happens when a religious form, such as Kali, developed within these precolonial, colonial and postcolonial psychopolitical contexts enters the very differently structured complexities of a Western culture such as the United States? From this perspective, one must question, I think, how the psychocultural resolutions that Kali embodies satisfactorily resolve anything for us today, especially in the West, where individuality and the sacrality of the human person are non-negotiable values that few of us would wish to sacrifice to anyone or anything, including a goddess, and where masculinity and femininity are generally structured along different lines. Moreover, I have to wonder how social justice and stability within a liberal democracy could ever be built on the symbolic sacrifices of so many identities, be they male or female or otherwise. I also fail to see how the desexualization of symbolic castration or the (un)consciousness of maternal absorption can function as viable answers in our postmodern world. Perhaps such

Sinha has recently published, in which multiple decapitated heads (which appear with severed phalluses throughout the series) display a remarkable calmness and peace in their severed state, as if this is precisely what they wished to be (Sinha 1993). I would not want to take this caveat too far—for more recent studies have uncovered significant elements of anxiety, suffering and threat in castration imagery (see, for example, Kakar 1981; Obeyesekere 1981, 1984; Courtright 1985; Berkson 1995; Hiltebeitel 1995, 1998, 1999; Kripal 1998b)—but it is nevertheless an important point to keep in mind. As with all symbolic phenomena, the symbolism of decapitation is overdetermined and multivocal.

solutions worked for the South Asian subcultures out of which they were developed. It is dubious at best that they can work in the postmodern West or in the larger global community. The Western heads of the goddess's garland must talk back. Union will come with our natural deaths anyway. Now it is time to speak.

Concluding Reflections: Listening in the Dark

So what are we to say? What are we to conclude from such auto-biographical and psychoanalytic musings? This talking head of the goddess's garland is left with the following tentative conclusions about its own specific 'Western' and 'male' perspectives.

First and most importantly, I would insist on the intellectual and religious integrity of the talking Western male head. Both feminist and postcolonial Indological discourse too often imply the demonization of the Western male, as if every Western male, past or present, were identical in his intentions, thought systems and conclusions (or as if even an ill-intentioned Western male might not have some genuinely accurate observations to make). Certainly Westerners, male or female, must be very careful about what they claim to know or understand about Indian sexualities and their encoding in Hindu mythology, ritual and mysticism, for, as psychoanalysis has taught us, all of these phenomena are rooted deeply in child-rearing and social processes to which the Westerner has little, if any, access (which is to say that psychoanalysis has a powerful and well-developed sense of the Other). From an experiential perspective, these are closed doors. But this does *not* mean: (1) that nothing can be known about these phenomena; (2) that the Western gaze is without its own merits, or, more perversely, (3) that the Westerner has no right to look at all. A word about each of these oft-implied claims is in order.

Clifford Geertz, following Robert Solow, once remarked with respect to objectivity that the fact that a completely antiseptic operating room is practically impossible does not imply that one should operate in a gutter. There are, in other words, degrees of objectivity, and it is specious to argue that, since complete objectivity is impossible, no degree of objectivity is possible (Geertz 1973: 30). The same, I think, is true of cross-cultural or comparative understanding: simply because complete cross-cultural understanding is impossible (but who completely understands even his or her own culture?) does not mean that no cross-cultural understanding is possible. With respect to our present discussion, we are all deeply indebted to South Asian thinkers such as Girindrasekhar Bose, Sudhir Kakar and Gananath Obeyesekere for teaching us, from both the inside and the outside, about the complexities of Indian sexuality and its structuring of the goddess traditions. Certainly no Western male has access to the intimacies of Indian family life as these thinkers did and do. But presumably this is at least one reason that they wrote—to give us some access, to help us to understand. Clearly, then, unless we are prepared to argue that cultures are solipsistic entities incapable of genuine external communication and that these writers wrote entirely in vain, we must admit that Western males can know something and perhaps quite a bit about such phenomena through the critical discourse and theoretical reflections of those 'on the ground', whether they be indigenous actors or, to a different degree, trained anthropologists.

But even the indigenous analyst or anthropologist is not entirely indigenous (Narayan 1993). The truth of the matter is that the theoretical gazes of thinkers such as Bose, Kakar and Obeyesekere are also Western gazes, for their visions have been disciplined, trained and honed through Freud's theorizing and its multiple, and often conflicting, developments in the later psychoanalytic traditions. They see what they see both because they were raised within a South Asian culture (as insiders) and because they have mastered a Western theoretical tradition (as outsiders). Moreover, it is also important to keep in mind that Western anthropologists and hermeneuts embody a very similar dual identity, even if their 'inside' and 'outside' statuses are often reversed in the mirror of cross-cultural scholarship. The history of psychoanalytic discourse on Hinduism can thus be imagined as a double mirror into which Western and South Asian thinkers have gazed in order to better understand both the Other and themselves. The psychoanalytic study of Indian culture, in other words, is constituted by a dual Western–South Asian perspective; it is dialectical to the core, an inside turned out, an outside turned in, a series of human mirrors reflecting other human mirrors. The same, of course, can be said about any number of contemporary Indological methods, including and especially feminism and postcolonial theory. There is no pure

'Western' or 'South Asian' perspective here either, although the power of this particular hermeneutic tradition would collapse if the relative autonomy and integrity of either perspective were denied. Like the indigenous South Asian gaze, then, the Western (psychoanalytic) gaze has its own merits, and these should not be denied.

Very much related to the implied assumptions that the Westerner cannot know or has nothing important to offer the discussion is the political claim that he or she has no right to know. I have often heard this view—usually framed in the technical vocabulary of postcolonial theory—voiced in contexts where a particular hermeneutic, psychoanalysis for example, attempts to understand the human being across cultures or times or, more radically, advances claims that the indigenous culture might deny. I must confess that I find this move particularly deleterious and almost completely out of touch with the global, postmodern realities of our contemporary world. Nevertheless, I take it quite seriously and so have honored it through four years of writing and speaking (Kripal 1998a, 1998c, forthcoming). Speaking confessionally once again, it was Hinduism that came to me, even when I was seemingly 'safely' tucked away in a segregated Catholic community, through the channels of devotional and scholarly monographs, talks, and translations of classical scriptures (most of which were produced and promulgated by Hindus). I was the converted one. It was Hinduism that made me into a double being, a self now permanently exiled from its own indigenous tradition. That I or any hundreds of thousands of other Westerners answer this experience with years of study, extended stays in India and our own integral and deeply personal appropriations (be they academic, religious, artistic or cultural) hardly makes us the symbolic demons we are sometimes painted out to be. It simply makes us citizens of what is now a global village trying to figure out what it all means, or could mean.

Add to this the historical fact that modern global Hinduism is largely a product of indigenous South Asian traditions and their interactions with Western forms of thought, and one begins to glimpse even further the absurdity of the solipsistic position. The truth is that the only walls that exist now are those that are anxiously built up by what we have come to call 'fundamentalist' movements to protect people from the psychological, social and political realities of our emerging global community. Such a reactionary response is no doubt understandable as a response to suffering of the deepest and most poignant kind (that is, the loss of a traditional worldview) (Kakar 1996), but it carries its own drastic social price, that is, the Balkanization of the species and a disturbing outbreak of ethnic and religious violence. Any theoretical position that insists on what is essentially an identity politics (only South Asians can speak of South Asia, only Hindus can speak of Hinduism, only Christians can speak of Christianity, only women can speak of feminism, and so on) can only contribute to this fracture.

So much for the Western nature of the talking head. But what about its maleness? What might this historically conditioned and socially constructed maleness have to say about the goddess Kali as a divine feminist? Certainly to the extent that feminism attempts to deconstruct and go beyond the contemporary social register in order to envision and ultimately construct an alternate world to live in, the Tantric Kali appears to offer some hope, for she too transgresses in order to transcend. No somatic, emotional or social boundary seems too much for her to cross (her rituals often involve the ingestion of forbidden substances—meat, alcohol, drugs—and the performance of forbidden sexual acts), and we can hear her wild, unsocialized laughter behind and within the antinomian scenes that light up the texts with such overwhelming colors—her tongue is sticking out, *at us*. And this is liberating in its own way. So too with her uninhibited sexuality and iconic sensuousness. Are not these divine models for at least the potential affirmation of female sexuality as something grounded in the very nature of reality? I cannot help thinking, by striking contrast, of my own indigenous tradition here, Roman Catholicism, in which the Godhead is imagined as three-males-in-one and the only *Ur*-female is a virgin mother. How, may I ask, can an actual, historical human female find sexual and gender affirmation in a mythical model that insists on being *both* a virgin *and* a mother? Talk about a problem.[12] The problems of the Western male's Kali seem almost mild in comparison.

12. The Virgin Mary, like the South Asian goddesses, presents the psychoanalytic thinker with some very familiar psychosexual and oedipal dilemmas. For discussions of these, see especially the powerful studies of Michael Carroll (Carroll 1986, 1992).

But there *are* still problems, and I think that we must be very careful here, even wary, and ask ourselves why it is that a goddess like Kali comes to represent all that is fearful, dangerous, sexual and seductive within the Shakta tradition. Surely this only reifies, and on a cosmic plane at that, the very stereotypical, and potentially misogynist, categories that feminist philosophies attempt to deconstruct once and for all. I suspect, and very strongly, that we are dealing here with male constructions, male fears and male solutions, which in the end are not really solutions at all, at least for us today, after the revelations of the feminist and psychoanalytic gazes. Consequently, it seems to me that any woman who uncritically assumes such religious solutions does so at her own, very considerable feminist risk.[13]

Nor do the problems magically disappear for Western males who want to appropriate Kali's truths for themselves. In some sense, they become even worse. Decapitated heads (not to mention what they might symbolize) tend to make a man, any man, more than a little nervous. Certainly the Western ethos of individualism is hardly commensurable with the decapitating/castrating and I-destroying maternal absorption that chops at the center of Kali's cultus. Nor, I suspect, can Kali's psychologically split meanings survive long in a culture whose child-rearing practices are so different than those of South Asia. Western males are not raised by Indian mothers and fathers within extended families. Consequently, their oedipal resolutions are normally quite different. Moreover, the societies into which they are socialized are structured along radically different principles—Western societies tend to be highly individualistic and egalitarian, whereas South Asian societies tend to be more community-centered and hierarchical (Dumont 1980). There are clear advantages and disadvantages to each of these cultural arrangements, and we need not engage in stereotypical generalities or cross-cultural preaching to realize that a religious form born in one will not easily translate into the other.

More radically, let us try to imagine for a moment a sexually unconflicted homosexual Ramakrishna who did not associate Kali

---

13. The esoteric and antinomian structure of Tantric ritual should also give us considerable pause. We are hardly dealing here with religious practices that could be easily appropriated within *any* public society—that is precisely why they are 'secret'.

with anguished decapitation, the bliss of childlike surrender or the renunciation of adult sexuality—say, in the manner of a well-adjusted gay man living openly in modern society. Once we do this, however, I think that we must immediately admit to ourselves that we can no longer imagine the famous ecstatic mystic who tried to cut his own head off with Kali's sword for his 'dark' sexual desires, who insisted on becoming a sexless Child before a sexless Mother, who went into hundreds of trance states, usually before beloved male disciples or feared sexualized women, and who preached against the impurities and spiritual dangers of heterosexual contact with the female body. Psychologically and historically speaking, socially recognized, 'canonized' mystical accomplishment of this sort seems to demand psychosexual conflict of the deepest sort. Remove the conflict and you remove the ecstasies and visions and teachings. It is not for nothing that Ramakrishna's own culture consistently, even vociferously called him 'mad' in his own day with a long list of Bengali terms loaded with pathological connotations. There is real wisdom here, and at least the possibility of real compassion (which can only begin when the denial of real suffering ends). But here again we encounter a very deep, perhaps insurmountable structural problem with incorporating traditional Tantric spirituality in the West: *pace* its modern popularizers, such spirituality often presupposes a cultural system that denies, displaces and sublimates sexualities that many of us now wish to see expressed, socially legitimated and sacralized. Put most baldly, our own modern conceptions of social and sexual justice would render impossible the kinds of psychosexual mechanisms that have driven much of Tantric spirituality.

Consequently, I doubt very much that the South Asian Kalis, as they stand and dance now, can find a stable home within contemporary public American culture. There will, of course, always be Western individuals who will find profound and lasting meaning in the goddess (I have corresponded at some length with two particularly gifted American Kali-mystics who have encountered the goddess within a cross-dressing transsexual identity and hallucinogenically catalyzed visions, respectively [Kripal forthcoming]), but, for some time at least, such rare individuals—rather like the actively heterosexual Christian mystics Blake and Boehme before them—will do so in spite of and not because of the larger culture.

This is not to say, however, that Westerners cannot or should not appropriate Kali in their own religious lives. With McDermott (1996), I consider it to be presumptuous for a historian of religion to declare, as if from on high, what the history of a particular religious form should or must be. It is one thing to try to understand or to interpret. It is quite another to dictate. My own goal here is to caution, nuance and discipline a process that will proceed regardless of my or any other theorist's objections. I want to problematize, not absolutize. The truth of the matter is that Kali is a dramatically colorful and astonishingly provocative deity who combines within her mythology and iconography powerful themes that many Westerners, male and female, academic and lay, are now existentially struggling with on the deepest of levels—the nature of human sexuality and gender, the essential violence of reality and the meaning of erotic mysticism. If the seeming heterosexuality and feminism of Kali allow them to do so more effectively and meaningfully, then so be it.

In the end, however, one cannot possibly adopt a spirituality whose sexual patterns are different than or, worse, in conflict with one's own, and today especially, with the social realities of radical religious pluralism and the self-reflexive capabilities of the modern and postmodern subjectivities, it is quite easy to find oneself a stranger or misfit in one's own native tradition. Ramakrishna was fortunate because the stunning plurality of his Hindu culture generously offered him multiple sexual patterns and spiritual possibilities: he could thus be a Child of the Mother, reject the Tantric (hetero)sexual Hero, and delight as Radha the female lover of Krishna, all at the same time. Many traditional Westerners are not so fortunate, and their options are often quite limited. Perhaps Kali is popular in the West today precisely because she offers other spiritual-sexual possibilities for these individuals. Certainly, it is up to those who make her their own, within or across or despite cultures, to determine her future histories—feminist, misogynist, homosexual, heterosexual, transsexual or otherwise. Until then, however, we would do well to bend our ears a bit closer to the goddess's breast and listen carefully to what her garland of talking heads whisper in the dark. Even if they speak in wildly disparate voices, they speak nonetheless, and their words carry the force of some conviction and more than a little experience.

Bibliography

Berkson, Carmel
1995   *The Divine and the Demoniac: Mahisa's Heroic Struggle with Durga* (New Delhi: Oxford University Press).

Blake, William
1975   *The Marriage of Heaven and Hell* (with an Introduction and Commentary by Geoffrey Keynes; Oxford: Oxford University Press).

Bose, Girindrasekhar
1956   'The Genesis and Adjustment of the Oedipus Wish', reprinted in Vaidyanathan and Kripal (eds.) 1998: 21-38.

Bose, Girindrasekhar, and Sigmund Freud
1997   *The Beginnings of Psychoanalysis in India: Bose–Freud Correspondence* (Calcutta: Indian Psycho-Analytical Society, [1964]).

Bradford, Nicholas
1983   'Transgenderism and the Cult of Yellama: Heat, Sex, and Sickness in South Indian Ritual', *Journal of Anthropological Research* 39.3: 307-322.

Caldwell, Sarah
1995   'Oh Terrifying Mother: The Mudiyettu Ritual Drama of Kerala, South India' (PhD dissertation, University of California, Berkeley).

Carroll, Michael P.
1986   *The Cult of the Virgin Mary: Psychological Origins* (Princeton, NJ: Princeton University Press).
1992   *Madonnas That Maim: Popular Catholicism in Italy Since the Fifteenth Century* (Princeton, NJ: Princeton University Press).

Carstairs, G.M.
1957   *The Twice-Born: A Study of a Community of High-Caste Hindus* (Indianapolis: Indiana University Press, 1957).
1983   *Death of a Witch: A Village in North India, 1950–1981* (London: Hutchinson).

Carstairs, G.M., and R.L. Kapur
1976   *The Great Universe of Kota: Stress, Change and Moral Disorder in an Indian Village* (Berkeley: University of California Press).

Christ, Carol
1994   'Symbols of Goddess and God in Feminist Theology', in Carl Olson (ed.), *The Book of the Goddess: Past and Present* (New York: Crossroad): 231-51.

Cohen, Lawrence
1995   'The Pleasures of Castration: The Postoperative Status of Hijras, Jankhas and Academics', in Paul R. Abramson and Steven D. Pinkerton (eds.), *Sexual Nature, Sexual Culture* (Chicago: University of Chicago Press): 276-304.

Courtright, Paul
1985   *Ganesa: Lord of Obstacles, Lord of Beginnings* (New York: Oxford University Press).

Delaney, Carol
1998   *Abraham on Trial: The Social Legacy of Biblical Myth* (Princeton, NJ: Princeton University Press).

Dumont, Louis
1980   *Homo Hierarchicus: The Caste System and Its Implications* (Chicago: University of Chicago Press).

Eilberg-Schwartz, Howard
1994   *God's Phallus: And Other Problems for Men and Monotheism* (Boston: Beacon Press).

Freud, Sigmund
1933   *New Introductory Lectures on Psycho-Analysis*. XXII. *The Standard Edition of the Complete Psychological Works of Sigmund Freud* (trans. and ed. James Strachey; London: Hogarth Press, 1964).

Geertz, Clifford
1973   *The Interpretation of Cultures* (New York: Basic Books).

Goldman, Robert P.
1978   'Fathers, Sons, and Gurus: Oedipal Conflict in the Sanskrit Epics', *Journal of Indian Philosophy* 6: 325-392.

Gross, Rita
1994   'Hindu Female Deities as a Resource for the Contemporary Rediscovery of the Goddess', in Carl Olson (ed.), *The Book of the Goddess: Past and Present* (New York: Crossroad): 217-30.

Hartnack, Christiane
1998   'Vishnu on Freud's Desk: Psychoanalysis in Colonial India', reprinted in Vaidyanathan and Kripal (eds.) 1998: 81-106.

Hawley, John Stratton
1996   'Prologue: The Goddess in India', in Stratton and Wulff (eds.) 1996: 1-28.

Hawley, John Stratton, and Donna Marie Wulff (eds.)
1996   *Devi: Goddesses of India* (Berkeley: University of Caifornia Press).

Hiltebeitel, Alf
1995   'Dying before the *Mahabharata* War: Martial and Transsexual Body-building for Aravan', *The Journal of Asian Studies* 54.2: 447-73.
1998   'Hair Like Snakes and Mustached Brides: Crossed Gender in an Indian Folk Cult', in Alf Hiltebeitel and Barbara Miller (eds.), *Hair: Its Power and Meaning in Asian Cultures* (Albany: State University of New York Press).
1999   'Kuttantavar: The Divine Lives of a Severed Head', in Elisabeth Schömbucher and Claus Peter Zoller (eds.), *Ways of Dying: Death and Its Meanings in South Asia* (Heidelberg University South Asian Institute Studies, 33; Delhi: Manohar).

Kakar, Sudhir
1981   *The Inner World: A Psycho-Analytic Study of Childhood and Society in India* (New Delhi: Oxford University Press, 2nd edn).
1989   'The Maternal Feminine in Indian Psychoanalysis', *International Review of Psycho-Analysis* 16: 335-362.
1996   *The Colors of Violence: Cultural Identities, Religion, and Conflict* (Chicago: University of Chicago Press).

Kripal, Jeffrey J.
1998a   'Pale Plausibilities: A Preface for the Second Edition', in *Kripal* 1998b.
1998b   *Kali's Child: The Mystical and the Erotic in the Life and Teachings of Ramakrishna* (Chicago: University of Chicago Press, 2nd edn).
1998c   'Mystical Homoeroticism, Reductionism, and the Reality of Censorship: A Response to Gerald James Larson', *Journal of the American Academy of Religion* 66.3: 627-35.
forthcoming 'Teaching Hindu Tantrism with Freud: Transgression as Critical Theory and Mystical Technique', in Diane Jonte-Pace (ed.), *Teaching Freud in Religious Studies* (Atlanta: Scholars Press).

Kurtz, Stanley N.
1992   *All the Mothers Are One: Hindu India and the Cultural Reshaping of Psychoanalysis* (New York: Columbia University Press).

Levenson, Jon
1993   *The Death and Resurrection of the Beloved Son* (New Haven: Yale University Press).

McDermott, Rachel Fell
1996   'The Western Kali', in Hawley and Wulff (eds.) 1996: 281-313.

Nanda, Serena
1990   *Neither Man Nor Woman: The Hijras of India* (Belmont: Wadsworth).

Nandy, Ashis
1983   *The Intimate Enemy: Loss and Recovery of Self Under Colonialism* (New Delhi: Oxford University Press).

Narayan, K.
1993   'How Native is a "Native" Anthropologist?', *American Anthropologist* 95: 671-86.

Obeyesekere, Gananath
1981   *Medusa's Hair: An Essay on Personal Symbols and Religious Experience* (Chicago: University of Chicago Press).
1984   *The Cult of the Goddess Pattini* (Chicago: University of Chicago Press).
1990   *The Work of Culture: Symbolic Transformations in Anthropology and Psychoanalysis* (Chicago: University of Chicago Press).

O'Flaherty, Wendy Doniger
1980   *Women, Androgynes, and Other Mythical Beasts* (Chicago: University of Chicago Press).

Parsons, William B.
1999   *The Enigma of the Oceanic Feeling: Revisioning the Psychoanalytic Study of Mysticism* (New York: Oxford University Press).

Ricoeur,
1970   *Freud and Philosophy: An Essay on Interpretation* (New Haven: Yale University Press).

Roy, Parama
1998   *Indian Traffic: Identities in Question in Colonial and Postcolonial India* (Berkeley: University of California Press).

Schjelderup, Harald, and Kristian Schjelderup
   1932   *Über drei Haupttypen der relgiosen Erlebnisformen und ihre psychologische Grundlage* (Berlin: W. de Gruyter).
Schuchard, Marsha Keith
   1998   'Emmanuel Swedenborg: Deciphering the Codes of a Celestial and Terrestrial Intelligencer', in Elliot R. Wolfson (ed.), *Rending the Veil: Concealment and Secrecy in the History of Religions* (New York: Seven Bridges Press): 177-207.
Sinha, Indra
   1993   *The Great Book of Tantra: Translations and Images from the Classic Indian Texts with Commentary* (Rochester, Vermont: Destiny Books).
Spratt, Philip
   1966   *Hindu Culture and Personality: A Psychoanalytic Study* (Bombay: Manaktalas).
Vaidyanathan, T.G., and Jeffrey J. Kripal (eds.)
   1998   *Vishnu on Freud's Desk: A Reader in Psychoanalysis and Hinduism* (New Delhi: Oxford University Press).

Rajeswari Sunder Rajan

Real and Imagined Goddesses: A Debate

Is the Goddess a feminist? There are many voices that join this debate, identifiable, broadly, as those of Indologists and South Asia area studies experts in the Western academy from different fields (religion, anthropology, philosophy, psychology, language and culture, history), whose disinterested scholarship and academic discussion of the Hindu goddess is given a political edge by being addressed in this pointed fashion;[1] and those of Hindu worshipers, Hindu 'nationalists', feminists of varying hues, left secularists and others who are located within contemporary social movements and politics in India, for whom the goddess is, as we might expect, primarily a symbolic resource. Thus the implications of the 'is' in the question 'Is the Hindu Goddess a feminist?' would differ, from the universal present tense indicating a perpetual condition or an indication of abstract potentiality (as it were, *can* the Hindu goddess be feminist?) in the former instance, to a historical present tense in the latter, our contemporary context, local and global, within which the question would resonate with the deployment and role of a majority religion's idiom in a post-colonial 'secular democracy', India.

Despite the different locations of these voices, in response to the question they may be allied in and through their common perception of the goddess's 'feminism'. One section of respondents would be agreed that the goddess 'is', indeed, a feminist, that a feminist is a good thing for a goddess to be, and that this position is enabling, that is, it is in the interests of women, India, Hinduism and Indian

---

1. I refer here especially to those who took part in the panel titled 'Is the Goddess a Feminist?' at the Religion in South Asia Panel at the November 1994 American Academy of Religion Annual Meeting in Chicago; the papers from that panel now form part of this book. This essay, in modified form, appears under the title 'Is the Hindu Goddess a Feminist?' in *Economic and Political Weekly* 33.44 (Oct. 31, 1998) and in Marianne DeKoven (ed.), *Feminist Locations* (Rutgers, NJ: Rutgers University Press, forthcoming).

women. From the other side, for reasons that I shall be rehearsing shortly, the conclusion will be called into question. I shall focus on the disagreement centering on the last claim, but shall treat certain other definitions as starting points and assume certain ideas to be consensual: one, that 'feminist' here will mean 'pro-woman', 'empowering women'; two, that the Hindu goddess is unique in that Hinduism is the only contemporary world religion that has a tradition and continuing practice of goddess worship; three, Hindu goddess worship is radical in so far as the goddess is not inscribed in the mainstream of deities and her devotees are drawn largely from lower castes, women and even non-Hindus, thus clearing certain spaces of alternative belief and practice in the monolith of Brahminical Hinduism; and finally, that it is not only the existence and worship of the goddess, but also her representations in 'feminist' ways—as complementary 'female principle', as autonomous female agent, or as powerful cosmic force—that are under discussion here as aspects of her 'feminist' recuperation.

To talk of 'the' Hindu goddess as if she were a single or composite figure is, of course, already problematic.[2] The debate over the meaning of the goddess would have to take into account the range and diversity of her representations, the sheer number of goddesses, major and minor, mainstream and 'local', that are to be found in the pantheon. David Kinsley's *Hindu Goddesses* provides a useful list and also a chronological history of the evolution of various goddess figures, and John Grimes's essay on Hindu goddesses constructs a taxonomy based on their different functions, provenance and attributes. One direction for the discussion to take would be to examine the distinctive attributes of different goddesses, or the anthropological aspects of their cults and worship, in order to decide upon their greater or lesser potential for feminist appropriation. It would be generally agreed that despite the great symbolic value and veneration bestowed on the consorts of the trinity, the goddesses Lakshmi, Saraswati and Parvati, it is the autonomous constructions of female divinity such as Kali, Durga and their numerous spin-offs who are representative of *stri shakti* (woman-power), and are therefore of relevance to this discussion. I shall sidestep the more nuanced and elaborate discriminations that

---

2.   The figure of 'Mahadevi' or the Great Goddess is discussed by Kinsley (1986: 132-50). Grimes (1993), however, stresses the diversity of goddesses.

this discussion would call for. As I clarified earlier, even if one does not dispute the claim that these goddesses belong to the 'radical' rather than mainstream—hence more patriarchal—tradition of Hindu social and religious practice, the implications of such radicalism are open to contestation.

In my view, the recuperation of the Hindu goddess, or of a Hindu goddess, as feminist is problematic at the present historical juncture both for its assumption of an undifferentiated 'woman-power' and for its promotion of a certain radicalized Hinduism. Some Indian feminists, among whom I count myself, would be cautious of buying into the constituency of 'women' by extending the scope and politics of contemporary Hinduism. I shall however first briefly rehearse both sides of the debate over the question, even though the arguments are likely to be familiar ones. I shall push them further by interrogating their politics: who is saying this? who is opposing it? what is at stake here? what interests can we discern in the investment in the goddess? what are the grounds of skepticism? These will lead to the elucidation of my argument in the concluding section of the paper.

Those who assert that the Hindu goddess is feminist celebrate, first, the Hindu religion's richness and plurality of traditions. In contrast to the singular patriarchal god of the Judeo-Christian tradition, Vedic Hinduism had female dieties and (arguably) a matriarchal world view. Joanna Liddle and Rama Joshi are quoted frequently in this context:

> The worship of the mother goddess does not constitute a matriarchy, but it does constitute a matriarchal *culture*, in the sense that it preserves the value of women as life-givers and sources of activating energy, and it represents the acknowledgement of women's power by women and men in the culture (1986: 55).

When a community's object of worship and veneration is female, it is logical to expect that women in general benefit by sharing that elevated status. The widespread acceptance, even valorization of positive constructions of femininity in goddess figures must serve as enabling models for women that would supplement, contest, or displace the more prevalent models of female meekness, subordination, and obedience (in the form and in the service of *pativrata*) derived from the mythological Sita–Savitri–Anasuya paradigm. Their dissemination via popular cultural forms like folk theatre, mythol-

ogy, song and dance performances, oral story-telling, and cinema
has assisted the rise and dominance of women political leaders like
Indira Gandhi or folk heroines like Phoolan Devi; or, at least, such
women have been accommodated and accepted within the cognitive frame provided by goddesses or the allied figure of the *virangana*, the heroic woman in 'history, myth, and popular culture'
(see Hansen 1988). In Hinduism, gender stereotypes are broken
down in the attribution of power to a female divinity, whether
such power be negative (unruly, destructive, sexually unbridled) or
positive (maternal, protective, asexual). Finally, the phenomenon
of 'possession' (by the spirit of the goddess) may be used by some
women to effectively resist oppression or devaluation in the family
by laying claim to spiritual prowess. And even where the goddess is
not a resource she is a solace to women.

The connections suggested here, between goddesses and women
in Indian society, have been questioned. The distinction is made
between the feminization of certain attributes—righteousness, justice, wealth, learning—or more accurately their embodiment in the
female form, and the elevation of strong or aberrant women with
these attributes to divinity. The goddess is a product of the first
process, not the second. The implication of this distinction lies in
this: that the symbolic valuation of forms is not a reflection of the
actual material and historical conditions in which they take shape.
If we locate the indices of the status of women in the latter, that is,
in female sex-ratios, life expectancy, literacy, income, subjection to
violence, equality of opportunity, legal equality, then the evidence
shows that societies that 'have' goddesses—and women leaders—
score poorly on these counts.[3] That the ideological promotion of
powerful female models does not contribute to ordinary women's
well-being may be contrary to certain feminist expectations, but it
appears to be an empirically valid finding. Tracy Pintchman (1993)
resolves her puzzlement over this contradiction by describing wom-
en's status in India as 'ambiguous'. But the divide between goddesses and women as social beings can be maintained by patriarchy
without any sense of contradiction. Furthermore, although unconventional women may find sanction for their behavior through

---

3.   Grimes points out that 'there is no stronghold of goddess-worship found
in Kerala', which has the highest literacy rate, the highest ratio of women to
men, and the second highest age of marriage for women in India (1993: 136).

reference to goddesses, goddesses are rarely invoked as explicit
role models in the socialization of girls (unlike certain heroines
such as Sita or Savitri).

Women's empowerment as 'goddesses' also meets with rational
and 'modern' skepticism of the kind made memorable in Satyajit
Ray's film, *Devi*. Ray highlights as well the patriarchal investments
in this transformative process and poignantly evokes the cost to the
young girl—the sacrifice of 'normal' conjugal life, sanity, and finally
life itself—that result from the pressures of the role she is obliged
to play as the *devi* of her father-in-law's fantasies. These arguments
raise the more substantial issue of certain kinds of power—individualistic, absolute, aggressive, or anarchic, and in certain contexts,
the power of authoritarian politics or fascistic social movements—
in relation to women, and specifically to women's putative *agency*,
to which I shall return.

The arguments can be taken further, on both sides; but I want to
move here into questions of identity, location and their politics:
who speaks? from where? to what ends or purposes?

The 'feminist' Hindu goddess, or more accurately the claim for the
progressive potential of the goddess for women's liberation, is to
be found chiefly in the following sites of discourse: South Asian
studies scholarship in the Western academy, which is largely reflected in this volume; Hindu 'nationalism'; radical Indian feminism
of a certain kind, and, allied with it, Gandhian secularism. These are
widely separated locations, and each operates with a distinctive
voice and politics that cannot be collapsed into the others; nevertheless, the connections and overlaps among their arguments draw
them into a single discursive field. I shall try briefly to identify the
different sites in what follows.

I begin with the Hindu goddess-scholars from various fields engaged, as Alf Hiltebeitel put it, in 'scholarly reflexivity', the 'attempt
to think about one's relation to what one studies'. This relationship
he frankly admits to be one of 'complicity'.[4] Apart from the gener-
alized complicity—the identification with the objects of one's study
that is an aspect of such studies—the scholars are also responsive
to recent calls to 'think difference' relativistically in ethnographic

---

4.   See Introduction. The comments there on scholarly complicity by both
editors draw on Hiltebeitel's opening remarks at the 1994 panel (see n. 1).

fieldwork, to refuse to see solely through ethnocentric lenses. The main consequence of this is a displacement of the earlier view of women in Indian society as universally exploited and submissive—which is now regarded as an unacceptable inferiorization of Hindu culture—through attempts instead to 'recover' the spaces of their autonomy and the resources of their positive self-images, and to identify their 'agency'. The goddess and her worship are a means to establishing these. Some of this results in what Bernard Williams has called 'vulgar relativism', an uncritical, naive and patronizing acceptance of other cultures' viewpoints that are unacceptable to one's own. The obverse of this, the temptation to idealize non-Western societies as a 'resource' to meet the inadequacies of Western philosophies and lifestyles, is also visible in some of the interpretations: the goddess clearly meets one such lack, especially among feminist theologians (see, for example, Gross 1978). But relativism is a complex position, and it is treated complexly for the most part in judging the question of the Hindu goddess's 'feminism'. There is the bold deployment of the deliberate anachronism of the term 'feminism' itself and the attempt to achieve commensurability between the non-Western 'feminine principle' that the goddess represents, and contemporary Western 'feminism'—both moves that push beyond the relativizing exercise. Apart from the ethnographic evidence of studies of the worshipers themselves (in many cases women) in specific regions of India which support a favorable interpretation of the impact of the goddess (e.g. Erndl 1993), these scholars also, interestingly, draw support from Hindu nationalist rhetoric, from the work of Indian feminists, and from aspects of the Indian women's movement in more visibly ideological ways.[5] This locates their interest in their 'subject' within the frames of feminist inquiry and contemporary subcontinental politics.

Hindu Indian nationalists in the nineteenth century and in the subsequent decades of the Indian freedom movement promoted the image of the militant goddess/heroic woman towards several ends: as a propagandistic and reformist measure for elevating both Hindu women's and Hinduism's self-image and status, as in the Arya Samaj's programs; to mobilize women to participate in the struggle; and above all to provide an inspirational symbolic focus—as in the

5.   Hansen (1988) and some of the papers presented at the panel (see n. 1) are examples.

evolution of the figure of Bharat-mata, 'Mother India'—for national and communal identity. By and large South Asian scholars have been sympathetic to and have endorsed these ends. In contrast to their acceptance, Gayatri Spivak has alerted us to the possibility that, in their resistance to the imperialist effacement of 'the image of the luminous fighting Mother Durga', nationalist (male) elites were simultaneously perpetuating a 'reverse ethnocentrism' (1985: 129). Feminist historians in India have identified the development of the myth of the 'advanced' Aryan (upper-caste) woman in nationalist historiography in the second half of the nineteenth century as belonging to the same ideological configuration (see Chakravarti 1990). Present-day Hindu 'nationalist' parties have produced aggressive women leaders and set up strong organizational structures for women volunteers for similar purposes and based on similar arguments, although in the quite different context of electoral politics and organized religious revivalism in the postcolonial nation state. The actual modalities of the formation of women leaders in the organized Hindutva movement, centered around the *shakti/* goddess ideology, have been investigated in detail by Paola Bacchetta (1994). I shall be returning to Hindutva feminism in the last section of this paper; before I do so, I shall attend to feminist 'uses' of the goddess in other fields.

The Indian women's movement of the mid-1970s, initiated by urban middle-class professional women (for the most part), invoked 'traditional Indian' (read: Hindu) symbols in some cases as a means of diluting if not countering the Western bias of 'feminism'.[6] The goddess figure, or in a more diffuse way the concepts of *stri shakti* and the 'feminine principle', were resorted to in order to mobilize women around women's issues: thus the logo and name of India's first feminist press, Kali for Women. Soon this was to be placed consciously on the agenda of some feminists. Madhu Kishwar, for instance, editor of *Manushi* (a journal of 'women and society'), declared her non-allegiance to 'feminism' as a sign of her refusal of all -ism ideologies, and began instead to explore 'our cultural traditions' to 'identify their points of strength and use them creatively to combat reactionary and anti-woman ideas' (Kishwar and Vanita [eds.] 1984: 47). As part of this trend *Manushi* has carried articles on women *bhakti* (devotional) poets,

6.   Agnes (1995: 139) has advanced this explanation.

on Gandhi's relevance for women, on women's negotiations with religious worship and practices like austerity, goddess cults, *bhakti*, spirit-possession, and so on.

Gail Omvedt links this to a radical rethinking of theory and practice in the Indian women's movement in the 1980s, which had earlier been tied mainly to a left tradition which rejected religion outright as 'patriarchal'. The new perspective, she argues, had some 'profound implications':

> On one hand, the idea of the 'feminine principle' challenged traditional Marxism by posing the nature-maintaining, subsistence-based rural peasant woman against the male industrial worker who embodied the 'proletarian vanguard'; on the other, it questioned the feminist tendencies to locate violence in the family, in the relations of women against men, by stressing the 'feminine principle' as something that men and women both could unite around. The notion of *stri shakti* similarly implied not so much a separate women's movement as the leading role of women in various popular movements, helping these movements to transcend some of their own limitations. As with the slogan 'the liberation of women and men through the awakening of women's power', it was a significant departure from the tendency of both urban feminists and party women to depict women as primarily victims (1993: 226).

Omvedt expresses the confidence that within this redefined attitude to 'religion/ethnicity/culture', traditional gender resources could be drawn upon by women without subscribing to, indeed while actively opposing, Hindu communalism.

Omvedt draws mainly upon the examples of the struggles of rural women in the Shetkari Sanghatana in Maharashtra for property rights and political representation, and of hill women in the Chipko movement in Uttar Pradesh for forestry rights and preservation of natural resources. In the influential work of Vandana Shiva (1989) on the Chipko and similar struggles against the widespread depredations of the environment in the name of 'development' (which include anti-dam struggles), nature is celebrated as *prakriti*, the feminine principle, women as its representatives, and their power in collective struggle as *stri shakti*.

This position on women and religion is closely related to those working from within what we may call a Gandhian secular tradition, which recuperates or freely recasts the symbols and idiom of *sanatana dharma* ('the eternal dharma') in 'progressive', univer-

sal—i.e. non-communal—ways, and exploits their affective potential for communal coexistence and harmony. Gandhi's use of Sita as
symbol for women in the nationalist movement has been discussed
by Madhu Kishwar (1986). More recently, Ramachandra Gandhi's
Sita's Kitchen (1992), a philosophical and historical treatise written
in the aftermath of the Ayodhya dispute, expounds the overlooked
Sita tradition in Hindu, Jain and Buddhist folklore and philosophy as
an argument to counter the militant masculinity of the new Hindutva movements and their streamlining of a canonical Hinduism.
Here too women are associated with their tribal origins, with nature, nurture, and hence motherhood, preservation, and pacifism.

The question about the Hindu goddess's feminism is embedded,
as we can see, within a larger question about the instrumentality of
religion in the postcolonial nation, both for a 'secular' politics and
for women's struggles in mass movements. It thus goes far beyond
any narrowly focused, decontextualized approach. In the following
section I shall problematize some of the connections between the
Hindu goddess and feminism, between religion and women that
have been made here, and the locations, theoretical and political,
from where disagreement is articulated.

There are unresolved theoretical issues for feminism, among which,
the question of power—women's access to it especially in political
life, their modes of exercising it, the ethics of domination versus
democracy—is increasingly recognized as central. I have rehearsed
in more detail elsewhere the feminist debates over the meaning of
'power' for women. Radical feminists repudiate 'male' values and
spheres of power, and valorize in their place women's 'traditional'
qualities of care, sacrifice, and sustenance in family and community; while other feminists argue that women's equality calls for
struggle and requires participation in and control of the existing
structures of political power.[7] Both arguments are deployed in
support of the feminism of the goddess: the former in the celebration of *prakriti*, nature as feminine principle, and the latter of
shakti, the autonomous force of the destructive goddess principle.
The problem with women's embrace of alterity is that it is based on
an essentialized concept of femaleness, which is also an idealized
one; the difficulty with the argument for power is that it is often

7.   See my chapter on Indira Gandhi in Sunder Rajan (1993: 103-28).

conceptualized as anarchic rather than as embedded in political process.[8]

Power is in both cases an instrument of 'agency'. Agency (autonomous action by the individual or collective subject) tends to be regarded as an inherently radical force or attribute of women and other subordinated groups, and therefore the recovery of their agency in the study of society, culture, and history has been uncritically pursued as a politically correct objective.

But women's 'agency' (like their 'empowerment') can neither be viewed as an abstraction, nor celebrated as an unqualified good. Agency is never to be found in some pure state of volition or action, but is complexly imbricated in the contradictory structures of patriarchy. In her extended reflections on the questions of women's 'consent, agency and the rhetorics of incitement' formulated in the context of contemporary Hindutva feminism, and more specifically in light of the phenomenon of its aggressive women leaders and ideologues, Kumkum Sangari observes that patriarchal sanction for women's participation in political life in India is at present most readily forthcoming in 'conservative, indigenist or right wing formations' (1993: 868). We must therefore be alert to the implications of 'who or what is women's agency on behalf of' and ask whether 'all modes of empowerment for women are equally desirable' (1993: 870-71). We also need to recognize that the celebration of a certain kind of 'feminism' as one that is always already available in 'our tradition' serves the function of pre-empting 'Western' feminist demands even as it simultaneously aggrandizes the scope and politics of that tradition and co-opts women's agency for its own ends.[9]

Omvedt anticipates some of the objections to locating women's struggles in India within the framework of *stri shakti* from a left feminist secular orientation:

> didn't the concept of *stri shakti,* with its reference to sometimes bloody mother goddess traditions, imply too much of an endorsement of power and violence? Wasn't it too readily being picked up

8.   For a discussion of popular Hindi cinema in which the protagonists are avenging women, see my chapter 'Name of the Husband' in Sunder Rajan (1993: 83-102). Their prototype is the figure of Kali.

9.   For a more extended discussion, see my chapter 'Real and Imagined Women' in Sunder Rajan (1993: 129-46).

by conservatives who could twist it to see women's ability to endure
all kinds of oppression as a symbol of magnificent power? Didn't
Hindu nationalists have a tradition of appealing to mother goddesses? Wasn't it a Rajput defender of the sati-murder of Roop
Kanwar who said 'Sati is shakti, the power that upholds the universe'? And wasn't the related theme of *virangana* the historical
tradition of heroic women queens who had taken arms against one
or other invader or oppressor, simply an endorsement of feudalism
as well as warfare? Could the question of empowerment be separated from that of violence? (1993: 216).

If, in Omvedt's opinion, 'by 1988–89, the need to do so was compelling' (1993: 216),[10] then in the following years the issue was
once again open to urgent reconsideration following the BJP-
instigated destruction of the Babri Masjid and their subsequent
riots.

Women's involvements in certain movements of the Hindu right
have been examined with care and detail in several essays in a
recent volume on that subject edited by Tanika Sarkar and Urvashi
Butalia (1995). As these essays demonstrate, the membership of
women in large numbers in the Sangh *parivar*, the promotion of
'feminist' as well as 'traditional' roles for women by the RSS organization, the xenophobic rhetoric of Hindutva propagated by Sadhvi
Rithambra and Uma Bharati, women *sanyasin* leaders in the VHP
and BJP respectively, and women's active participation in the Bombay and Surat riots, are related phenomena.[11] In another post-
Ayodhya collection of feminist essays, *Against All Odds*, Gabriele
Dietrich marks this as a traditional moment in feminist politics in
India. The subjectivity and agency of a Hindu feminist ('Kamalabehn'), as shaped within the ideological and organizational structures of the Rashtra Sevika Samiti, are studied by Paola Bacchetta in
the same volume, and reveal in particular the instrumentality of the
goddess in her self-fashioning. Kamalabehn rationalizes her para-
military activity as follows: 'Did Kali fight the rakshasas with her

10. Omvedt gives the following reasons for the urgently felt need to
redefine women's 'empowerment' at the decade's end: political representation
for women in legislatures and local boards was being talked about; women
themselves were seeking entry into these areas; 'conventional left politics' was
dead-ended, and revolutionary violence was being questioned (1993: 216-17).

11. See in particular the essays in Sarkar and Butalia (eds.) 1995 by Basu,
Sarkar, Banerjee and Setalvad.

hands? All our goddesses are armed. Why should I not be armed?'
(Bacchetta 1994: 144). As a militant Hindu woman committed to
ridding the 'Hindu nation' of the Muslim 'enemy', she finds her
model in 'Kali's ridding of the world of evil in the form of demons
in the *Devi Mahatmya*' (p. 153).

Goddess-inspired Hindu feminism is problematic not only for reasons having to do with recent majoritarian communalism in India.
Flavia Agnes has pointed out that Hindu religious symbols and practices treated as an unquestioned secular 'norm' have a tendency to
alienate women in the movement who belong to minority communities (1995: 139). More recently, Kancha Ilaiah, launching a '*shudra*
critique' of 'Hindutva philosophy, culture and political economy',
has called for a disassociation of what he terms the *dalitbahujan*
caste and community from allegiance to Hinduism. The question of
the feminism of the *Hindu* goddess is subject to a different orientation in light of this disavowal. Although Ilaiah's argument may be
(merely) polemical in this regard,[12] his representation of the non-
Hindu Dalit goddess is politically more in consonance with the
goals of a secular and democratic feminism:

> What is their [Dalits'] notion of Pochamma [a popular *dalitbahujan*
> goddess in Andhra Pradesh, typical of local village deities all over
> India]? She is the person who protects people from all kinds of dis-
> eases; she is a person who cures the diseases. Unlike Sita, her gender
> role is not specified. Nobody knows about Pochamma's husband.
> Nobody considers her inferior or useless because she does not have
> a husband. The contrast [with] Lakshmi and Saraswathi…is striking.
> Pochamma is independent. She does not pretend to serve any man.
> Her relationship to human beings is gender-neutral, caste-neutral and
> class-neutral… She herself relates to nature, production and pro-
> creation… The people can speak with her in their own tongues…
> (1996: 92).

12. In his review of Ilaiah's book, D.R. Nagaraj questions the model of
'binary opposition' that Ilaiah creates between Hindu and *dalitbahujan*
deities. On the contrary, he argues, Shudra goddesses may be praised in Sanskrit *shloka*s and Brahman deities appear in Shudra temples, and he refers to
the 'competent' anthropological work that is available in this 'double phenomenon'. He reads this as a sign of 'the radical energies of the dalits to
transform the experience of intimate enmity' (1996: 7). Kinsley's book does
indeed carry a chapter on 'village goddesses' (1986: 197-211).

Ilaiah regards the influence of Hindu goddesses upon upper-caste women in Indian society as pernicious, particularly as it emerged in their aggressive opposition to the Mandal reforms in 1990. This antagonism jeopardizes the possibility of alliances between Dalit movements and women's movements (1996: 78).

These sites then—broadly, the left, left feminist, and Dalit movements—are ones from which caution about the recuperation of the Hindu goddess, and of Hinduism in general as a radical progressive force for social change, is articulated. This essentially rational and skeptical attitude reflects a belief in what D.R. Nagaraj calls the 'emancipatory potential of the project of modernity', a belief that is mainly a result of the 'qualitative change in the lives of the dalits' (and, we may add, of women) brought about by the 'modern institutions of polity and social engineering' (1996: 8). But the pristine days of that uncomplicated belief may now be over. Both religious 'tradition' and secular 'modernity' have become fraught, contradictory, and complex realities, and their identities as separate and oppositional are difficult to maintain. Critiques of enlightenment reason and of projects based upon its premises, including secular modernity, science, and post-colonial nation-statehood, are growing in influence. The struggle for meaning (of the goddess, in this instance) has been joined on religious terrain, as I have pointed out, and folk myths, *bhakti* syncretic faiths, goddess worship, and other 'little' traditions have been resurrected and recast for their rich possibilities of contesting and subverting the hegemonic Hindutva ideology in the making. Strategically, radical and now left secular movements feel the need to wrest religion from the sole domination of the right and to exploit the spaces within a plural and living tradition of Hinduism for progressive purposes.[13]

But the contemporary politics of Hindutva are, as seems increasingly clear, expansionist and adaptable, and show themselves to be (selectively) incorporative of various 'progressive' elements in the political interests of enlarging Hindutva's appeal to women, lower castes, and even other minority communities. Feminist activists/intellectuals, as I have indicated, have been particularly alert to these moves. In a 'modernizing' post-colonial nation, the authority of majoritarian religious discourse and practice can only be coun-

13. The activities of Sahmat have been particularly noticeable in this sphere.

tered, it seems to me, by a clear-cut and visible secular alternative. And to privilege religion as the sole available idiom of the social would be to surrender the hard-won gains of democratic and secular struggles in post-Independence India. Finally, for 'elite' intellectuals to recommend the 'use' of religious symbols in social movements for change, in the absence of personal religious conviction—whether as a capitulation to religion's perceived appeal to the 'masses', or as a show of identification with them—is, literally, bad faith.

Questioning whether the Hindu goddess is a feminist therefore leads us to the discovery of the many ramifications of feminism as it is found in the intertwined contexts of religion, politics, and social movements in India today.

Bibliography

Agnes, Flavia
1995	'Redefining the Agenda of the Women's Movement within a Secular Framework', in Sarkar and Butalia (eds.) 1995: 136-57.

Bacchetta, Paola
1994	'All our Goddesses are Armed: Religion, Resistance and Revenge in the Life of a Militant Hindu Nationalist Woman', in Bhasin *et al.*, (eds.) 1994: 133-57.

Banerjee, Sikata
1995	'Hindu Nationalism and the Construction of Woman: The Shiv Sena Organises Women in Bombay', in Sarkar and Butalia (eds.) 1995: 216-32.

Basu, Amrita
1995	'Feminism Inverted: The Gendered Imagery and Real Women of Hindu Nationalism', in Sarkar and Butalia (eds.) 1995: 158-80.

Bhasin, Kamia, *et al.* (eds.)
1994	*Against All Odds: Essays on Women, Religion and Development from India and Pakistan* (New Delhi: Kali for Women).

Chakravarti, Uma
1990	'Whatever Happened to the Vedic Dasi? Orientalism, Nationalism and a Script for the Past', in Kumkum Sangari and Sudesh Vaid (eds.), *Recasting Women: Essays in Colonial History* (New Brunswick: Rutgers University Press): 27-87.

Dietrich, Gabriele
1994	'Women and Religious Identities in India after Ayodhya', in Bhasin *et al.* (eds.) 1994: 35-50.

Erndl, Kathleen M.
1993	*Victory to the Mother: The Hindu Goddess of Northwest India in Myth, Ritual and Symbol* (New York and Oxford: Oxford University Press).

Gandhi, Ramachandra
 1992   *Sita's Kitchen: A Testimony of Faith and Inquiry* (New Delhi: Penguin Books).
Grimes, John
 1993   'Feminism and the Indian Goddess: Different Models', in Smart and Thakur (eds.) 1993: 126-43.
Gross, Rita
 1978   'Hindu Female Deities as a Resource for the Contemporary Rediscovery of the Goddess', *Journal of the American Academy of Religion* 46.3: 269-92.
Hansen, Kathryn
 1988   'The *Virangana* in North Indian History, Myth and Popular Culture', *Economic and Political Weekly* (April 1988): 25-33.
Hiltebeitel, Alf
 1994   Opening Remarks at Religion in South Asia Panel, 'Is the Goddess a Feminist?', American Academy of Religion Annual Meeting, Chicago, November.
Ilaiah, Kancha
 1996   *Why I am Not a Hindu: A Sudra Critique of Hindutva Philosophy, Culture and Political Economy* (Calcutta: Samya).
Kinsley, David
 1986   *Hindu Goddesses: Visions of the Divine Feminine in the Hindu Religious Tradition* (Berkeley: University of California Press).
Kishwar, Madhu
 1986   *Gandhi and Women* (Delhi: Manushi Prakashan).
Kishwar, Madhu, and Ruth Vanita (eds.)
 1984   *In Search of Answers: Indian Women's Voices from Manushi* (London: Zed Books).
Liddle, Joanna, and Rama Joshi
 1986   *Daughters of Independence: Gender, Caste and Class in India* (London: Zed Books).
Nagaraj, D.R.
 1996   'The Pathology of Sickle Swallowing'. Review of Ilaiah 1996. *Book Review* 10.10 (October): 7-8.
Omvedt, Gail
 1993   *Reinventing Revolution: New Social Movements and the Socialist Tradition in India* (New York: M.E. Sharpe).
Pintchman, Tracy
 1993   'The Ambiguous Female: The Conception of Female Gender in the Brahmanical Tradition and the Roles of Women in India', in Smart and Thakur (eds.) 1993: 144-59.
Sangari, Kumkum
 1993   'Consent, Agency and the Rhetorics of Incitement', *Economic and Political Weekly* (May) 1: 867-82.
Sarkar, Tanika
 1995   'Heroic Women, Mother Goddesses: Family and Organisation in Hindutva Politics', in Sarkar and Butalia (eds.) 1995: 181-215.

Sarkar, Tanika, and Urvashi Butalia (eds.)
    1995   *Women and the Hindu Right: A Collection of Essays* (New Delhi: Kali for Women).
Setalvad, Teesta
    1995   'The Woman Shiv Sainik and her Sister Swayamsevika', in Sarkar and Butalia (eds.) 1995: 223-44.
Shiva, Vandana
    1989   *Staying Alive: Women, Ecology and Development* (New Delhi: Kali for Women).
Smart, Ninian, and Shivesh Thakur (eds.)
    1993   *Ethical and Political Dilemmas of Modern India* (London: Macmillan).
Spivak, Gayatri C.
    1985   'Can the Subaltern Speak? Speculations on Widow-Sacrifice', *Wedge* 7.8 (Winter/Spring): 120-30.
Sunder Rajan, Rajeswari
    1993   *Real and Imagined Women: Gender, Culture, Postcolonialism* (London: Routledge).

Index of Authors

Agnes, F. 275, 280
Agrawala, V.S. 214
Aurobindo, S. 207-209, 211, 225, 229

Babb, L.A. 84, 192, 222, 223
Bacchetta, P. 14, 275, 279, 280
Banerjee, S. 175, 279
Basu, A. 14, 279
Beane, W.C. 216, 225
Beauvoir, S. de 132
Bellah, R. 197
Berkson, C. 255, 257
Berreman, G.D. 17, 96
Berry, K. 92, 100
Bhattacharya, N.N. 37, 40
Bhattacharya, S.R. 118
Biardeau, M. 116-18
Blackburn, S.H. 113
Blake, W. 244, 263
Bose, G. 251, 256, 259
Briggs, G.W. 39, 40
Brown, C.M. 36, 140, 141, 192, 216
Buitenen, J.A.B. van 52
Burton, A. 176
Butalia, U 279
Bynum, C.W. 190, 191, 196

Caldwell, S. 241
Carroll, M.P. 254, 261
Carstairs, G.M. 251, 252
Chakravarti, U. 92, 275
Chhachhi, S. 99
Chitnis, S. 141, 143, 145
Christ, C.P. 97, 187-91, 241
Cixous, H. 130
Coburn, T.B. 32, 211, 213-15, 217, 226
Cohen, L. 240, 256, 257
Collins, A. 20, 21, 55, 59, 117, 118
Courtright, P. 257
Coward, H. 39, 44

Daly, M. 187, 195, 196

Daniel, S.B. 147
DasGupta, S.B. 34, 37, 44
De, S.K. 27
DeKyoven, M. 269
Ded, L. 30
Delaney, C. 254
Derrida, J. 132
Desikachar, T.K.V. 204
Devi, M. 21, 118, 119
Dietrich, G. 279
Dobia, B. 20
Doniger, W. 70
Dumont, L. 185, 262
Dyczkowski, M.S.G. 38, 41, 42

Edgerton, F. 115
Eilberg-Schwartz, H. 245
Eliade, M. 205, 206
Eller, C. 199
Erndl, K.M. 11, 12, 16-19, 21, 22, 85, 91, 92, 94, 95, 195, 223, 274

Freud, S. 250, 251, 259

Gadon, E.W. 197
Gandhi, R. 277
Geertz, C. 189, 190, 206, 258
George, C. 170, 171
Ghanananda, S. 30
Gold, A.G. 70, 80, 193
Goldman, R.P. 66, 252
Goudriaan, T. 232
Grimes, J. 270, 272
Gross, R.M. 18, 20, 22, 106, 108, 111, 188, 196, 239, 274
Gupta, B. 212
Gupta, L. 98, 108, 133, 142, 195
Gupta, S. 30, 93, 167, 232

Hallstrom, L.L. 93
Handelman, D. 69
Hansen, K. 138, 139, 272, 274

Hardiman, D. 17
Harlan, L. 19, 69-71, 77, 80, 83, 86, 87
Harman, W.P. 221-25
Hawley, J.S. 239
Hiltebeitel, A. 12, 17, 20, 21, 62-64, 87,
    113, 115, 240, 256, 257, 273
Hoens, D.J. 232
Humes, C.A. 18-20, 123, 130, 144

Ilaiah, K. 280, 281
Inden, R. 56
Ions, V. 205
Iyer, R. 16

Jagadiswarananda, S. 208
Joshi, R. 92, 93, 98, 271
Jung, C.G. 212

Kakar, S. 192, 252-54, 256, 257, 259,
    261
Kapur, R.L. 251
Kaviraj, G. 52
Khanna, M. 94
King, M.L. 198
Kinsley, D. 196, 226, 270, 280
Kishwar, M. 275, 277
Klein, M. 252
Kohut, H. 55
Kripal, J.J. 18, 94, 247, 249-51, 257,
    260, 263
Kumar, N. 92
Kumar, R. 92, 96-99
Kurtz, S.N. 17, 19, 181, 183, 184, 252

Lacan, J. 55, 132, 133
Larson, G.J. 199
Larson, J. 118
Leenerts, C. 115
Leslie, I.J. 192
Levenson, J. 254
Levi Strauss, C. 132, 164
Lewis, I.M. 97
Liddle, J. 92, 93, 98, 271
Luther, M. 254

M.N.M. 75
Marglin, F.A. 18, 95, 175
Marriott, M. 52, 58, 59
Maynes, H. 76
McDaniel, J. 32, 93
McDermott, R.F. 14, 198, 227, 239,
    240, 250, 264

McKean, L. 14
Meena, V. 220
Mehendale, M.A. 115
Meister, M. 84
Menon, U. 14, 17, 18, 20-22, 153, 157,
    158
Mernissi, F. 107
Mohanty, B. 17
Mohanty, C.T. 92, 177, 178
Mookerjee, A. 208
Mus, P. 56

Nagaraj, D.R. 280, 281
Namjoshi, S. 99
Nanda, S. 256
Nandy, A. 174, 257
Narayan, K. 259
Narayan, U. 92
Nathan, L. 228
Nicholas, R. 56
Nikhilananda, S. 227
Nivedita, S. 228, 247

O'Flaherty, W.D. 20, 58, 62, 192, 212,
    214, 219, 220, 223, 256
Obeyesekere, G. 245, 247, 249, 255,
    257, 259
Omvedt, G. 96, 276, 278, 279
Ortner, S.B. 164

Parsons, W.B. 251
Patel, K.C. 94
Payne, E.A. 33
Pintchman, T. 17, 19, 21, 32, 53, 138,
    192, 272
Pollock, S. 121

Raheja, G.G. 70, 75, 193
Rajan, R.S. 14, 17, 277, 278
Ramanujan, A.K. 69, 161, 164, 222,
    223
Ramaswamy, S. 15
Rastogi, N. 41
Ratté, L. 195
Rawson, P. 44
Reynolds, H.B. 137, 144, 163
Ricoeur, P. 91, 190, 191, 247
Robinson, S. 211
Rogers, C. 55
Rolland, R. 250, 251
Roy, P. 247
Rudolph, L. 83

Rudolph, S.H. 83
Sangari, K. 278
Sarkar, T. 279
Savigliano, M.E. 176
Sax, W. 72
Schjelderup, H. 254
Schjelderup, K. 254
Schuchard, M.K. 245
Seely, C. 228
Sen, R. 228
Sen, S. 31
Setalvad, T. 279
Sharma, S. 87
Shastri, J.L. 218, 219
Shaw, M. 17, 20, 21, 169, 171, 172
Sherma. R.D. 19, 28
Shinn, L.D. 191, 192
Shiva, V. 92, 98, 276
Shulman, D. 118, 192, 223
Shweder, R.A. 14, 17, 18, 20-22, 153, 157, 158
Singh, M. 83
Sinha, I. 257
Solow, R. 258
Spencer, A.M. 227
Spivak, G. 118-20, 275

Sponberg, A. 167
Spratt, P. 251
Srinivasan, A. 175
Stewart-Wallace, J. 30
Suzuki, M. 114
Svoboda, R.E. 209

Tambs-Lyche, H. 72, 75, 76
Taneja, L. 118
Thadani, G. 99
Thompson, E.J. 227
Turner, V. 190, 191

Vaidyanathan, T.G. 250, 251
Vanita, R. 275
Vimalananda, S. 210

Wadley, S.S. 108, 147, 192
Weber, M. 245
Wehr, D.S. 212
Weinberger-Thomas, C. 87
Williams, B. 274
Woodroffe, J. 208, 209, 225
Wulff, D.M. 239

Young, K. 26